Mountains of Injustice

MOUNTAINS of INJUSTICE

Social and Environmental Justice in Appalachia

Edited by
Michele Morrone and Geoffrey L. Buckley
Foreword by Donald Edward Davis • Afterword by Jedediah S. Purdy

OHIO UNIVERSITY PRESS • ATHENS

Ohio University Press, Athens, Ohio 45701
ohioswallow.com
© 2011 by Ohio University Press
All rights reserved

Printed in the United States of America
Ohio University Press books are printed on acid-free paper ∞ ™

Hardcover   18 17 16 15 14 13 12 11   5 4 3 2 1
Paperback   20 19 18 17 16 15 14 13   5 4 3 2 1

First paperback printing in 2013
ISBN 978-0-8214-2043-0

Library of Congress Cataloging-in-Publication Data
Mountains of injustice : social and environmental justice in Appalachia / edited by
Michele Morrone and Geoffrey L. Buckley ; foreword by Donald Edward Davis ;
afterword by Jedediah S. Purdy.
    p. cm.
Includes bibliographical references and index.
ISBN 978-0-8214-1980-9 (hc : alk. paper)
1. Environmental justice—Appalachian Region. 2. Social justice—Appalachian Region.
3. Appalachian Region—Environmental conditions. 4. Appalachian Region—Social
conditions. I. Morrone, Michele, 1962– II. Buckley, Geoffrey L., 1965–
GE235.A13M68 2011
363.700974—dc23
                                                                                2011022501

CONTENTS

Contents

FOREWORD

On September 27, 2010, several thousand protesters marched in Washington, D.C., demanding an end to the practice of mountaintop removal coal mining. Ranging in age from twelve to seventy-two, most of the marchers were from the Appalachian region, and many came directly from the communities directly impacted by the practice. In front of the White House, where the march ended, more than one hundred individuals were arrested, ending what many observers called the largest protest against mountaintop mining in our nation's history. For those attending the rally, the objective was clear: tell the president that his administration should honor its own regulations and scientific findings. If the Environmental Protection Agency finds that slicing the tops off mountains does irreversible harm to Appalachia's ecosystems and watersheds, then such mining practices should be immediately stopped.

Unfortunately, neither the arrests nor the subsequent government reports documenting the environmental hazards of mountaintop removal mining put a stop to the controversial practice. Nor was this the first widely publicized environmental injustice faced by mountain residents. For more than a century, Appalachia has been a major battleground between those who live and work in the mountains and those who have perennially profited from the vast natural resources of the region.

In fact, one of the first environmental lawsuits in the United States was *Madison et al. v. Ducktown Sulphur, Copper & Iron Co. et al.*, which in 1904 pitted North Georgia residents angry over the devaluation of their lands against a large copper smelter operating in nearby Tennessee. The suit argued that the emissions coming from the smelters were killing forests and orchards over the border as well as making local residents ill. Although the mountain farmers were defeated in the initial lawsuit, the case would eventually make its way to the U.S. Supreme Court. In 1915 the court ruled in favor of the Georgia plaintiffs, a bittersweet ending to a decade-long battle. By that date, much of the mountain landscape was already irreversibly scarred by toxic smoke, forcing most of the remaining landholders to permanently leave the area.

Environmental and social injustice in Appalachia predates *Madison v. Ducktown*, however. By the 1890s excessive soil erosion and flooding in the region initiated considerable discussion among local residents, conservationists, and lumbermen regarding the precise role of standing timber in preventing floods and the loss of valuable topsoil. In many counties, more than half the total surface area was owned by absentee timber barons, individuals who might clearcut entire headwater forests without any regard for those small landholders living downstream. After considerable public debate, there was little doubt that injudicious lumbering was causing major flooding in Appalachia, and in some cases, even the loss of life. It wasn't until several tragic floods in West Virginia and Kentucky in 1907 that federal legislation was proposed to protect mountain forests and those living along major floodplains. After hearing testimony from industry spokesmen, conservationists, and local residents, Congress passed the Weeks Act in 1911, authorizing the federal purchase of "forested, cut-over, or denuded lands within the watersheds of navigable streams," lands that would later become America's first eastern national forests.

Ironically, the creation of more than seven million acres of public preserves in Appalachia during the 1920s and 1930s did not fully stop the destruction of mountain forests. Perceived largely as timber reserves by the U.S. Forest Service, these public lands were heavily logged once again as lumber demands rose after World War II. In fact, large-scale timbering in Appalachia's national forests continued for several decades, resulting in legislative efforts by conservation groups across the region to restrict those management practices. In 1975 a West Virginia citizens' group filed a lawsuit in U.S. District Court to enjoin the Forest Service from clearcutting mountain forests, the most common technique for harvesting timber on public lands. Their lawsuit halted logging in the mountain region for many months, ultimately leading to the passage of the National Forest Management Act, in 1976.

Although there has been considerable legislation passed at the federal level regarding the protection and management of public lands in Appalachia, environmental legislation regarding the protection of privately held lands has been less than uniform. In the coalfields, where individual states were historically responsible for regulating coal-mining practices, regulatory agencies and their statutes remained woefully inadequate. In the 1960s, Kentucky residents Jink Ray and Widow Combs chose to sit in front of company bulldozers in order to stop the destruction of their homes. By the early 1970s, several well-organized grassroots groups were beginning to successfully challenge environmental and social injustices in Appalachia, among them Save Our Cumberland Mountains and Kentuckians for the Commonwealth.

In 1972 representatives from no fewer than ten national and regional organizations testified at congressional hearings focusing on the environmental abuses caused by the surface mining of coal. By 1974 their activities were coordinated within the Coalition against Strip Mining, a national alliance composed of local citizen's groups, farmers, sportsmen, and environmentalists. Their highly coordinated political activism eventually led to the passage of the Surface Mining

Control and Reclamation Act of 1977, which finally brought all surface mining activities in Appalachia under federal enforcement. Since the late 1980s, however, newer technologies, including gigantic dump trucks, earthmoving equipment, and draglines, increased the scale of surface coal mining more than tenfold. This practice, known as mountaintop removal, is of such a large scale that entire mountaintops are now removed in order to access the underlying coal seams.

Appalachia also became the target of large solid and hazardous waste conglomerates during the 1980s, absentee firms who saw the region as a potential dumping ground for garbage that could not be legally placed elsewhere. Soon afterward, citizens from across Appalachia began challenging the permitting of landfills and hazardous waste incinerators. One of the most celebrated cases involving a fight against a toxic landfill occurred in Bumpass Cove, Tennessee, an environmental battle that was captured in the award-winning documentary *You Got to Move* (1985).

Without question, the social and political efforts of the 1970s and 1980s forced many state and national policymakers to enact legislation that would benefit Appalachian communities and the environment upon which their survival is often paramount. In some cases, when legislation failed or went unenforced, grassroots groups stepped in to force a new generation of legislators to pass additional laws or to demand better enforcement of existing ones. Since the 1990s, a growing number of grassroots environmental groups have, in fact, been successful in passing local, state, or federal legislation designed to protect the environment, health, and well-being of Appalachian communities. This fact should not go unnoticed, as their success challenges the erroneous assumption that mountain residents are largely passive and quiescent when confronting environmental and social injustices.

In the twenty-first century, new community and activist groups have emerged across Appalachia, providing citizens with an important voice on a wide range of issues, from the siting of industrial parks and nuclear-weapons waste disposal facilities to forest management and mountaintop removal coal mining. Without a doubt, numerous environmental and social injustices still persist in the region, as is documented throughout this volume. Many of the contributors do us an incredible service, not only providing important documentation about important regional struggles but placing these cases studies within the context of the maturing environmental justice field. *Mountains of Injustice* opens up new territory for scholars of Appalachia and provides those working on the topic of environmental justice new insights into the social and political origins of ecological destruction.

Donald Edward Davis

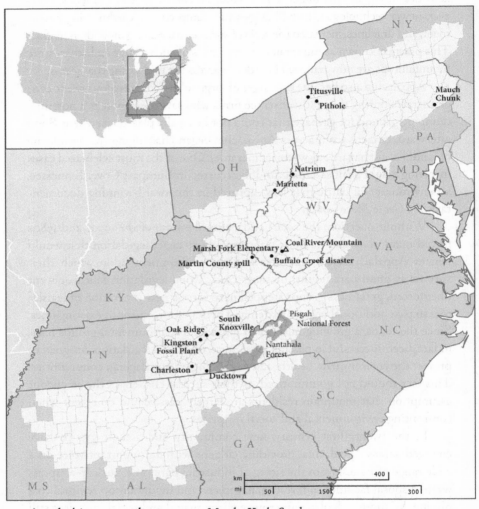

Appalachian county locator map. *Map by Karla Sanders.*

INTRODUCTION

Environmental Justice and Appalachia

MICHELE MORRONE AND GEOFFREY L. BUCKLEY

> Now all of the issues of environmental racism and
> environmental justice don't just deal with people of
> color. We are just as much concerned with inequities in
> Appalachia, for example, where the whites are basically
> dumped on because of lack of economic and political
> clout and lack of having a voice to say "no" and that's
> environmental injustice.
>
> Robert Bullard

ON DECEMBER 22, 2008, AN EARTHEN DAM AT A WASTE
retention pond in Roane County, Tennessee, broke, sending more than 1.1
billion gallons of coal fly ash slurry into nearby streams, flooding hundreds
of acres, and damaging numerous homes and other structures. The slurry—a
by-product of the burning of coal—contained high levels of heavy metals
and other harmful contaminants. The spill, which occurred at the Tennessee
Valley Authority's Kingston Fossil Plant, was reported to be the largest of its
type in U.S. history.[1] Regrettably, for residents of rural Appalachia, it was not
an unusual event.

Just eight years earlier, on October 11, 2000, a coal sludge impoundment in
Martin County, Kentucky, burst through an underground mine, discharging
an estimated 306 million gallons of sludge into two tributaries of the Tug Fork

River. The collapse of this impoundment, owned and operated by a subsidiary of the Massey Energy Company, polluted hundreds of miles of streams and fouled the drinking water of more than twenty-seven thousand residents. According to the U.S. Environmental Protection Agency, the spill was thirty times larger than the eleven-million-gallon oil slick produced by the *Exxon Valdez* accident, in 1989, and one of the worst environmental disasters to take place east of the Mississippi River.[2]

Then there was Buffalo Creek. Early on a Saturday morning in 1972, just as local residents were getting up to make breakfast, a series of coal slurry impoundment dams belonging to the Pittston Coal Company failed, overwhelming more than a dozen mining communities situated in a narrow valley in Logan County, West Virginia. The torrent of coal wastewater unleashed on these unsuspecting communities killed 125 people, injured hundreds more, and left many thousands homeless. Decades later, survivors still suffer from nightmares and other traumas associated with the tragedy.[3]

Today, there are hundreds of waste impoundments of various types, both large and small, scattered across the Appalachian region. For every major incident that has taken place over the past four decades, dozens of minor ones have occurred but have not been reported. Some of these are small spills that degrade local streams; others are underground leaks that taint drinking water supplies. For residents of Appalachia's coalfields, it is the price they pay for living in an "energy sacrifice zone."[4]

Unfortunately, waste impoundments are not the only environmental "disamenities" Appalachian residents must tolerate. Other undesirable land uses, including chemical factories, waste treatment facilities, and landfills pose health and safety risks as well. With regard to the latter, author Elizabeth Royte points out that as of 2002, Pennsylvania—the most populous state in the Appalachian region—was importing "10 million tons of waste per year from neighboring states, more than any other state in the union."[5] Air pollution from dozens of coal-fired power plants and the social and environmental consequences of the mining process itself only add insult to injury.

While giant corporations, utilities, and regulatory agencies deserve much of the blame for the current state of the environment, they are not solely responsible for the crisis. Though we are loathe to admit it, it is our collective "pursuit of quick and easy profit and the insatiable demand for cheap energy" that create the conditions that make another spill—like the ones that occurred in Tennessee, Kentucky, and West Virginia—almost inevitable.[6] Likewise, our desire for low-cost goods all but assures a future in which more peaks are lost to mountaintop removal, more children are exposed to harmful chemicals and tainted water supplies, more species are pushed to the brink of extinction, and more communities disappear from the map.

As long as those of us who live far away from these "landscapes of production" are still able to enjoy the benefits of an inexpensive and uninterrupted flow of energy, we will turn a blind eye to the environmental destruction that takes place in the hills and hollows beyond our gaze. Truth be told, most of us do not care where chemical plants, utilities, or landfills are located, so long as it is not near us. Perhaps author Guy Davenport was right: distance negates responsibility.[7] Or as Jeff Goodell phrases it, "One of the triumphs of modern life is our ability to distance ourselves from the simple facts of our own existence."[8] But these facilities have to be placed somewhere. Where they locate, and why, necessarily brings to the fore issues of environmental justice.

As Christine Meisner Rosen has shown, questions about fairness and the siting of locally unwanted land uses have been with us a long time.[9] Starting in the 1980s, however, researchers began to delve more deeply into the matter. Perhaps the best known of these early studies was the United Church of Christ's *Toxic Wastes and Race in the United States*. Focusing primarily on U.S. cities, these early reports indicated that hazardous waste sites were more likely to be found in communities of color than in white communities.[10] It was suggested that one of the reasons for this disproportionate distribution of potentially hazardous facilities was that minority and low-income communities did not possess the political or economic power to defend their neighborhoods. Social activists decried the injustice of exposing disenfranchised populations to environmental harms and began referring to this practice as environmental racism.

Over the next two decades, social scientists and activists experimented with different scales and units of analysis and employed more sophisticated spatial and statistical techniques to reveal patterns of injustice in urban America. Once preoccupied with the distribution of unwanted land uses and whether or not these "disamenities" were deliberately placed in minority and low-income areas, environmental racism evolved to consider the role that "white privilege" played in creating patterns of injustice. In effect, this new approach allowed researchers to examine more closely how institutionalized racism and "a social system that works to the benefit of whites" permitted predominantly white residents to attract a greater share of amenities to their neighborhoods while deflecting disamenities elsewhere.[11]

In 2007 the United Church of Christ updated its seminal 1987 report. Researchers found that the inequities noted in 1987 were still prevalent twenty years later and may, in fact, have become even worse. Although their ability to effectively oppose the introduction of unwanted land uses into their neighborhoods has improved considerably, communities of color and low-income communities still shoulder a greater burden when it comes to the distribution of these facilities and activities. The problem has been exacerbated by years of government cuts to programs that were designed specifically to address such environmental justice issues.[12]

Along with possible exposure to pollution from day-to-day operations at industrial plants and waste facilities, recent scholarship suggests that accidents may place minority and low-income populations at greater risk. Investigating accident frequencies at industrial facilities in the Los Angeles area, Lisa Schweitzer concluded that the past is a good predictor of the future; that is, by examining records of past accidents, it is possible to draw conclusions about the likelihood of future accidents. Since many accidents occur in minority and low-income communities, she argues that community officials should incorporate historical accident data into the land use planning process. Thus, it may be possible to minimize environmental injustice by paying attention to the potential for environmental accidents.[13]

A key question that arises with the siting of any locally unwanted land use is, How will this facility or activity affect the health of the local community? Although a substantial literature exists on the relationship between environmental health and various demographic variables, including socioeconomic status (SES), again, relatively little research has focused on rural areas, although these populations are more likely to suffer from harmful exposures.[14] A 2005 report in the *American Journal of Preventive Medicine* divided the United States into eight regions based on demographic characteristics including education, income, population density, and homicide rates. The area identified as "poor whites living in Appalachia and the Mississippi Valley" was found to have higher mortality rates among young and middle-aged inhabitants than some developing countries.[15] In addition, studies have shown that cancer levels are often higher in Appalachian counties than in non-Appalachian counties, although this may be attributable to higher levels of tobacco use and unhealthy lifestyles.[16]

This book contributes to the environmental justice discourse in at least three ways. First, by examining the impacts that industrial activities have had on rural communities it addresses an important shortcoming in the field. As noted earlier, most environmental justice work to date has had a decidedly urban bias. Second, while Appalachian scholars and activists have made important contributions in the past—especially when it comes to documenting community resistance and the environmental impacts of industrialization—relatively few of these studies have been contextualized as justice issues.[17] And third, in highlighting the connections between rural and urban, both implicitly and explicitly, we endeavor to show that the dualism is an artificial one, and that our landscapes of consumption and landscapes of production are inextricably intertwined.

Mountains of Injustice is divided into three parts. The three chapters in part 1, "Perspectives," establish the historical and regional context for the rest of the book. In chapter 1, Stephen Scanlan presents us with an introduction to the field of environmental justice. According to Scanlan, persistent poverty and uneven economic development are closely linked to environmental alteration and, as such, must take center stage in any discussion of environmental injustice in Appalachia. In the second chapter, Brian Black explores the "ethic of extraction" that drives our insatiable demand for resources, especially fossil fuels. Against the backdrop of western Pennsylvania's coal- and oilfields, Black tracks the development of Appalachia's "energy landscape," from its colonial origins to its boomtown phase and then, finally, to its demise. In the end, he suggests the possibility of a brighter future, albeit one that does not include a revival of the coal or oil industry. In chapter 3, Nancy Maxwell investigates environmental exposure and health disparities in Appalachia. Her data-rich analysis compares Appalachia to the rest of the country and shows that the counties in the region suffer from environmental burdens at higher levels than counties in other parts of the United States. Ironically, her research reveals that Appalachian counties with higher socioeconomic status also exhibit higher levels of environmental pollution, as indicated by industrial production.

While history and data help frame the environmental justice dialogue, it is the narratives of those who live in Appalachia that personalize the issue. Relying primarily on archival data, contributors to part 2, "Citizen Action," shine the spotlight on local residents, both past and present, who have fought diligently over the years to protect their families, homes, and communities from environmental ruin. In chapter 4, Chad Montrie reminds us that opposition to strip mining in Appalachia has deep roots. Along the way, he recounts the stories of Widow Combs and Uncle Dan Gibson, traces the emergence of organizations like the Appalachian Group to Save the Land and People, and reconstructs the path that ultimately led to passage of the Surface Mining

Control and Reclamation Act of 1977. Reading Montrie's chapter, one gains a better appreciation for the role that politics and compromise play in shaping environmental decisions. One also understands why the present regulatory system has failed to achieve its goals and why citizens groups continue to agitate for "mountain justice."

In the next chapter, Kathryn Newfont dispels the notion that Appalachian residents are antienvironment. Rather, she shows that a different brand of conservation holds sway in the eastern mountains, in this case, western North Carolina. In tracking the development of the Western North Carolina Alliance's campaign against clearcutting in the Pisgah and Nantahala national forests, she shows how residents responded to a strategy that appealed to their sense of fairness regarding access to the area's timber resources. Newfont also puts to rest the myth that open-space issues are primarily urban in nature. In chapter 6, John Nolt tells the story of a community that epitomizes the hazards of facility siting. He begins by recounting the death of a woman who succumbed to cancer after working for years, unprotected, at a radioactive-waste management facility. Her death ignited a two-decade struggle to clean up the hazardous site. His firsthand account is compelling because it reminds us that similar struggles are playing out in small communities across Appalachia.

The chapters in part 3, "In Their Own Words," are constructed largely around interviews conducted with citizen activists over the course of several weeks in the fall of 2008. In chapter 7, Michele Morrone and Wren Kruse profile six environmental activists who have dedicated significant portions of their lives to defending their homes from the by-products, hazards, and wastes generated by large industrial operations. Of primary concern are the "siting decisions" that follow "a path of least resistance," placing vulnerable and exploited populations at risk.[18] They are motivated by a deep sense of injustice that their communities are subject to such end-point pollution because they are poor, disenfranchised, and, perhaps, just because they are Appalachian. In chapter 8, Geoff Buckley and Laura Allen focus on the practice of mountaintop removal—a textbook example of "start point" environmental injustice. While the struggles of these five activists described in this chapter differ from those featured in the preceding chapter, their reasons for battling big business—in this case, companies engaged in a particularly destructive form of surface mining—are no less compelling. Nor are they less moving. And, as Rebecca R. Scott notes in her recent book, *Removing Mountains*, the stakes are high: "In no time at all thousands more acres of the Appalachian Mountains will be dismantled and reclaimed as flattops with rolling grasslands and scrubby shrublands, a brand-new ecosystem to replace the mixed hardwood forest."[19] Finally, this volume concludes with an afterword by Jedediah Purdy in which he examines our relationship with nature and explores our creation of "sacrifice zones."

Appalachia is an area of great natural beauty. While some have viewed the area's natural assets—mountains and valleys, forests and streams, abundance of plant and animal life—as amenities worthy of protection and conservation, others have surveyed the area with an eye toward resource extraction and energy production. Historically, it is the latter perspective that has guided our approach to resource management in the region for more than 150 years.[20] While the extraction of mineral resources, in particular, fueled America's industrial revolution, most of the wealth it generated flowed outside the region.[21] Today, mining continues, albeit using very different methods. One thing has not changed, however. Residents still must contend with the environmental damage that goes hand in hand with such activities. Likewise, they must deal with the risks associated with living in close proximity to other locally unwanted land uses, such as manufacturing that uses large amounts of toxic chemicals. It is high time that those of us who benefit from the extraction of raw materials and the production of manufactured goods acknowledge the true cost of our consumption.

Notes

1. "Coal Ash Spill Revives Issue of Its Hazards," *New York Times*, December 25, 2008, A1, A17; "Ash Flood in Tennessee Is Found to Be Larger Than Initial Estimates," *New York Times*, December 27, 2008, A8.

2. Shaunna Scott, Stephanie McSpirit, Sharon Hardesty, and Robert Welch, "Post Disaster Interviews with Martin County Citizens: 'Gray Clouds' of Blame and Distrust," *Journal of Appalachian Studies* 11, nos. 1–2 (2005): 7–29; David Kohn, "The 300-Million-Gallon Warning," *Mother Jones* 27, no. 2 (March–April 2002): 22–25.

3. Lynda Ann Ewen and Julia A. Lewis, "Buffalo Creek Revisited: Deconstructing Kai Erikson's Stereotypes," *Appalachian Journal* 27, no. 1 (1999): 22–45.

4. Jedediah S. Purdy, "Rape of the Appalachians," in *Appalachia: Social Context Past and Present*, ed. Phillip J. Obermiller and Michael E. Maloney, 4th ed. (Dubuque: Kendall/Hunt, 2002), 208–14.

5. Elizabeth Royte, *Garbage Land: On the Secret Trail of Trash* (New York: Back Bay Books, 2005), 63.

6. Ronald D. Eller, *Uneven Ground: Appalachia since 1945* (Lexington: University Press of Kentucky, 2008), 248.

7. Quoted in Erik Reece, *Lost Mountain: A Year in the Vanishing Wilderness: Radical Strip Mining and the Devastation of Appalachia* (New York: Riverhead Books, 2006), 58.

8. Jeff Goodell, *Big Coal: The Dirty Secret Behind America's Energy Future* (Boston: Houghton Mifflin, 2006).

9. Christine Meisner Rosen, "Noisome, Noxious, and Offensive Vapors, Fumes, and Stenches in American Towns and Cities, 1840–1865," *Historical Geography* 25 (1997): 49–82.

10. General Accounting Office, *Siting of Hazardous Waste Landfills and Their Correlation with Racial and Economic Status of Surrounding Communities* (Washington, DC: GAO, 1983); United Church of Christ, Commission for Racial Justice, *Toxic Wastes and Race in the United States* (New York: Public Data Access, 1987); Robert D. Bullard, *Dumping in Dixie: Race, Class, and Environmental Quality* (Boulder: Westview, 1990).

11. Laura Pulido, "Rethinking Environmental Racism: White Privilege and Urban Development in Southern California," *Annals of the Association of American Geographers* 90, no. 1 (2000): 12–40.

12. Robert D. Bullard, Paul Mohai, Robin Saha, and Beverly Wright, *Toxic Wastes and Race at Twenty, 1987–2007: Grassroots Struggles to Dismantle Environmental Racism in the United States*, Report Prepared for the United Church of Christ Justice and Witness Ministries (Cleveland: United Church of Christ, 2007).

13. Lisa Schweitzer, "Accident Frequencies in Environmental Justice Assessment and Land Use Studies," *Journal of Hazardous Materials* 156, nos. 1–3 (2008): 44–50.

14. Steven G. Prus, "Age, SES, and Health: A Population Level Analysis of Health Inequalities over the Lifecourse," *Sociology of Health and Illness* 29, no. 2 (March 2007): 275–96; Anthony J. McMichael, "The Urban Environment and Health in a World of Increasing Globalization: Issues for Developing Countries," *Bulletin of the World Health Organization* 78, no. 9 (2000): 1117–26.

15. C. J. L. Murray, S. Kulkarni, and M. Ezzati, "Eight Americas: New Perspectives on U.S. Health Disparities," *American Journal of Preventive Medicine* 29, suppl. 1 (2005): 4–10.

16. Mary Ellen Wewers, M. Katz, Darla Fickle, and E. D. Paskett, "Risky Behaviors among Ohio Appalachian Adults," *Preventing Chronic Disease* 3, no. 4 (October 2006), http://www.cdc.gov/pcd/issues/2006/oct/06_0032.htm.

17. For more than forty years, Appalachia has proved fertile ground for environmental research. With respect to environmental history, several excellent volumes exist. See, for example, Donald Edward Davis, *Where There Are Mountains: An Environmental History of the Southern Appalachians* (Athens: University of Georgia Press, 2000); Ronald D. Eller, *Miners, Millhands, and Mountaineers: Industrialization of the Appalachian South, 1880–1930* (Knoxville: University of Tennessee Press, 1982); Ronald L. Lewis, *Transforming the Appalachian Countryside: Railroads, Deforestation, and Social Change in West Virginia, 1880–1920* (Chapel Hill: University of North Carolina Press, 1998); Timothy Silver, *Mount Mitchell and the Black Mountains: An Environmental History of the Highest Peaks in Eastern America* (Chapel Hill: University of North Carolina Press, 2003). Meanwhile, an impressive body of work has been assembled by anthropologists, historians, political scientists, and sociologists who seek to explain poverty, uneven economic development, and environmental alteration in the region while at the same time accounting for the power and control of outside forces. See, for example, Allen W. Batteau, *The Invention of Appalachia* (Tucson:

University of Arizona Press, 1990); Wilma A. Dunaway, *The First American Frontier: Transition to Capitalism in Southern Appalachia, 1700–1860* (Chapel Hill: University of North Carolina Press, 1996); Eller, *Uneven Ground*; Helen Lewis, Linda Johnson, and Donald Askins, eds., *Colonialism in America: The Appalachian Case* (Boone, NC: Appalachian Consortium Press, 1978); Barbara Rasmussen, *Absentee Landowning and Exploitation in West Virginia, 1760–1920* (Lexington: University Press of Kentucky, 1994); Paul Salstrom, *Appalachia's Path to Dependency: Rethinking a Region's Economic History, 1730–1940* (Lexington: University Press of Kentucky, 1994); David S. Walls and Dwight B. Billings, "The Sociology of Appalachia," *Appalachian Journal* 5, no. 1 (1977): 131–44; John Alexander Williams, *West Virginia and the Captains of Industry* (Morgantown: West Virginia University Library, 1976). Others, including Eller, Reece, Robert Armstead, and John Gaventa, have trained their sights more narrowly, concentrating on the social and environmental impacts of extractive industries, such as mining. Eller, *Miners, Millhands*; Reece, *Lost Mountain*; Armstead, *Black Days, Black Dust: The Memories of an African American Coal Miner* (Knoxville: University of Tennessee Press, 2002); Gaventa, *Power and Powerlessness: Quiescence and Rebellion in an Appalachian Valley* (Urbana: University of Illinois Press, 1980). Still others have explored the many and varied ways that Appalachian residents have stood their ground and resisted the destruction of their homes and communities, shattering the stereotype of the weak and fatalistic mountaineer. Especially notable are Dwight B. Billings, Gurney Norman, and Katherine Ledford, eds., *Confronting Appalachian Stereotypes: Back Talk from an American Region* (Lexington: University Press of Kentucky, 1999); Stephen L. Fisher, *Fighting Back in Appalachia: Traditions of Resistance and Change* (Philadelphia: Temple University Press, 1993); Chad Montrie, *To Save the Land and People: A History of Opposition to Surface Coal Mining in Appalachia* (Chapel Hill: University of North Carolina Press, 2003).

18. Robert J. Brulle and David N. Pellow, "Environmental Justice: Human Health and Environmental Inequalities," *Annual Review of Public Health* 27, no. 1 (2006): 103–24; David N. Pellow, "The Politics of Illegal Dumping: An Environmental Justice Framework," *Qualitative Sociology* 27, no.4 (2004): 511–25; David N. Pellow, *Resisting Global Toxics: Transnational Movements for Environmental Justice* (Cambridge, MA: MIT Press, 2007).

19. Rebecca R. Scott, *Removing Mountains: Extracting Nature and Identity in the Appalachian Coalfields* (Minneapolis: University of Minnesota Press, 2010), 1.

20. Eller, *Miners, Millhands*; Williams, *Appalachia*.

21. John Gaventa, "The Political Economy of Land Tenure: Appalachia and the Southeast," in *Who Owns America? Social Conflict over Property Rights*, ed. Harvey M. Jacobs (Madison: University of Wisconsin Press, 1998), 227–44.

PART ONE

Perspectives

ONE

The Theoretical Roots and Sociology of Environmental Justice in Appalachia

STEPHEN J. SCANLAN

A ROMANTIC VIEW OF APPALACHIA MOST LIKELY conjures up images of rolling and forested foothills that give rise to the ancient mountains that form the backbone of the region. One might think about abundant wildlife, spring wildflowers, fall foliage, and numerous rivers and streams that crisscross the landscape, providing life, scenic beauty, and opportunities for exploration. It is a land prized for its ruggedness and isolation, a region where in many places it seems as if time has stood still. In getting lost in its wonders, one may seem far removed from the sights, sounds, and fast pace of modernity and all that city life and technology bring. This is the Appalachia that many have called home and is the root of their rich cultural heritage. This is the Appalachia of magnificence and splendor that has a priceless intrinsic value.

From an environmental perspective, however, romantic images are only that. Although its beauty is abundant and its landscape offers an escape to the natural world, Appalachia is anything but far removed from the sights, sounds, and fast pace of modernity. In fact, with regard to how important Appalachia is to the U.S. economy, the region is not isolated at all but intimately connected. Thus, as Joyce Barry notes, seemingly geographic isolation in Appalachia does not equate to being disconnected.[1] In fact, its geography and natural resources have fueled modernity and made economic development possible in the United States. Timber from Appalachian forests produced the charcoal that stoked the iron ore furnaces central to the country's early industrial growth. Coal from its mountains has heated and provided electricity for millions of people and powered the nation's factories. Stone from its quarries and clay from its hillsides have paved the country's highways and streets and provided bricks that built cities and homes. Appalachian people have sometimes given their lives to stoke the fires of the nation's economy—often with only minimal reward for their effort and risk.

It is clear Appalachia's role in American history has altered its romantic landscape. Mountaintops are removed and hillsides stripped for the resources that lie on and beneath their surface. The air and water becomes polluted, wetlands are filled and degraded, and biodiversity is threatened by resource extraction, industrialization, and urbanization. The landscape gives way to smokestacks, oil wells, and gas line rights-of-way and is altered by dams and development.

Environmental Justice, Resource Extraction, and Facility Siting

Environmental justice as a social issue has emerged out of a social movement that many believed was not addressing the needs of people of color, the poor, or the working class.[2] Environmental concerns were seen as too ecocentric and environmentalists were criticized for not paying enough attention to the cultural, economic, political, and societal concerns linked to environmental degradation. There was general agreement that the planet was indeed in peril, but with strictly ecological concerns come a need to understand the human causes and consequences of environmental harm. Environmental justice makes environmental concerns more anthropocentric by bringing human elements more fully into the discussion.[3] The result of integrating humanity with the environment has led anthropologists, geographers, historians, political scientists, and sociologists to enter the conversation with their colleagues in the environmental and natural sciences.

The environment does not exist independent of human activity and the most important consideration for environmental justice is the distribution of environmental harms.[4] These harms arise from decisions that are intertwined with politics and economics and result in the detrimental impacts of resource extraction in particular. Whether it is coal, natural gas, oil, or timber, their extraction alters natural ecosystems and the lives of individuals living in the proximity of such operations. Hazards come in the form of water pollution from acid mine drainage, flash floods from pillaged hillsides and mountaintops, noise, and the generation and disposal of waste from such processes. Harms and environmental injustices also come from locating potentially dangerous facilities and disposing of hazardous and toxic wastes. Facility siting increases vulnerability to industrial accidents, chemical discharges, spills, and other disasters. In addition, increased exposure to polluted air and water could ultimately result in health disparities in the form of higher than average rates of asthma, birth defects, and cancers. Environmental problems and potential related health outcomes connected to resource extraction and siting decisions cannot be understood without also giving attention to the underlying system of social stratification accompanying them.[5]

Inequality is the core concern regarding environmental justice, with people of color being the focus of the first analyses of this issue.[6] The overlapping of environmental inequality with racial injustice gave rise to environmental racism, a term coined by the Reverend Dr. Benjamin E. Chavis. Chavis argues that environmental racism involves a variety of processes, including "racial discrimination in environmental policy-making, enforcement of regulations and laws, the deliberate targeting of communities of color for toxic waste disposal and the siting of polluting industries."[7] In his view, environmental racism "is racial discrimination in the official sanctioning of the life-threatening presence of poisons and pollutants in communities of color. And, it is racial discrimination in the history of excluding people of color from the mainstream environmental groups, decision-making boards, commissions and regulatory bodies."[8]

Robert Bullard updates Chavis in defining environmental racism as "any policy, practice, or directive that differentially affects or disadvantages (whether intended or unintended) individuals, groups, or communities based on race or color. Environmental racism combines with public policies and industry practices to provide benefits for whites while shifting costs to people of color."[9] By noting beneficiaries in his definition, Bullard emphasizes the importance of relative inequalities between groups and that environmental well-being, like any other societal reward, is stratified, thus creating winners and losers in its distribution.

Definitions such as these speak not only to the maldistribution of environmental hazards and their consequences but also imply unequal access to power and institutionalized inequality in the broader political economy. Such ideas move research and policymaking to additional forms of inequality that incorporate class, space, status, and power, which some claim are as important, if not more important than race alone.[10] Debates concerning the role of race and class have resulted in more inclusive notions of "environmental justice" and *the EPA's definition*

this has been the approach taken by government agencies such as the United States Environmental Protection Agency (EPA). Race remains central to examining environmental inequality, but considering only environmental racism neglects other forms of stratification and injustice.

The inclusiveness of the EPA's approach is found in its definition of environmental justice: "the fair treatment and meaningful involvement of all people regardless of race, color, national origin, or income with respect to the development, implementation, and enforcement of environmental laws, regulations, and policies."[11] The phrases "fair treatment" and "meaningful involvement" reinforce the Chavis and Bullard definitions. The former means that "no group of people should bear a disproportionate share of the negative environmental consequences resulting from industrial, governmental and commercial operations or policies."[12] The latter means that "(1) people have an opportunity to participate in decisions about activities that may affect their environment and/or health; (2) the public's contribution can influence the regulatory agency's decision; (3) their concerns will be considered in the decision making process; and (4) the decision makers seek out and facilitate the involvement of those potentially affected."[13]

It is becoming increasingly clear that the definition of environmental justice is not just about disproportionately distributed hazards but access to power and having a voice in preventing unfair practices. Existing political economic structures therefore need correction; otherwise disenfranchised groups will continue to fall prey to the search for the path of least resistance that is the centerpiece of environmental injustice.

Sound policy, local empowerment, and altering the political-economic structures that create environmental inequality are especially important for Appalachia, for although race certainly has a place in the dynamics of the region, historically its geography, assumed isolation, and stark poverty have been considered defining characteristics.[14] Although the history of the United States is wrought with many instances of environmental inequality, injustice, and racism,[15] many associate a 1982 siting dispute involving the location of a hazardous waste landfill in Warren County, North Carolina, as the defining moment of the environmental justice social movement.[16] African Americans in Warren County challenged the construction of the landfill, and even though they lost and the landfill became operational, their legal battle ultimately brought outside attention to the issue of environmental racism.[17]

The Warren County case spawned further analysis of this issue nationally, leading to ground-breaking research, such as a 1983 U. S. General Accounting

Office (GAO; renamed the Government Accountability Office in 2004) study of hazardous waste landfill siting in the South; a landmark 1987 United Church of Christ study of the spatial relationship between hazardous waste sites, race, and socioeconomic characteristics of communities; and a book-length sociological analysis of environmental justice, *Dumping in Dixie*, that examined siting disputes in Alabama, Louisiana, Texas, and West Virginia.[18] All these works questioned structural inequalities and human decisions that discriminated against minorities and the poor. A fundamental argument in all the early research is that policymakers listened to people of wealth and privilege when they proclaimed, "Not in my backyard," forcing many of these potentially hazardous facilities onto those with less power to prevent them.[19]

With regard to Appalachia specifically, there has been much research on the environmental impact of mountaintop removal coal mining and the movements for justice that has emerged to challenge the government and big coal.[20] This work is framed in the power dynamics and political economy of resource extraction, drawing on the legacy of mining in the Appalachian region and its dependence on the industry despite mining's ecological destruction.[21] Additional work on environmental justice in the region has examined siting concerns, most notably the analysis of a case involving the location of a hazardous waste incinerator in Ohio and the political battles that ensued.[22] Other research has looked at health disparities associated with poverty and environmental burdens in the region.[23] Siting patterns that appear to target specific groups of populations, especially when these decisions lead to negative environmental and health consequences for vulnerable groups, call for explanations of why such patterns exist, and demand to take steps to address them.[24]

Resource extraction in general and mountaintop removal mining in particular are important issues that raise questions with regard to the disproportionate share of environmental harm experienced by those who live in such environs. Communities whose trees are pillaged, hillsides and mountaintops devastated, and rivers and streams polluted live in the middle of what could be considered the most significant environmental tragedy in Appalachia, if not the entire United States, making the region a "national sacrifice area" as described by Jessica Azulay.[25]

Mountaintop removal is "indigenous to Appalachia" in that it can occur only where the mountains rise from the earth, concealing the coal residing within them. Thus, the citizens who call those mountains home are victims of the misfortune of living in the midst of an energy source that has fueled the global economic engine. As long as coal continues to electrify our homes and power our factories, acquiring as much as possible, cheaply and quickly, will be the top priority of coal and utility companies, regardless of the environmental consequences of extracting it. The injustice of this cannot simply be reduced to the accident of circumstance that pits extraction of a valuable resource against the lives of citizens who happen to live in the way of acquiring it. The injustice of mountaintop coal removal requires a hard look at the history of Appalachia, specifically the dominance and power wielded by the coal industry and its supporters over an exploited citizenry.[26]

With regard to facility siting, institutionalized inequality connected to gender, race and ethnic, or spatial considerations are fundamental to the decision-making processes at work. Siting disputes are based on calculated decisions that humans make. Identifying a location for a hazardous facility is not restricted to where various resources have to be extracted from the earth and those experiencing such an injustice must ask, "Why in my backyard?" Answering this for Appalachia necessitates understanding its history and the political economy of both the region and the larger global system—an economy that has left its people powerless, poor, and more vulnerable to the harmful consequences of environmental injustice.[27]

It is due to the nature of siting decisions that claims of environmental injustice are sometimes controversial—particularly with regard to allegations of classism or racism. Despite the evidence of environmental injustice, debates over the question whether environmental hazards "come to" specific groups or vice versa indicate that causal direction is not always clear.[28] In addition there are debates regarding whether race versus class or some other form of stratification best explains environmental injustice. For these reasons, framing a siting decision as an environmental justice issue includes both the siting process and the historical context of the communities before and after the hazards became public controversies.

Understanding local history is essential for examining environmental justice, hence the importance of case studies and comparative-historical approaches in this literature.[29] In addition, much research regarding these concerns is methodological and theoretical, revealing that units of analysis, measurement of variables, geographic settings, the time frame, and the source of data and its reliability and validity can all affect findings.[30] When theories about why environmental injustice exists are combined with accepted and sound research methods, we may be able to take steps to resolve disparities through collective action and policymaking.

Poverty and Political Economy in Appalachia:
Theoretical and Historical Context

Contrary to stereotypes and beliefs about its homogeneity, Appalachia is a diverse region the boundaries of which are difficult to pin down.[31] Indeed, "there are numerous territorial definitions of Appalachia based on such wide-ranging criteria as topography, geography, history, demography, culture, and popular images."[32] There are actually "many Appalachias" with much cultural, economic, and geographic diversity characterizing the region.[33] A range of industries employ workers throughout Appalachia including manufacturing, farming, prisons, retirement facilities, steel, textiles and apparel, and tourism, in addition to coal and timber production.[34]

Even with a diverse economy, the persistent poverty of the region can sometimes be assumed to be its defining characteristic.[35] Although some progress has been made, deep pockets of poverty linger and Central Appalachia in particular remains the "Other America" as described by Michael Harrington.[36] Appalachia typifies "poverty amidst plenty" in that intense poverty—coupled with lack of control over local institutions and development and high rates of emigration among young people—contrasts starkly with a vast abundance of natural resources, economic potential, and a wealth in scenic beauty.[37] This is an essential context for examining environmental justice.

One of two approaches has typically been taken to explain poverty in Appalachia: one structural and the other cultural. The structural perspective is based on larger patterns of underdevelopment or dependent development in the region, while cultural theories argue that poverty is transmitted across and ingrained in the lifestyles of generations of "mountain folk."[38] Critics of the latter argue that the cultural approach blames the victims for their plight and does not account for the exploitation and lack of economic development believed responsible for the region's poverty. These critics opt for structural approaches that I present from multiple perspectives: the regional development model, internal colonialism,[39] and the core-periphery model of development.[40]

The regional development model is concerned with "providing economic and social overhead capital, training people for skills for new industrial and service jobs, facilitating migration, and promoting the establishment or relocation of privately-owned industries through a growth center."[41] In the absence of regional development, Appalachian poverty will remain high until such mechanisms are established to lift up the region. Internal colonialism is more calculating and critical of the capitalist system, emphasizing domination from powerful outside corporate interests who seek to establish control and prevent autonomous development of the subordinate internal colony of Appalachia. In this regard, the development and prosperity of other parts of the United States, such as cities, is only possible because of the exploitation of the internal colony and its citizens, be it for cheap labor, natural resources, or locating hazards. As for the core-periphery model and what has been called the new economic geography, the emphasis is on how the geography of a region and its economic offerings structure its relationship with other regions in the country and even the world. The end result is a spatial organization of the economy divided between innovative, high-growth urban cores and lagging rural peripheries.[42] The former are service-, industry-, and technology-driven while the latter are dominated by agriculture and resource extraction, for which the geography of the rural economy is most suited.

Environmental justice, resource extraction, and siting issues fit with each of the structural theories because job creation and economic development often justify decisions despite their environmental harm. Similarly, because Appalachia has much wealth in the form of coal, timber, and other resources, its geography opens the door for potential ecological exploitation that favors urban centers that are seeking to generate economic growth. As with dependence on the extraction of coal as a source of much-needed jobs and revenue, siting facilities producing, storing, or disposing of toxic materials are likely to be less controversial in depressed areas with few employment opportunities.

When people are suffering because they cannot earn a living, economic development can become more important than environmental protection. The initial proposal for construction of a hazardous waste incinerator in the Appalachian community of East Liverpool, Ohio, touted it as a boon to the local economy that would create jobs and heal the wounds of the city's deindustrialization.[43] East Liverpool reinforces the need to examine the political-economic opportunity structure and "the path of least resistance," connecting with Bullard, who notes that waste disposal companies viewed the South as a "push-over, lacking community organization, environmental consciousness, and with strong and blind pro-business politics,"[44] creating a context in which people were not willing to risk fighting back.[45] Regional development is desirable among policymakers and poverty activists, but this approach can lead to unsustainable and irreversible decisions that sacrifice equity and the environment for economic growth.

As for internal colonialism, critics of exploitation experienced by the poor and persons of color argue that the economic development process in Appalachia is no different than the dynamics of global colonial dominance, be it classic imperialism or the corporate capitalist variant of the modern world system. Although typically applied to the global transfer of toxic waste, parallel patterns of such toxic colonialism are prevalent within the United States, with impoverished or minority communities being the targets.[46] A telling example is the disproportionate number of dangerous military facilities located near American Indian lands, exposing this population to hazards such as nuclear testing or the storage of unexploded ordnance.[47] The internal colony may be powerless to resist or, paralleling the development model, may decide to accept such hazards to generate revenue. Whether chosen or not, once lands are degraded, additional damage is likely to follow as the cycle of exploitation continues.[48]

With regard to internal colonialism, it is therefore important to consider the "political-economic opportunity structure" of the region inviting to capitalist interests that likely would meet stronger opposition in more viable communities.[49] Bullard describes this as a form of "economic blackmail," noting that "in a desperate attempt to attract new industry and jobs . . . many poor communities in the South relaxed their enforcement of pollution and environmental regulations or simply looked the other way when violations were discovered. . . . When questions were raised by concerned citizens, the argument of jobs for local residents . . . was used to quell dissent."[50]

With regard to the core-periphery model, environmental justice is less about regional development or exploitation associated with the other approaches. The concern here has more to do with the injustice of having to address the environmental concerns that are a consequence of the geographical hand dealt to a region. Because the economies of rural peripheries are more dependent on natural resources, there is greater vulnerability of ecological harm. The unequal distribution of such harm based on geographic circumstances attracts the attention of those concerned with environmental justice. From this perspective, therefore, being a coal-mining region is certain to have environmental damages associated with such geographies. Regardless of the type of environmental destruction, injustices are relevant even if someone is not viewing their presence from a more critical capitalist-exploitation point of view. A central question could be whether such harms can be dismissed simply because that is the region's place within the overall economy. Environmental injustice is thus a result of the same dynamics that create the gap in economic development between the core and periphery: spatial variation in the geography and ecology of a region.

Explanations for poverty and the political economy of Appalachia complement perspectives accounting for inequality experienced from the interactions

[handwritten margin note:] Can environmental injustice apply to just human? Ex animals Plants?

[handwritten note at bottom:] does envi. Injustice create poor or does poor attrat Injustice?

of environment and society. One of these theoretical considerations is the treadmill of production, which is a perspective used to explain environmental degradation and injustice resulting from the capitalist system of production and consumption.[51] Using a Marxist-ecology perspective, this approach questions the compatibility of capitalism and environmental well-being, given the exploitative dynamics of such an economic system.[52] This perspective argues the earth is in peril because of the placement of profit over ecology, even if the former is destroyed by the latter and therefore ultimately not sustainable.

Treadmill of production theorists argue that dramatic systemic change is needed not just to slow down ecological damage but to reverse patterns before it is too late. Modernity greatly impacts the human "ecological footprint,"[53] and we are on a treadmill of increased extraction and natural resource use as the economy operates. To grow, package, transport, and market the food we eat, to produce and fuel the cars we drive, to build the cities we live in, and to provide the technology and conveniences we depend on in our daily lives, modern industrial societies use energy and raw materials at an unprecedented rate. The treadmill is created by capitalism, which drives the consumption it needs to survive and is constantly marketing the replacement for existing, often adequate goods. Not only does such a system require a great deal of energy and raw materials—the implications of which are especially significant for Appalachia—it also generates massive amounts of pollution and waste. Furthermore, there is a great deal of inequality to consider as to who benefits and who suffers from treadmill processes. In considering waste management, patterns suggest that hazardous materials are sent "south," be it first in U.S. communities inhabited by persons of color or the poor, or increasingly to developing countries desperately in need of revenues and often powerless to prevent the exportation of toxics to their homelands.[54] This is ultimately a question of inequality and powerlessness. Globalization has created a "global village dump" that in addition to exacerbating public health and environmental harms in other countries has detrimental effects within the United States as well.[55] Siting disputes in Appalachia can reflect these same dynamics, for example, connecting development models and internal colonialism to the treadmill of production.

Mountaintop removal and hazardous facility siting issues in Appalachia specifically highlight the disparity in power between the region's citizens and those who make the decisions that shape their lives and impact the environment. Whether examining this from a development, internal-colonialism, core-periphery, or treadmill-of-production perspective the region's history is rooted in environmental injustice.

The Injustice of Mountaintop Removal

Mountaintop removal mining has attracted increased attention as an important socioeconomic, environmental, and political issue,[56] making it a point of contention and resistance from those seeking to achieve justice in their communities.[57] It is beyond the scope of this chapter to present a comprehensive discussion of the literature, so what follows is intended to highlight significant elements while providing a snapshot of mountaintop removal mining in the region.

Mountaintop removal mining, or what is often referred to as mountaintop mining with valley fills (MTM/VF), is "a surface mining practice involving the: removal of mountaintops to expose coal seams, and disposing of the associated mining overburden in adjacent valleys—'valley fills.'"[58] Expanding on this definition, the EPA describes five steps that constitute mountaintop removal mining, which includes removing layers of rock to access the coal seam and placing the "spoils" of this process in an adjacent valley, and then seeding the former mountain.[59]

Not surprisingly, others describe the practice using more critical language. There are other elements of mountaintop removal that include clearcutting or burning all vegetation, use of large amounts of explosives, road construction, and processing and washing coal before it is shipped away creating the need to store large amounts of coal sludge (slurry).[60] Mountaintop removal mining has grown immensely over the last three decades and is now "the dominant driver of land-use change in the central Appalachian ecoregion of the United States" with the process concentrated in eastern Kentucky, southern West Virginia, western Virginia, and parts of Tennessee.[61] According to John Mitchell, the use of mountaintop removal mining has expanded so fast that monitoring has failed to even keep track of the total area affected, though one common estimate is that if practices continue unabated until 2012, "it will have squashed a piece of the American earth larger than the state of Rhode Island."[62]

With regard to ecological and environmental justice concerns, mountaintop removal has numerous impacts on both the local ecosystems in which it occurs and the health and quality of life of the residents living in its wake.[63] Extracting coal using this practice is fraught with destruction, devastation, and degradation as described by Butler and Wuerthner,[64] who use visual imagery and citizen narratives to analyze "coal's deadly legacy" for the health of the environment. Others note the disruption in the daily lives of citizens in terms of declining property values, encroachment upon private property, dried-up wells or contaminated water, damage to homes, and personal health issues.[65]

Taking impacts a step further, perhaps most damaging to some is the loss of emotional and spiritual attachment to the mountains that the Appalachian citizens call home. With strong historical, family, and cultural ties to the land that have been reinforced generation after generation, there are real emotional scars left on individuals. Larry Gibson is one such example, waging a long battle against the coal companies from encroaching on his land and refusing to sell it to them, claiming that he owes it to the generations buried before him in family plots on the land that has been in his family for more than 220 years, desiring to walk on the earth that they trod on and listen as the woods speak to him.[66] In a similar vein Janet Keating alludes to the sense of self and identity that she derives from the land: "When I think about a sense of place, what comes to mind is mountains, rivers, and forests, my life experiences, generations of family and friends, the Appalachian culture that spawned me—its politics and history. While all those things undoubtedly helped me develop a sense of place, my deepest connections are with nature and the land."[67]

The citizens of Appalachia therefore struggle with the multitude of impacts from mountaintop removal mining, and many distrust both the government and big coal to protect them, as they feel powerless to fight the mining industry's negligent, unregulated practices. The most infamous example of big coal's negligence was the 1972 Buffalo Creek disaster, detailed by Kai Erikson in *Everything in Its Path*, which killed 125 people, injured a thousand more, and left thousands homeless. Heavy rains put pressure on the earthen dam securing a "gob pond" of mining waste, causing it to break and send a wall of thick black water gushing through the mountain hollow, destroying all in its wake. The dam was an integral part of the Buffalo Mining Company's strip-mining practices, and its parent company, Pittston Coal, claimed that the spill was clearly a natural disaster, an act of God. State and federal officials disagreed, however, ultimately finding Buffalo Mining negligent in its violation of numerous safety standards.[68] But the win was only a small victory for the citizens of Appalachia, with little consequence, in that the hazard remains widely prevalent and the practices of big coal largely unaltered.

One report notes that over five hundred similar ponds are dotted throughout the Appalachian region,[69] and similar spills occurred in Martin County, Kentucky, in 2000 and Roane County, Tennessee, in 2008 among others. One precarious situation is located near Marsh Fork Elementary School, in the Coal River Valley of Raleigh County, West Virginia. The school is located in the heart of coal country, with hazards of the industry literally outside its back door, including a silo that collects processed coal from the neighboring mining operations less than a hundred yards away. In addition, the school is situated a mere twelve hundred feet below a massive sludge impoundment, and blasts from active mining processes continue. Local residents have filed a lawsuit against Massey Energy, the owner of the mine, arguing that hundreds of children have been exposed to toxins associated with the coal dust that inevitably drifts into the school yard. Furthermore, parents have been fighting for six years for a new school, located away from the mining operations. After strong grassroots efforts and much fundraising, which included a $1 million donation from Massey, their movement has been a success. In making the donation, Massey noted the new elementary was needed because of the school's age and location in the floodplain of the Coal River, not because of the potential dangers cited in the case against them.[70] Questions of environmental justice such as this define the challenges faced by the citizens of Appalachia with regard to resource extraction and mountaintop removal mining, calling into question the power structures and stratification characterized by the region.

Big coal has used a powerful campaign to encourage support for its practices. With billboards, print ads, television, and the Internet,[71] the coal industry has sought to "greenwash" the damage it has done to the environment and continues to do, let alone the injustices experienced by the people.[72] The industry argues that mountaintop removal is the most efficient means of obtaining coal, thus keeping electricity, steel production, and other costs down. Furthermore, they claim that mountaintop removal is much safer than underground mining and that land reclamation and other environmental efforts are reducing harms and actually benefiting the region. What makes their arguments so effective is the power that coal wields in Appalachia and the legacy of influence on politics and environmental policy.

Mountaintop removal mining can take place only where the coal seams lie on the ground. However, critics note that just because the coal is there does not mean that it absolutely has to be extracted in such a destructive way, if at all. A fair question therefore is, apart from the geological considerations determining where coal is located and thus where mountaintop removal takes place, what are the social, economic, and political factors that actually allow it to occur? After all, the Clean Water Act and the Surface Mining Reclamation Act were both intended to prohibit the destructive process, so what is it about the dynamics of the political economy that condones the process? Critics of mountaintop removal mining argue that the practice is a new form

What if no MTR? then prices soar and these ppl don't have electricity??

of exploitation of natural resources that in many ways reflects the notion of the internal colony discussed above. The practice has little concern for the colony that it benefits from, beyond the resources it can take from it. In this sense, it is the other America not just because of its poverty but what the rest of the country does there at the expense of the Appalachian citizenry.

According to Richard Drake, modern corporate capitalism gave Appalachia a role early on in the history of industrialization in the United States: as a producer of fossil fuels and other resources.[73] The powerlessness of the citizenry and the poverty of the region can thus keep Appalachia dependent on the employment opportunities available from mining and its spin-off economic impacts.[74] This is the case even today when the mining industry employs a fraction of what it has in the past—a change due mainly to mechanization and shifts to surface-mining practices that has increased coal productivity at the expense of employment numbers.[75] Great dependency on the remaining jobs still exists, contributing to a path of least resistance in the presence of environmental injustice. This path is characteristic of the destructive practices of mountaintop removal mining and its effects on citizens and their communities. It has been reliance on coal and other natural resources that keep many would-be challengers silent on the issue, fearful of harming what little economic opportunity the region has. As long as the treadmill of production demands the acquisition of cheap energy to fuel the consumption drive of modern economies, the environmental impacts of mountaintop removal mining will be deemed acceptable.

The power dynamics of the region and what John Gaventa has described as the quiescence imposed on the citizens of Appalachia by the powerful interests of the coal industry and support from elected officials help explain how exploitation, mountain removal mining, and environmental injustice are allowed to occur.[76] According to Gaventa, power is not simply the idea of carrying out one's will despite the resistance of others in the classic Weberian political sociological notion.[77] Power involves two additional dimensions that determine who is involved in the discussion of issues and what issues are on the agenda. Dwight Billings nicely summarizes Gaventa's perspective on these "faces of power" in Appalachia noting that not only are elites able to win decisions, they can block challenges to their power by limiting participation in decision-making arenas and prevent challenges from ever arising to begin with "as to determine the very *wants* of the people they rule and their sense of what is *possible or not*."[78] With regard to the environmental movement in general, or environmental justice specifically, the struggle against mountaintop removal is one involving not just winning the concessions that are the ultimate goal but being able to raise the issue or gaining access to the power structures that enable victory. To outsiders the quiescence of the people, despite the history of exploitation and grievances, may appear to be apathy or lack of will, when in reality patterns of class dominance have set the agenda and dictated any resistance or lack thereof—a common pattern in a range of issues pertaining to power struggles in the United States.[79]

History has shown that the citizens of Appalachia have been anything but quiescent, and this is certainly the case now with regard to environmental justice and the fight to end mountaintop removal mining. The coal industry, for example, has prompted its fair share of labor struggles, often bloody and violent, which are prime examples of rebellion against the power structures of the region. These include not only struggles for power by workers attempting to organize and gain concessions from corporate ownership, but also fights with and within organizations like the United Mine Workers.[80] The history of activism has occurred well beyond the coalfields, however, and it is the diversity of struggle and the quest for justice on multiple fronts that provide a foundation on which movements for environmental justice are occurring today.[81]

Grassroots organizing around civil rights, community development, employment, poverty, and race, class, and gender issues, for example, reflect important cultural contexts in which political opportunity structures have enabled the fight against mountaintop removal mining to have a strong presence. There is a growing literature examining movements against mountaintop removal mining.[82] And whether it be the fight of lone individuals and single communities or a variety of organizations—such as Appalachia Rising, Appalachian Voices, Coal River Mountain Watch, Kentuckians for the Commonwealth, Mountain Justice, Southern Appalachian Mountain Stewards, or the West Virginia Highlands Conservancy—that have taken up the cause, the citizenry is becoming increasingly mobilized, making the issue not just of interest to Appalachia but to wider audiences who are paying more attention to the destructive impacts of this form of mining.

Facility Siting in Appalachia: Patterns, Cases, and Dynamics

Action levied against mountain removal mining carries over into struggles concerning facility siting. An important starting point for examining environmental justice with regard to facility siting is the EPA's database on Superfund sites.[83] "A Superfund site is any land in the United States that has been contaminated by hazardous waste and identified by the Environmental Protection Agency (EPA) as a candidate for cleanup because it poses a risk to human health and/or the environment."[84] Typically these sites are in "uncontrolled" or abandoned areas and their presence potentially exposes people and the environment to risks from contaminants. Superfund sites include accident sites, chemical production and disposal facilities, contaminated waterways, foundries and metals facilities, landfills and waste disposal sites, mining operations, and tanneries among many others, including those connected with the U.S. military.[85]

More than 11,500 hazardous waste are distributed throughout the United States, nearly 1,600 of which are on the EPA's National Priorities List (NPL), which contains the most dangerous sites as determined by the agency itself.[86] Although Appalachia covers only 5.4 percent of the area of the United States and contains 8.4 percent of the population, the region is home to 9.2 percent of the country's Superfund sites and 7.9 percent of the sites on the NPL. In addition, toxic sites are dispersed throughout the region; 260 (62.4%) of the counties in Appalachia contain one or more Superfund sites.

Not only do Superfund sites have a disproportionate presence throughout Appalachia, but many are among the most hazardous in the country. According to the Center for Public Integrity there are thirty-five Appalachian Superfund sites on their 2007 list of the EPA's most dangerous, comprising 6.8 percent of the 517 national sites examined—a value disproportionately higher than the geographic area covered by Appalachia.[87] Contrary to what one may assume, these sites are not concentrated in mining or extractive industries. They represent hazards from a variety of sources, including military sites like the Anniston Army Depot, in Alabama, and an army ordnance facility in Point Pleasant, West Virginia. There are also chemical facilities in Hagerstown, Maryland, Lock Haven, Pennsylvania, and Dover, Ironton, and Salem, Ohio; landfills and waste disposal areas in Hickory Township, Pennsylvania, and Saltville and Selma, Virginia; a refinery in Wellsville, New York; salvage yards in Marietta, Ohio, and Fairmont, West Virginia; and the U.S. Department of Energy's Oak Ridge Reservation, in Tennessee. Numerous other sites were *brought to* the people of Appalachia, leaving behind hazards resulting in blighted ecosystems and unhealthy populations.

According to the pollution information site and monitoring group Scorecard,[88] there are 128 counties in the United States considered the most hazardous based on four burdens that define environmental injustice: cancer risks from hazardous air pollutants, releases of toxic chemicals, Superfund sites, and facilities emitting smog and fine-particle pollution. Ten of these counties

(7.8 percent) are in Appalachia,[89] further evidence that the region has a disproportionately higher share of environmental hazard. Furthermore, using indicators for race and ethnicity, poverty, education, and job classification, these counties reveal an unequal burden of environmental hazards and risk.

This story of exposure to environmental burdens and health disparities is repeated throughout Appalachia, where citizens attempt to explain the death of a loved one from a rare cancer or a child born with a birth defect. As factories close and industry moves to other parts of the world, the legacy of environmental hazards are left for the communities to either fight to clean up or learn to live with. There are communities desperate for jobs, hosting the waste generated in far-off places. Besides the challenges that arise from coal mining and other extractive industries there are numerous other "hotspots for injustice" related to environmental inequality and facility siting in a variety of forms that merit potential scrutiny as well.

The difference in the contemporary cases of siting facilities in Appalachian communities is that people are starting to fight their location. This is a significant societal change, especially considering the theoretical framework of environmental justice discussed above. The following are just a few of the many specific examples:

Arkwright, South Carolina. Citing the prevalence of cancers and other diseases, residents in a predominantly African American community have acted against a closed fertilizer plant they claim released toxic chemicals and concealed information regarding environmental risks.[90]

Belpre, Cutler, Little Hocking, and Vincent, Ohio. Residents in these communities have been exposed to the chemical perfluorooctanoic acid, or C8, a suspected carcinogen that has contaminated the drinking water. The unhealthy level of C8 revealed in a sample of residents has been attributed to the production of Teflon at a nearby DuPont plant across the river, in West Virginia. Municipalities and social movement organizations such as Ohio Citizen Action have waged an ongoing battle with DuPont on this issue through legal channels and public outcry and awareness campaigns.[91]

Birmingham, Alabama. Citizens have challenged the reopening of the New Georgia Landfill, located within the Fultondale community of mostly minority and disproportionately poor citizens who fear groundwater contamination and the pollution of Five Mile Creek. At one point this waterway was one of the worst in the state.[92]

Chattanooga, Tennessee. Residents of the Alton Park–Piney Woods community have demanded cleanup of coal tar deposits contaminating Chattanooga Creek—remnants from World War II-era munitions manufacturing—or government-funded relocation if the Superfund site is not addressed. Residents cite higher rates of cancer, emphysema, and other diseases, with one local activist likening the situation to genocide.[93]

Cheshire, Ohio. The residents here were bought out by American Electric Power in a multimillion-dollar settlement because of persistent toxic releases from a coal-fired power plant. In part because of recent memories of this incident and its consequences, residents in neighboring Meigs County have been challenging the siting and construction of a similar power plant, though this facility recently received the last permit needed for construction.[94]

Erie, Pennsylvania. Opponents have challenged the construction of a tire-burning power plant, claiming it would be the world's largest and most dangerous tire incinerator, releasing unhealthy levels of nitrous oxide, sulfur dioxide, volatile organic compounds, and other particulate matter in a neighborhood of public housing units occupied by persons of color and the poor.[95]

Kenova, West Virginia. Already citing three other chemical plants in the area and higher rates of infant mortality, infertility, and lung diseases, residents in this community—with a household poverty rate of 37 percent—have protested the potential siting of a new chemical plant in the neighboring town of Neal.[96]

Rock Hill, South Carolina. Residents of the Hagins–Fewell neighborhood have obtained federal funds through the EPA's Environmental Justice Pilot Program—one of sixteen cities nationwide at the time—for cleanup and redevelopment of a long-neglected site of the once-prosperous Arcade Mill destroyed by fire and left in rubble and a shell of a structure contributing to blight and decay in the community.[97]

West Anniston, Alabama. Residents of the mostly poor and African American community have protested the presence of both a chemical plant producing cancer-causing polychlorinated biphenyls (PCBs) and the siting of a chemical weapons incinerator at the Anniston Army Depot with the potential discharge of not only PCBs but dioxins, heavy metals, mustard gas, and nerve gas.[98]

The question at the heart of this handful of cases and numerous others in Appalachia is, why are these communities targets for facilities? The communities share many characteristics that are defined in theories of environmental injustice, including (1) high percentages of persons of color or the poor and working class; (2) exposures to environmental risks that adversely affect the health of the citizens; (3) economic blackmail, challenging citizens to weigh risk versus employment opportunities and economic development; (4) manufacturing, processing, and disposal facilities that are part of the treadmill of production and that have ecological consequences for communities that host such practices; and (5) powerlessness, which potentially results in collective action.

Taking these dynamics into consideration, facility siting must be examined with regard to the harm experienced by these and other communities throughout Appalachia. Beyond Superfund sites awaiting classification on the NPL and eventual cleanup, there are facilities throughout the region that expose people of color and the poor to hazardous environmental conditions. These groups suffer harmful consequences from these "patterned inequalities,"[99] from poor health to the emotional burden of raising families and living in hazardous communities. Furthermore, when people perceive that they are powerless to take part in the decision-making processes that place harmful facilities in their communities or fail to clean up the ones that already exist, the environmental injustice is further reinforced through the failings of democratic principles of equal rights and protection.

Toxic colonialism is thus a reality for many communities in Appalachia. Locating hazardous facilities in poor or minority communities and perpetuating a society in which certain social segments have no option but to live in the face of environmental risk is a grave injustice that demands vigilance.

Decisions about mountaintop removal mining and facility siting must incorporate an environmental justice framework[100] that works toward developing sustainable communities where economic development, the environment, and social justice are equally valued. Such a perspective empowers all citizens with regard to the quality of life desired and the degree to which the lives of individuals in Appalachia and beyond can be reasonably free of environmental burdens and risk.

Just as people of color have taken hold of the reigns of political activism through the civil rights movement and the early years of the environmental racism/environmental justice movement, so too can the people of Appalachia

Compares env. injustice to civil rights
good connection?

take or expand action to challenge environmental inequality. Although poverty and inequality of many kinds are grounded in exploitation and the broken promises associated with isolation and powerlessness, environmental injustice in the region is likely to be increasingly challenged as the activism shifts from a localized, grassroots effort of a handful of communities, like those noted above, to a connected network that instead of proclaiming, "Not in my backyard," shouts, "Not in anyone's backyard." The legacy of activism rooted in Appalachia can be a powerful force that overcomes the legacy of powerlessness and quiescence of the past.[101]

This question of power, powerlessness, and exploitation cannot be ignored. A community of elites and their corporations and banks, whose primary interest is in maintaining the status quo of the economic system, uses its power to dominate think tanks and policy discussion and planning, control the media and shape public opinion, and dominate elections and governance.[102] Such considerations are important in that not only is environmental injustice about disproportionate harm experienced by the poor and persons of color, but also a maldistribution of benefits from decision-making processes that occur. Too little attention has been paid to the benefits receive by corporations from challenging environmental regulations by seeking policy that would enhance their operations and effectively enable them to wield power over the lower classes.[103] Corporate dominance has a large role in environmental politics and injustice, and interests are shared by, and power is concentrated in, a variety of industries.[104] Other than what can be strategically placed in corporate responsibility statements, clever advertising, and imagery on their Web sites and in the media to persuade the public differently, environmental justice is not on the corporate community's agenda because of the need to keep the treadmill running.

A path of least resistance applies to mountaintop removal mining and siting disputes because of an imbalance of power between decision makers and those whose voices dare not risk the consequences of challenging that power. This path parallels colonialism and the dominance of the hinterlands by the metropolis, resulting from an acquiescent colony that empowers the colonizer deemed legitimate in its actions.[105] Mountaintop removal mining is touted as legitimate because it is safer than underground mining, a hazardous waste incinerator is legitimate because a community needs regional development, a military munitions storage depot is legitimate because a community needs jobs, and a toxic landfill is legitimate because a community needs tax revenues for its schools. The communities accept the risks because they may not have other alternatives. In the meantime they play their part in the production

22

treadmill, providing the resources that fuel the system and a place to dispose of its by-products. Appalachia, like many other places thus pays the environmental price for its powerlessness, ultimately enabling the rest of us to benefit from the use of the treadmill.

The treadmill of production and the unequal rewards and risks that result from the modern political economy cannot be sustained. When coupled with and reinforced by internal colonialism and promises of economic development the consequences are detrimental for both the natural environment and the citizens who must unequally bear the environmental burdens of the system. Appalachian citizens have a right to demand not only that their land not be pillaged and their streams filled in but also that hazardous industrial sites not be in their communities. Environmental justice is not only about fairness and equity with regard to who shoulders the ecological burdens but about reducing, if not outright eliminating, those burdens and creating a fair and sustainable society that enables citizens to live free of hazards and risks. It is about real opportunity and the creation of a just society that recognizes the value in maintaining the human security of all its citizens, both today and in the future. It is about human rights and democratic principles that when properly tended will name and shame those who benefit from exploiting others. It is about paying attention to the contributions of Appalachia and its citizens and the price they have paid to help put the United States and the world in the position it is in today.

Notes

1. Joyce Barry, "Mountaineers Are Always Free? An Examination of the Effects of Mountaintop Removal in West Virginia," *Women's Studies Quarterly* 29, no. 1/2 (2001): 116–30.

2. Julian Agyeman, Robert D. Bullard, and Bob Evans, eds., *Just Sustainabilities: Development in an Unequal World* (Cambridge, MA: MIT Press, 2003); Bullard, ed., *Confronting Environmental Racism: Voices from the Grassroots* (Boston: South End Press, 1993).

3. Sharmistha Bose, "Environmental Justice Framework: A Case from the Mining Sector," *Gender, Technology, and Development* 8, no. 3 (2004): 407–12.

4. Chuck Laszewski, "The Sociologists' Take on the Environment," *Contexts* 7 (2008): 20–24.

5. J. Timmons Roberts, "Global Inequality and Climate Change," *Society and Natural Resources* 14, no.6 (2001): 501–9.

6. Robert J. Brulle and David N. Pellow, "Environmental Justice: Human Health and Environmental Inequalities," *Annual Review of Public Health* 27, no. 1 (2006): 103–24; Michael Fisher, "Environmental Racism Claims Brought under Title VI of the Civil Rights Act," *Environmental Law Review* 25, no.2 (1995): 285–334; Diane Sicotte, "Dealing in Toxins

on the Wrong Side of the Tracks: Lessons from a Hazardous Waste Controversy in Phoenix," *Social Science Quarterly* 89, no. 5 (2008): 1136–52.

7. Benjamin E. Chavis, foreword to Bullard, *Confronting Environmental Racism*, 3–5.

8. Ibid., 3.

9. Robert D. Bullard, ed., *The Quest for Environmental Justice: Human Rights and the Politics of Pollution* (San Francisco: Sierra Club Books, 2005).

10. Furjen Denq, D. H. Constance, and Su-Shiow Joung, "The Role of Class, Status, and Power in the Distribution of Toxic Superfund Sites in Texas and Louisiana," *Journal of Poverty* 4 (2000): 81–100.

11. U.S. Environmental Protection Agency (USEPA), "Environmental Justice: Basic Information," http://www.epa.gov/compliance/ej/basics/index.html (accessed March 10, 2011).

12. Ibid.

13. Ibid.

14. Perceptions of poverty and isolation are in some ways a product of the creation of the Appalachian Regional Commission to bring economic development of the region and the effort of the federal poverty programs to call attention to the region's plight. In this sense, the region was "discovered" by the rest of the country and seen through this lens, thus sometimes leading to stereotyping and misunderstanding the complex history of the region and its people intertwined with underdevelopment and the type of industrialization that occurred there. See Jeff Biggers, *The United States of Appalachia: How Southern Mountaineers Brought Independence, Culture, and Enlightenment to America* (Emoryville, CA: Shoemaker and Hoard); Ronald D. Eller, *Uneven Ground: Appalachia Since 1945* (Lexington: University Press of Kentucky, 2008); Thomas Kiffmeyer, *Reformers to Radicals: The Appalachian Volunteers and the War on Poverty* (Lexington: University Press of Kentucky, 2008).

15. David N. Pellow, *Garbage Wars: The Struggle for Environmental Justice in Chicago* (Cambridge, MA: MIT Press, 2004); Pellow, *Resisting Global Toxics: Transnational Movements for Environmental Justice* (Cambridge, MA: MIT Press, 2007).

16. Environmental justice as an issue and the movement of the same name go hand in hand. In this chapter, however, I give little attention to the social movements responding to environmental inequality. For discussion and theoretical perspectives on this movement and its connection to environmental justice issues, see Melissa Checker, *Polluted Promises: Environmental Racism and the Search for Justice in a Southern Town* (New York: NYU Press, 2005); Daniel Faber and Deborah McCarthy, "The Evolving Structure of the Environmental Justice Movement in the United States: New Models for Democratic Decision-Making," *Social Justice Research* 14, no. 4 (2001): 405–21; Eileen Maura McGurty, "Warren County, NC, and the Emergence of the Environmental Justice Movement: Unlikely Coalitions and Shared Meanings in Local Collective Action," *Society and Natural Resources* 13, no. 4 (2000): 373–87; Achim Schluter, Peter Phillimore, and Suzanne Moffatt, "Enough Is Enough: Emerging 'Self-Help' Environmentalism in a Petrochemical Town," *Environmental Politics* 13, no. 4 (2004): 715–33; David Schlosberg, *Defining Environmental Justice: Theories, Movements, and Nature* (New York: Oxford University Press, 2007).

17. McGurty, "Warren County."

18. Robert D. Bullard, *Dumping in Dixie: Race, Class, and Environmental Quality* (Boulder: Westview, 1990); U.S. General Accounting Office, *Siting of Hazardous Waste Landfills and Their Correlation with Racial and Economic Status of Surrounding Communities* (Washington, D.C.: U.S. General Accounting Office, 1983); United Church of Christ, Commission for Racial Justice, *Toxic Waste and Race in the United States: A National Report on the Racial and Socio-economic Characteristics of Communities with Hazardous Waste Sites* (New York: United Church of Christ Commission for Racial Justice, 1987).

19. Brulle and Pellow, "Environmental Justice"; Pellow, "The Politics of Illegal Dumping: An Environmental Justice Framework," *Qualitative Sociology* 27, no. 4(2004): 511–25; Pellow, *Resisting Global Toxics.*

20. See Shirley Stewart Burns, *Bringing Down the Mountains: The Impact of Mountaintop Removal on Southern West Virginia Communities* (Morgantown: West Virginia University Press, 2007); Burns, Mari-Lynn Evans, and Silas House, eds., *Coal Country: Rising Up against Mountain Removal Mining* (New York: Sierra Club Books, 2009); Julia Fox, "Mountaintop Removal in West Virginia: An Environmental Sacrifice Zone," *Organization and Environment* 12, no. 2 (1999): 163–83; Bryan T. McNeil, "Searching for Home Where Mountains Move: The Collision of Economy, Environment, and an American Community" (PhD dissertation, University of North Carolina, Chapel Hill, 2005); Chad Montrie, *To Save the Land and People: A History of Opposition to Surface Coal Mining in Appalachia* (Chapel Hill: University of North Carolina Press, 2003); Erik Reece, *Lost Mountain: A Year in the Vanishing Wilderness: Radical Strip Mining and the Devastation of Appalachia* (New York: Riverhead Books, 2006).

21. See Geoffrey L. Buckley, *Extracting Appalachia: Images of the Consolidation Coal Company, 1910–1945* (Athens: Ohio University Press, 2004); Eller, *Uneven Ground*; Jeff Goodell, *Big Coal: The Dirty Secret behind America's Energy Future* (Boston: Houghton Mifflin, 2007); John Alexander Williams, *Appalachia: A History* (Chapel Hill: University of North Carolina Press, 2001).

22. Thomas Shevory, *Toxic Burn: The Grassroots Struggle against the WTI Incinerator* (Minneapolis: University of Minnesota Press, 2007).

23. Michele Morrone, "Environmental Justice and Health Disparities in Appalachia, Ohio," in *Environmental Change and Human Security*, ed. Peter H. Liotta, David A. Mouat, William G. Kepner, and Judith Lancaster (New York: Springer, 2008), 299–323.

24. See also Robert D. Bullard, "Solid Waste Sites and the Black Houston Community," *Sociological Inquiry* 53, no. 2/3 (1983): 273–88; Jim F. Couch, Peter M. Williams, Jon Halvorson, and Keith Malone, "Of Racism and Rubbish: The Geography of Race and Pollution in Mississippi," *Independent Review* 8, no. 2 (2003): 235–47; Furjen, Constance, and Joung, "Class, Status, and Power"; Stephen B. Huebner, "Storm Clouds over the Environmental Horizon," *Society* 36, no. 3 (1999): 57–67; Timothy Maher, "Environmental Oppression: Who Is Targeted for Toxic Exposure?" *Journal of Black Studies* 28, no. 3 (1998): 357–67; McGurty, "Warren County"; Lani Merritt, "Common Cause: A Comparative Case Study of Alabama Communities against Landfills," *Southern Rural Sociology* 17 (2001): 134–58; Jennifer M. Norton, Steve Wing, Hester J. Lipscomb, Jay S. Kaufman, Stephen W. Marshall, and Altha J. Cravey, "Race, Wealth, and Solid Waste Facilities in North Carolina," *Environmental Health Perspectives* 115, no. 9 (2007): 1344–50; David N. Pellow,

Adam Weinberg, and Alan Schnaiberg, "The Environmental Justice Movement: Equitable Allocation of the Costs and Benefits of Environmental Management Outcomes," *Social Justice Research* 14, no. 4 (2001): 423–39; Sicotte, "Dealing in Toxins".

25. Jessica Azulay, "West Virginia, National Sacrifice Area," *Znet*, http://www.zcommunications.org/contents/47076 (accessed September 17, 2010).

26. See Burns, *Bringing Down the Mountains*; McNeil, *Searching for Home*; Montrie, *Save the Land*.

27. Dwight B. Billings and Kathleen M. Blee, *The Road to Poverty: The Making of Wealth and Hardship in Appalachia* (New York: Cambridge University Press, 2000); Cynthia M. Duncan, *Worlds Apart: Why Poverty Persists in Rural America* (New Haven: Yale University Press, 1999); John Gaventa, *Power and Powerlessness: Quiescence and Rebellion in an Appalachian Valley* (Urbana: University of Illinois Press, 1980).

28. Huebner, "Storm Clouds"; Eric J. Krieg, "The Two Faces of Toxic Waste: Trends in the Spread of Environmental Hazards," *Sociological Forum* 13, no. 2 (1998): 3–20.

29. Krieg, "Two Faces."

30. See Douglas L. Anderton, Andy B. Anderson, John Michael Oakes, and Michael R. Fraser, "Environmental Equity: The Demographics of Dumping," *Demography* 31, no. 2 (1994): 229–47; Melissa Checker, "From Friend to Foe and Back Again: Industry and Environmental Action in the Urban South," *Urban Anthropology* 34, no. 1 (2005): 7–44; Couch et al., "Racism and Rubbish"; Furjen, Constance, and Joung, "Class, Status, and Power"; Eric J. Krieg, "Methodological Considerations in the Study of Toxic Waste Hazards," *Social Science Journal* 35, no. 2 (1998): 191–201; Krieg, "Two Faces."

31. Ronald L. Lewis, "Beyond Isolation and Homogeneity: Diversity and the History of Appalachia," in *Appalachia: Social Context Past and Present*, ed. Phillip J. Obermiller and Michael E. Maloney, 4th ed. (Dubuque: Kendall/Hunt, 2002).

32. See Dwight B. Billings and Ann R. Tickamyer, "Uneven Development in Appalachia," in *Forgotten Places: Poor Rural Regions in the United States*, eds., Thomas Lyson and William W. Falk (Lawrence: University Press of Kansas, 1993), 7–29. The official definition of Appalachia is both geographic and political, arising out of the creation of the Appalachian Regional Commission (ARC) by the Appalachian Regional Development Act of 1965. The ARC defines the region as extending from fourteen counties in New York to twenty counties in northeastern Mississippi including all of West Virginia and parts of Alabama, Georgia, Kentucky, Maryland, North Carolina, Ohio, Pennsylvania, South Carolina, Tennessee, and Virginia. The region comprises 420 counties and is divided into three subregions by the ARC: Northern, Central, and Southern, but can be divided in other ways as well (see chapter 3 of this volume). Although predominantly rural, Appalachia claims cities such as Birmingham, Knoxville, and Pittsburgh, and numerous smaller metropolitan areas are dotted throughout the region.

33. Deborah Thorne, Ann Tickamyer, and Mark Thorne, "Poverty and Income in Appalachia," *Journal of Appalachian Studies* 10, no. 3 (2004): 341–57.

34. Elgin Mannion and Dwight B. Billings, "Poverty and Income Inequality in Appalachia," in *Population Change and Rural Society*, eds., William A. Kandel and David L. Brown (New York: Springer, 2006), 357–79.

35. Ibid.

36. Michael Harrington, *The Other America: Poverty in the United States* (New York: Macmillan, 1962); Susan Sarnoff, "Central Appalachia—Still the Other America," *Journal of Poverty* 7, no. 1/2 (2003): 123–39.

37. Patricia D. Beaver, "Participatory Research on Land Ownership in Rural Appalachia," in *Appalachia and America*, ed. Allen Batteau (Lexington: University Press of Kentucky, 1983), 252–66; Burns, *Bringing Down the Mountains*; Harrington, *Other America*.

38. Allen Batteau, "Rituals of Dependence in Appalachian Kentucky," in *Appalachia and America*, ed. Batteau (Lexington: University Press of Kentucky, 1983), 142–67; Ulrich Beck, *Risk Society: Toward a New Modernity* (Thousand Oaks, CA: Sage, 1992).

39. David S. Walls and Dwight B. Billings, "The Sociology of Southern Appalachia," *Appalachian Journal* 5, no. 1 (1977): 131–44.

40. See Paul Krugman, "Increasing Returns and Economic Geography," *Journal of Political Economy* 99, no. 3 (1991): 483–99; Masahisa Fujita, Paul Krugman, and Anthony J. Venables, *The Spatial Economy: Cities, Regions, and International Trade* (Cambridge, MA: MIT Press, 2000); Tyrel G. Moore, "Core-Periphery Models, Regional Planning Theory, and Appalachian Development," *Professional Geographer* 46, no. 3 (1994): 316–31; David S. Walls "Internal Colony or Internal Periphery? A Critique of Current Models and an Alternative Formulation," in *Colonialism in Modern America: The Appalachian Case*, ed. Helen M. Lewis, Linda Johnson, and Donald Askins (Boone, NC: Appalachian Consortium Press, 1978), 319–49; Erik Wibbels, "Cores, Peripheries, and Contemporary Political Economy," *Studies in Comparative International Development* 44, no. 4 (2009): 441–49.

41. Walls and Billings, "Sociology of Southern Appalachia," 133.

42. Moore, "Core-Periphery Models," 318. See also John Friedmann, *Regional Development Policy: A Case Study of Venezuela* (Cambridge, MA: MIT Press, 1966).

43. Shevory, *Toxic Burn.*

44. Robert D. Bullard, "Environmentalism, Economic Blackmail, and Civil Rights: Competing Agendas within the Black Community," in *Communities in Economic Crisis: Appalachia and the South*, ed. John Gaventa, Barbara Ellen Smith, and Alex Willingham (Philadelphia: Temple University Press, 1990).

45. Bullard, *Dumping in Dixie.*

46. See Jennifer Clapp, *Toxic Exports: The Transfer of Hazardous Wastes from Rich to Poor Countries* (Ithaca: Cornell University Press, 2001); R. Scott Frey, "The Transfer of Core-Based Hazardous Production Processes to the Export Processing Zones of the Periphery: The Maquiladora Centers of Northern Mexico," *Journal of World Systems Research* 9, no. 2 (2003): 317–54.

47. Gregory Hooks and Chad L. Smith, "The Treadmill of Destruction," *American Sociological Review* 69, no. 4 (2004): 558–75.

48. Ibid.

49. Pellow, *Resisting Global Toxics.*

50. Bullard, "Environmentalism," 190–91.

51. See Kenneth A. Gould, David N. Pellow, and Allan Schnaiberg, "Interrogating the Treadmill of Production: Everything You Wanted to Know about the Treadmill but Were Afraid to Ask," *Organization and Environment* 17, no. 3 (2004): 296–316; Schnaiberg, *The Environment: From Surplus to Scarcity* (New York: Oxford University Press 1980);

Schnaiberg and Kenneth Gould, *Environment and Society: The Enduring Conflict* (New York: St. Martin's, 2000).

52. See Murray Bookchin, *The Ecology of Freedom: The Emergence and Dissolution of Hierarchy* (Montreal: Black Rose Books, 1991); John Bellamy Foster, *The Vulnerable Planet: A Short Economic History of the Environment* (New York: Monthly Review Press, 1999); Foster, *Marx's Ecology: Materialism and Nature* (New York: Monthly Review Press, 2000); Foster, *Ecology against Capitalism* (New York: Monthly Review Press, 2002); James R. O'Connor, *The Fiscal Crisis of the State* (New York: St. Martin's, 1973). 53. See Richard York, Eugene A. Rosa, and Thomas Dietz, "Footprints on the Earth: The Environmental Consequences of Modernity," *American Sociological Review* 68, no. 2 (2003): 279–300.

54. Pellow, *Garbage Wars*.

55. Gaventa, *Power and Powerlessness*.

56. See Burns, *Bringing Down the Mountains*; Burns, Evans, and House, *Coal Country*; Fox, "Mountaintop Removal"; McNeil, "Searching for Home"; Reece, *Lost Mountain*.

57. See Silas House and Jason Howard, *Something's Rising: Appalachians Fighting Mountaintop Removal* (Lexington: University Press of Kentucky, 2009); Penny Loeb, *Moving Mountains: How One Woman and Her Community Won Justice from Big Coal* (Lexington: University Press of Kentucky, 2007); Montrie, *Save the Land*; Michael Shnayerson, *Coal River: How a Few Brave Americans Took on a Powerful Company—and the Federal Government—to Save the Land They Love* (New York: Farrar, Straus and Giroux, 2008).

58. USEPA, "Mid-Atlantic Mountaintop Mining," http://www.epa.gov/region3/mtntop/ (accessed September 17, 2010).

59. Ibid.

60. For example, see iLoveMountains, "What Is Mountaintop Removal?" http://www.ilovemountains.org/resources#whatismtr (accessed September 15, 2010).

61. M. A. Palmer, E. S. Bernhardt, W. H. Schlesinger, K. N. Eshleman, E. Foufoula-Georgiou, M. S. Hendryx, A. D. Lemly, G. E. Likens, O. L. Loucks, M. E. Power, P. S. White, and P. R. Wilcock, "Mountaintop Mining Consequences," *Science* 327, no. 5962 (2010): 148–49; USEPA, "Mountaintop Mining."

62. John G. Mitchell, "Mining the Summits: When Mountains Move," *National Geographic Online*, http://ngm.nationalgeographic.com/2006/03/mountain-mining/mitchell-text (accessed September 17, 2010).

63. For a summary discussion of scientific data and empirical findings with regard to ecological losses, downstream impacts, human health impacts, and mitigation effects, see Palmer et al., "Mountaintop Mining." For an extensive discussion of environmental impacts including scientific studies and findings based on public comment, see USEPA, *Mountaintop Mining/Valley Fills in Appalachia: Final Programmatic Environmental Impact Statement*, http://www.epa.gov/region3/mtntop/pdf/mtm-vf_fpeis_full-document.pdf (accessed September 13, 2010).

64. Tom Butler and George Wuerthner, eds., *Plundering Appalachia: The Tragedy of Mountaintop-Removal Coal Mining* (San Rafael, CA: Earth Aware, 2009)

65. See Azulay, "West Virginia."

66. Larry Gibson, "This Land Will Never Be for Sale," in Burns, Evans, and House, *Coal Country*, 181–87.

67. Janet Keating, "A Sense of Place, a Sense of Self," in Burns, Evans, and House, *Coal Country*, 249–51 (quote, 249).

68. See Gerald M. Stern, *The Buffalo Creek Disaster: How the Survivors of One of the Worst Disasters in Coal-Mining History Brought Suit against the Coal Company—and Won*, 2nd ed. (New York: Vintage Books, 2008)

69. David Kohn, "The 300-Million-Gallon Warning," *Mother Jones Online*, http://motherjones.com/environment/2002/03/300-million-gallon-warning (accessed September 15, 2010).

70. See Brad Johnson, "Massey Offers $1 Million to Help BOE Build New Marsh Fork Elementary," *Register-Herald*, http://www.register-herald.com/todaysfrontpage/x769240837/Massey-offers-1-million-to-help-BOE-build-new-Marsh-Fork-Elementary (accessed September 16, 2010); WSAZ News Channel 3, "Funding OK'd to Replace Marsh Fork Elementary School," http://www.wsaz.com/news/headlines/88810672.html (accessed September 16, 2010).

71. For example, see industry Web sites with unclear sponsorship, such as http://www.miningusa.com/, or http://www.mountaintopmining.com/, as well as the National Mining Association's *Mountaintop Mining Fact Book*, http://www.nma.org/pdf/fact_sheets/mtm.pdf.

72. Laurie Winston, "Clean Coal Technology: Environmental Solution or Greenwashing?" (master's thesis, Ohio University, 2009).

73. Richard B. Drake, *A History of Appalachia* (Lexington: University Press of Kentucky, 2003).

74. See Billings and Blee, *Road to Poverty*; Burns, *Bringing Down the Mountains*; Eller, *Uneven Ground*.

75. See Rory McIlmoil and Evan Hansen, *The Decline of Central Appalachian Coal and the Need for Economic Diversification* (Morgantown, WV: Downstream Strategies, 2010.)

76. Gaventa, *Power and Powerlessness*. See also Goodell, *Big Coal*; Burns, *Bringing Down the Mountains*.

77. Gaventa, *Power and Powerlessness*; Goodell, *Big Coal*; Burns, *Bringing Down the Mountains*. See also Max Weber, *Economy and Society*, ed. Guenther Roth and Claus Wittich, trans. Ephraim Fischoff et al. (1922; New York: Bedminster Press, 1968).

78. Dwight B. Billings, "Supporting 'Conscious Hearts' and Oppositional Knowledge in the Struggle against Mountaintop Removal Coal Mining," *Journal of Appalachian Studies* 14 no. 1/2 (2008): 20–27 (quote, 24), italics in original.

79. G. William Domhoff, *Who Rules America? Power, Politics, and Social Change*, 5th ed. (Boston: McGraw-Hill, 2006).

80. See Biggers, *United States of Appalachia*; David Corbin, *Life, Work, and Rebellion in the Coal Fields: The Southern West Virginia Miners, 1880–1922* (Urbana: University of Illinois Press, 1989); Eller, *Uneven Ground*; Gaventa, *Power and Powerlessness*; Howard Burton Lee, *Bloodletting in Appalachia: The Story of West Virginia's Four Major Mine Wars and Other Thrilling Incidents of Its Coal Fields* (Morgantown: West Virginia University Press, 1969); Lon Savage, *Thunder in the Mountains: The West Virginia Mine War, 1920–21* (Pittsburgh: University of Pittsburgh Press, 1990); Robert Shogan, *The Battle of Blair Mountain: The Story of America's Largest Labor Uprising* (New York: Basic Books, 2006).

81. Biggers, *United States of Appalachia*; Stephen Fisher, ed., *Fighting Back in Appalachia: Traditions of Resistance and Change* (Philadelphia: Temple University Press, 1993).

82. See Burns, Evans, and House, *Coal Country*; Butler and Wuerthner, eds., *Plundering Appalachia*; House and Howard, *Something's Rising*; Loeb, *Moving Mountains*; McNeil, "Searching for Home"; Montrie, *Save the Land*; Shnayerson, *Coal River*.

83. Furjen, Constance, and Joung, "Class, Status, and Power."

84. USEPA, "Superfund: Frequent Questions," http://www.epa.gov/superfund/programs/recycle/faqs/index.html#1 (accessed March 10, 2011).

85. See Hooks and Smith, "Treadmill of Destruction"; Simon, "Corporate Environmental Crimes and Social Inequality," *American Behavioral Scientist* 43, no. 4 (2000): 633–45.

86. USEPA, "Superfund."

87. Center for Public Integrity, "Most Dangerous Superfund Sites," http://projects.publicintegrity.org/Superfund/HumanExosure.aspx (accessed March 10, 2011).

88. Scorecard, "The Pollution Information Site," http://www.scorecard.goodguide.com/ (accessed March 10, 2011).

89. The ten counties are Boyd County, Kentucky; Butler, Clinton, and Lycoming Counties, Pennsylvania; Calhoun, Jefferson, and Madison Counties, Alabama; Cortland County, New York; Hamilton County, Tennessee; Haywood County, North Carolina.

90. Associated Press, "Hundreds Sue, Saying Closed Fertilizer Plant Contaminated Environment," *Associated Press State and Local Wire*, November 13, 2002.

91. For C8 contamination, see Brian Farkas, "C8 Spreads through Water, Study Finds," *Charleston Gazette*, July 28, 2005; Ken Ward Jr., "Avoid C8 Water, Researcher Says," *Charleston Gazette*, August 16, 2005. For Ohio Citizen Action, see http://www.ohiocitizen.org/campaigns/dupont_c8/dupont_c8.html.

92. Katherine Bouma, "City Says Fultondale Landfill to Reopen: Opponents Feel Plan Would Violate Environmental Justice," *Birmingham News*, October 27, 2004.

93. Van Henderson, "Churches Push Environmental Concerns; Creek Here Gets Gore's Notice." *Chattanooga Free Press*, February 6, 1997; Henderson, "Relocating Homes Near Creek Urged," *Chattanooga Free Press*, March 11, 1997.

94. Adam Goodheart, "Something in the Air," *New York Times*, February 8, 2004; Michael Hawthorne, "AEP Agrees to Buy Out Entire Town: $20 Million Settlement Reached in Gallia County Plant Dispute," *Columbus Dispatch*, April 17, 2002; Hawthorne, "Cheshire: Death of a Village: Cleanup Lags for Decades," *Columbus Dispatch*, November 10, 2002.

95. Michael Scott, "Power Plant Becomes Hot Topic; Tire-Burning Facility Creates Controversy," *Cleveland Plain Dealer*, March 31, 2008.

96. Paul Nyden, "EPA Engineer Warns of Hazards from Proposed Wayne Plants," *Charleston Gazette*, November 18, 1994.

97. Caroline Brustad, "A Neighborhood Takes Stock: Once-Thriving Mill Village Assesses Its Strengths, Needs," *Herald* (Rock Hill, SC), July 18, 2003; Jason Foster, "City Council to Proceed with Cleanup of Former Textile Mill," *Herald*, April 30, 2003.

98. Rick Bragg, "Anniston Journal: From Trust in the Army to a Sense of Betrayal," *New York Times*, April 9, 1995; Bob Herbert, "Poor, Black, and Dumped On," *New York Times*, October 5, 2006; Ronald Smothers, "Plan to Destroy Toxic Weapons Polarizes a City," *New York Times*, September 24, 1992.

99. Simon, "Corporate Environmental Crimes."

100. The environmental justice framework is best understood by examining "The Principles of Environmental Justice" adopted by delegates to the First National People of Color Environmental Leadership Summit, October 24–27, 1991, in Washington, D.C. These documents are easily accessible online from Environmental Justice Net at http://www.ejnet.org/ej/.

101. See Biggers, *United States of Appalachia*; Gaventa, *Power and Powerlessness*.

102. See Domhoff, *Who Rules America?*

103. Simon, "Corporate Environmental Crimes."

104. Ibid.

105. Gaventa, *Power and Powerlessness*.

TWO

A Legacy of Extraction
Ethics in the Energy Landscape of Appalachia

BRIAN BLACK

WHEN EUROPEAN AMERICANS FIRST SET FOOT IN
Appalachia, they discovered a land rich in natural resources. They also observed
the region's American Indian occupants taking full advantage of this great
natural abundance. One resource they depended on was the gooey tar that
seeped through cracks in the earth in what is today northwestern Pennsylvania.
Over many centuries, Indian groups from Midwestern settlements stopped
regularly in this section of Appalachia to collect the tar-like oil for use as a skin-
coloring agent. They built cribbed pits that allowed oil to trickle out slowly and
accumulate over time. When they returned months later by boat, they used
blankets and containers to extract the oil. These Paleoindians collected only
enough to satisfy their needs. Their pattern of use—their ethic—was one of
inconspicuous consumption. The humans who arrived later would not be so
patient. Nor would their demands be satisfied so easily.

At first, the arrival of Euro-Americans did little to diminish the supply
of tar and oil. Although these early settlers were well aware that such deposits
existed, they were far more interested in the land's agricultural potential. Not
surprisingly, they judged the oily soils to be of poor quality for agriculture.[1]
Similarly, they paid little attention to the other fuel and nonfuel minerals found
throughout the region. More often than not, the Appalachian Mountains were

viewed in a negative light—as an impediment to movement and settlement. Indeed, the area of scattered settlement along the mountain range emerged as one of the first bona fide American frontiers by the late 1700s.

Industrialization changed everything. By the second half of the nineteenth century, coal, and later petroleum, had become America's fuels of choice—minerals that could be extracted from the earth and burned to generate power and profits. No longer treated as obstacles, the Appalachian mountain chain was now viewed as a great vault for carbon. Acquiring these fuel resources in sufficient quantities took time and required a complete reorganization of human activities and living patterns. This shift toward industrialization represents one of the great technological undertakings of human history. Although remarkable innovations converted inanimate energy into products of all types, at the most basic level industrialization was constructed on a foundation of shifting priorities and ethics. In addition to the remarkable social and commercial accomplishments of this era, the transformation of the Appalachians into the nation's greatest energy landscape also came with significant residual costs attached. Appalachia's energy landscape is one of the clearest expressions of a specific American environmental ethic: extraction.

Geographer Martin Pasqualetti has written generally about energy landscapes as an artifact of past cultural ethics and decision making. The importance of energy landscapes does not stop there. They help us create and organize a continuum of past decisions that might influence future alternatives. "Energy landscapes," he writes, "will continue to be compelling and in places dominating components of the earth's surface, and our reactions to them will continue coloring and steering our energy decisions, the direction and support of our technological research, the degree of land disruption we accept, and to some degree the nature of how we live our lives. The visibility of these landscapes, their scale and spread, and the frustration and intimidation we can feel in their presence has had a growing influence on our future energy decisions." As such, the Appalachians are closely tied to a broad swath of American energy history. They also hint at its energy future. Pasqualetti argues that the policy choices we make as a nation are often partly a "response to the landscape changes we see."[2]

Even so, a key feature of energy landscapes is separation. Whether a product of zoning, residential preference, or the supply of raw material, most often landscapes of energy production are not seen by most consumers. Mining operations are often carefully separated from population centers by design and by chance. To residents of the Appalachians, though, layers of American energy history are all too observable. By organizing this continuum of energy harvest in Appalachia, this essay seeks to close the gap between consumers of energy and this remarkable place that has provided Americans with power for generations.

The Ethic of Extraction

When European settlers arrived in America, after 1500, they stepped onto a continent that teemed with one of earth's great mixed forests, covering 360 million acres. Tree sizes during these early years suggest that North America's plant communities were stable and self-replicating ecosystems—they had existed for many years with minimal impact from other species, including humans. In the first decades of continental settlement, fishing yielded massive numbers of salmon, cod, sea bass, haddock, herring, lobster, mullet, crab, oysters, clams, and mussels. Flocks of passenger pigeons were estimated to total two billion birds. There were reports of wild turkeys that stood three feet tall and weighed as much as forty pounds. As settlers moved inland, they encountered a Plains buffalo population that ranged nearly the entire continent and numbered sixty million. Historians now caution that some of this bounty can be traced to the cultural hyperbole of settlers trying to rationalize their own actions and to entice others.[3] However, the natural bounty of North America was irrefutable. And yet, the process of making commodities in the New World had literally only skimmed the surface.

Once populations stabilized in North America, colonists began to view nature less as an enemy and more as an opportunity. Through the models of mercantilism and capitalism and the sacrifice of generations of settlers, the natural resources of North America could be converted into commodities to fuel a new economy. The formation of this unique American society, of course, begins in the late 1700s. The ideas of John Locke and Adam Smith organized the use of the natural environment in profoundly new ways: a beaver became a pelt, a white pine became a ship's mast, and a parcel of land became a source of food and trade. For resources to be construed as valuable, they needed to be linked to larger markets. Locke writes, "For I ask, What would a Man value Ten Thousand, or a Hundred Thousand Acres of excellent *Land*, ready cultivated, and well stocked too with Cattle, in the middle of the in-land Parts of *America*, where he had no hopes of Commerce with other Parts of the World, to draw *Money* to him by the Sale of the Product?"[4] Inherent in Locke's observation is the assertion that land had value—value that might be increased with proper "improvement." One of these forms of improvement, of course, was to link areas and resources into larger economic networks of trade. Although these essential ideas would undergird development in America through the nineteenth century, in the late 1700s Americans had just scratched the surface—quite literally—of North America's economic potential.

This same spirit of development spurred nineteenth-century Americans to dig below the land's surface in order to access the carbon-based resources packed away by the forces of geology. Ground zero for this effort was the Appalachian Mountains, with their abundant mineral resources. By 1820 an interest in energy production drew developers to the Appalachians. While many communities were designed to extract coal and other minerals, none did so like the town of Mauch Chunk, Pennsylvania, now known as Jim Thorpe. The town was built to demonstrate industrial processes to others involved in industry as well as to the general public. It was a celebration of extraction.

Mauch Chunk was owned and developed by the Lehigh Coal and Navigation Company from 1818 to 1831. If anthracite coal had not been found, the town of Mauch Chunk would have been much different. But in 1791, Philip Ginter discovered coal on Sharp Mountain. Then, in 1818, the Lehigh River became the center of anthracite transportation and Mauch Chunk emerged as an integral link along this shipping corridor. Roads were constructed to connect the primary coal mine to the river. In 1827 a new era in technology was ushered in when the wagon road was transformed into a gravity railroad. One of the nation's first small-scale rail lines, Mauch Chunk's railroad became known as the Switchback Gravity Railroad. From the mine's location at a higher elevation, the coal could then travel down the mountain by means of gravity. The empty cars were then hauled up the mountain by mules.[5]

All the coal from Summit Hill and Panther Valley arrived at the canal landing in this fashion. Then, in 1872, a large tunnel opened that ended the need for the gravity railroad. At approximately the same time, the gravity railroad was replaced for coal hauling by the steam locomotive–powered Panther Creek Railroad. This, however, did not end the gravity line's history. In 1874 developers purchased the switchback gravity railroad and made it the centerpiece attraction in Mauch Chunk, the tourist attraction of the industrial era. Eventually, the switchback railroad inspired the developers of roller coasters.

Historian John F. Sears contrasts Mauch Chunk with Niagara Falls, the other great tourist attraction of the Northeast, while also making an important statement about nineteenth-century tourists' interest in visiting industrial sites: "At Niagara Falls industry intruded on visitors' expectations of what they had come to see, but at Mauch Chunk it was an integral part of the scene."[6]

Historian David Nye refers to this attraction to a blighted landscape as the industrial or technological sublime.[7] For a nation emphasizing the development of its resources, extraction was a symbol of prosperity. An energy landscape such as Mauch Chunk flaunted the industrial future for all its visitors; however, it was an exception. Throughout Appalachia, companies located supplies of energy-producing minerals and devised methods and practices for quickly extracting them.

The scale and scope of this action overwhelmed knowledgeable observers such as the Vermont statesman George Perkins Marsh, a trained geographer. While acknowledging the need for human use of the natural environment, Marsh used his 1864 book *Man and Nature* to take Americans to task for their misuse and mismanagement of their national bounty:

> Nature, left undisturbed, so fashions her territory as to give it almost unchanging permanence of form, outline, and proportion, except when shattered by geologic convulsions. . . . In countries untrodden by man, the proportions and relative positions of land and water . . . are subject to change only from geological influences so slow in their operation that the geographical conditions may be regarded as constant and immutable. Man has too long forgotten that the earth was given to him for usufruct alone, not for consumption, still less for profligate waste. . . . But she has left it within the power of man irreparably to derange the combinations of inorganic matter and of organic life. . . . Man is everywhere a disturbing agent. Wherever he plants his foot, the harmonies of nature are turned to discords. . . . Of all organic beings, man alone is to be regarded as essentially a destructive power.[8]

Ironic?

In this passage, Marsh introduces an alternative ethic for land use. Radical for his time, Marsh's assessment foreshadows the words of historian William Cronon, who would observe over a century later, "Ecological abundance and economic prodigality went hand in hand: the people of plenty were a people of waste."[9]

The disturbance of the Appalachians by humans over the course of the next century and a half helped to power the economic development of the United States. The scars of this development also revealed the remarkable prescience of Marsh's perspective. Marsh was the first voice to openly suggest that there were alternative ethics for land use other than development and extraction. Later scholars shaped the field of environmental ethics. Of particular importance, during the same general time period that Americans constructed the Empire State Building, Hoover Dam, and some of the nation's early highways, a former Forest Service employee named Aldo Leopold penned an ethic that would inspire environmentalists for generations. Leopold's words suggested a new way of looking at humanity's place in the natural environment: "In short, a land ethic changes the role of *Homo sapiens* from conqueror of the land-community to plain member and citizen of it. It implies respect for his fellow-members, and also respect for the community as such."[10] Although this perspective draws inspiration from nineteenth-century romanticism, Leopold's "land ethic" was grounded in the new scientific understandings of the mid-twentieth century. Just as engineers taught us new, innovative ways to solve everyday problems, scientists, writers, and naturalists took the opportunity to better explain and consider the complexity of the human condition, particularly as it related to the natural world.

From these roots, contemporary scholars of philosophy have cordoned off a sphere of ethics organized around patterns and the extent of environmental impact and use. All societies practice environmental ethics. Some are more in tune with the limits and needs of the natural world, while others are less so. In contrast to Leopold's writing, the ethic for some cultures is to give no standing whatsoever to the natural world—they believe that natural resources exist solely for the use of humans. As Americans have tied land use so closely to capitalist ideas of profit over the last century, we have witnessed a dramatic increase in our ability to impact Earth. In certain areas of focused use, the severity of this impact has ushered in an entirely new range of environmental ethics that may leave resources or even entire regions permanently altered and, in some cases, uninhabitable for life.

There remains abundant life in the Appalachians. However, industrialization exacted a severe toll on these mountains that continues to play out today. I have given the ethic behind this land use a name: the ethic of extraction.[11] To varying degrees, many locales within the Appalachians have been subject to this ethic as their valuable minerals have been extracted particularly as a source of energy to help power the tremendous growth of the United States during the past century. The ethic of extraction expedites the acquisition of these energy resources over all other priorities, including the viability of human and animal communities, long-term habitation of the region, and the impact to the existing landscape. The spread of the ethic of extraction has often made the mining regions of Appalachia appear as a unique landscape of energy. For once we consider the entire life cycle of our high-energy existence, we recognize that it is a process that begins with extraction. Although the benefits are enjoyed widely, the costs are primarily exacted locally.

A market-based system does not allow a valuable item to remain a resource for all to access; instead, it becomes a commodity, which is predicated on and defined by the competition to acquire it. This development is governed by ethics that shape the strategies of companies and communities. The Appalachians have been defined by energy extraction, and thus it follows that the region has practiced an ethic of extraction—a set of strategic decisions that facilitate and simplify the ability of large corporations to mine and remove mineral resources. When the value of these resources became tied to energy production in the early and mid-1800s, greater supply was needed and the ethics of the industry were modified to accommodate and prioritize extraction. Many cultural details that we associate with Appalachia today derive from its transmutation into an energy landscape. This status sets Appalachia apart from any other region in the world.

In the case of the oil collected by Indian visitors, for instance, I am always met by incredulous responses when I ask national and international audiences where the first well of oil was struck. One of the reasons for this surprise is that northwestern Pennsylvania is no longer associated with the commodity that it birthed. This is at least partly related to a major tenet of the ethic of extraction: the flexibility of capital to focus in one locale until its usefulness is completed and then move on. When the companies extracting coal and petroleum have been focused on Appalachia, residents have prospered economically. But times change; for instance, although more coal than ever is taken from Appalachia, increased mechanization has brought significant sociological shifts. In the ethic of extraction, it follows that just as the energy landscape of Appalachia has been defined by active extraction, today much of the region suffers from the residual effects of that ethic, including poverty, abandonment, and pollution. Each of these developments represents a stage in the Appalachians' existence as a landscape of energy.

Boomtowns and the "Drawing Board City"

Cultural geographer John Brinckerhoff Jackson writes, "No group sets out to create a landscape. . . . What it sets out to do is to create a community, and the landscape as its visible manifestation is simply the by-product of people working and living, sometimes coming together, sometimes staying apart, but always recognizing their interdependence." He continues, "It follows that no landscape can be exclusively devoted to the fostering of only one identity."[12] Under Jackson's logic it would seem that a community is incapable of existing where it is organized under a single motivation. No built landscape better exemplifies this logic than the boomtown, particularly those that remain so completely dependent on the single entity under which they have been organized that they cease to exist when it is exhausted. Although many of Appalachia's extractive communities fit into this category, the oil boomtown—and particularly a Pennsylvania town known as Pithole—may best demonstrate the transience that permeates the ethic of extraction.

The development and history of Pithole tries our traditional definitions of terms such as *town, community,* and even *landscape.* Indeed, the place compares most easily to factoryscapes where each person and business relies entirely on the creation of a single product. In essence, the town's reason for being is unequivocally based on a single commodity. Is this then truly a town? Does it have any of the traditional earmarks of a community? And if it is devised on a drawing board by an economic developer interested only in extracting oil from the earth, can it even be called a culturally created landscape? Yet it is through exactly this testing of definitions that the boomtown phenomenon allows a penetrating foray into the ethics and values of the industry that took shape in the Oil Creek valley after the initial discovery of oil in Titusville, in 1859.

Production in the Oil Creek valley had been so great during the early 1860s that markets could not absorb it. This glut caused a sharp drop in price, which then led to massive abandonment of towns and leases in the region. With oil available in abundance, experiments in illumination and lubrication promised new markets soon. These applications merged with a widening of international markets to revive the industry. Finally, as 1865 began, profits exploded and foreign capital flooded into the area.[13] Petrolia, as the area came to be known, stood poised on the edge of economic boom. To cross that threshold, however, it needed a magnificent attraction to arouse national interest.[14]

With the infusion of investment, speculators began exploring areas beyond Oil Creek. During this 1864–65 push they pressed nearer and nearer to the two Holmden farms along Pithole Creek. Leases were taken out from the Holmden brothers and other surrounding farmers in late 1864.[15] The lessees then banded together to form the United States Petroleum Company. When the region's first well came in, timing was everything. Similar strikes had been made in the Oil Creek valley during the first five years of the oil boom, and boomtowns materialized around them to provide the goods and services that would be needed. When the Union army disbanded, in the early months of 1865, thousands of men flocked to the most likely source of jobs. As if staged as an act in a play, Pithole burst onto the scene, suddenly poised to boom as no town ever had.

By the end of the summer three thousand teamsters were on hand to drive the oil out of the Pithole area by wagon.[16] The only buildings in the immediate vicinity were the homes of the two Holmden brothers and a log cabin known as Widow Lyon's house. Such a setting left hordes of visitors and workers with no place to eat or stay. The Holmdens began serving meals to nearly two hundred visitors per day, with workers always eating first. In May 1865, Col. A. P. Duncan and George C. Prather, two businessmen from Oil City, purchased land adjacent to the oilfields. They were not interested in speculating for oil; their interest lay in creating a town to profit from the tremendous surge in local population.

After purchasing the land, Duncan and Prather laid out the drawing board city, and began letting leases. Even the first leases for property in the town reflect the predominance of the ethic of transience. Leases for a store or business cost $50 for six months, $100 per year, renewable for three years. This price allowed the leases to move briskly, but with one catch: at the expiration of the three-year agreement, the lessee had the privilege of removing the buildings that he had constructed or selling them to the owners of the land at the landowner's figure. Even if a business owner thought he or she might not be in this place permanently, they may have wished to have a sturdy or nicely kept building; however, with the knowledge that anything they built would basically return to the landowner from whom they rented, few worthwhile improvements would be made. The entire process of town settlement encouraged the tenant to think in short terms and quick profits.

Like all boomtowns, the community developed in a backward fashion. Whereas many towns settled in the American West put the infrastructure in place first and then developed out of and around it, these oil boomtowns postponed setting up the infrastructure in case the town did not last. For instance, no sanitation system existed in Pithole. "The whole place smells like a camp of soldiers with diarrhea," observed the correspondent for the *Titusville Morning Herald*.[17] Privies were insufficient and poorly maintained. Residents simply tossed garbage out of back doors to decompose. Many observers complained of the rank smell from carcasses of mules and horses discarded in the brush along the edge of roads.

Prices for food and other goods generally ran 15 to 20 percent higher than in Titusville.[18] Except during the apple harvest season, fresh fruit was virtually nonexistent at any price. But it was a lack of water that proved the bane of Pithole's existence. With none of the surface water suitable for human consumption, water became the most valuable commodity in the boomtown. Many of the oil companies privately piped water into their buildings from the nearby hills; however, inhabitants of Pithole were forced to purchase drinking water from peddlers in the streets. The crisis grew worse during September 1865, when water sold for fifty cents a barrel and five cents a pail, with some peddlers charging ten cents a pitcher.

Any symbols of the formation of a standard community, however, were always counterbalanced by the reality that Pithole existed as an oil camp, exceedingly dependent on the oil laborers and the crude that they would generate for lubrication and refinement into kerosene for illumination. By October a line of two-inch pipe had been laid in a trough stretching from Pithole to the Miller farm on the Oil Creek Railroad. A total of three pumps forced through eighty-one barrels of oil an hour, equivalent to three hundred teamsters working ten-hour days. Developers added a fourth pump, which, if run twenty-four hours, increased the capacity of the line to twenty-five hundred barrels a day. Later, a second pipeline was installed along the same path. Generally, oil was transported at $1 per barrel, which compared favorably with the teamster charge. This innovation was a great boon for the efficiency of extraction; however, it forced five hundred teamsters out of work in the first five weeks. Teamsters threatened the developers, sabotaged the line, and even set fire to some of the storage tanks of one company. Finally, with no other alternatives, teamsters cut their prices to $1.25 a barrel.

Regardless, pipelines and other technologies still shared a common weakness with the teamsters: they required a consistent supply of crude oil. By March 1866, Pithole's oil supply dwindled. With Pithole's supply suddenly cut in half, thousands of teamsters and other workers left town. That exodus crushed Pithole's commerce and hopes for permanence. Businesses began closing and services streamlined after only five or six months in existence. Such a fate befell many boomtowns. No effort was made to diversify industry to support the newly unemployed. Industrial rationalization would never allow such humanitarianism to penetrate the utilitarian logic of Petrolia. Pithole existed as the major supplier of oil and the industrial process took shape to get it out of this remote place—if one of these cogs failed, the entire operation would collapse. Like a patient attached to life support, the livelihood of every occupant of this town was directly connected to black gold.

Pithole reached its peak of production in October 1865. On the Thomas Holmden farm, there were eighty-one wells on seventy-nine leases. Only eleven of these wells were actually in production, three of them only marginally. Statistics show that the entire Pennsylvania oil region was producing about nine thousand barrels at this time, of which Pithole accounted for at least six thousand. Of the Pithole supply, over half came from just two wells. In a place where the product had become the rationale for every development, these two wells sustained the largest town in the oil region.

Even during its October peak, few voiced concern about wells running dry. Yet that would only be one of the problems confronting Pithole. From December 1865 through January 1866, Pithole experienced one fire per week. Finally, more than a thousand people gathered in Murphy's Theater to demand the installation of hydrants and the formation of a fire brigade. Their call went unheeded.[19] Arsonists, with a variety of motives, started most fires. The town tried to quash this practice by instituting a lynch law. But Pithole had no ability to cope with a large fire or even to notify its occupants in the event of one's occurrence.

In the end, local apathy and the inability to rally any sort of community sentiment thwarted attempts to stabilize the town. By spring 1866 the fire company had disbanded due to lack of support and interest.[20] Throughout the rest of 1866, Pithole experienced one fire after another. One June blaze claimed twenty buildings in the heart of town. Another fire in early August swept through the oilfields. Total losses were estimated as high as $3 million.[21] It seemed impossible that the town could continue—and indeed it could not.

People left Pithole en masse starting in late 1865. Business owners attempted to sell the grand hotels and found no takers. They held raffles to dispose of the fine properties and again found no takers. Finally, most were abandoned and others sold for scrap. By January 1866 the population had fallen to barely four thousand. Then the oil supply began giving out as well. In February 1867 another fire destroyed almost all the remaining businesses in Pithole. The oil region began a Pithole Relief Fund, and Horace Greeley came to speak on the town's behalf. The *Daily Record* discontinued publication in July 1868; the flash that was Pithole died. Founded on a drawing board in May 1865, the town had boomed and completely busted in little more than three years.

Ironically, the years that Pithole enjoyed success were too short to appear in the census records. In the 1860 census, Pithole, of course, did not exist; in the 1870 census, the town's population was down to 281. Falling between the cracks of the decennial census, the story of Pithole's boom was left to be told by those who lived it and observed it. By August 1877 the court of quarter sessions revoked the borough's charter. Pithole was struck from the face of the earth and ceased to exist.

By the late 1800s developers who had established Pithole within the framework of the ethic of extraction very likely would look at the empty field that was this great producer of the raw material of energy and see a "clean" job. It is just this approach to development, though, that contradicts Jackson's basic observations of community development. When Jackson wrote the following excerpt, he imagined a hypothetical site, possibly a hybrid of many. His insights, however, serve as an epigraph for a landscape that never fit his definition of community: "[The] condition of being part of nature brings with it certain responsibilities and restraints. To damage a system which allows an infinite number of life forms to coexist, to destroy what we cannot possibly replace, would not only be irresponsible, it would threaten our own survival."[22] The harvest of the Appalachians' bountiful energy resources has produced many communities with similarities to Pithole. Guided by the ethic of extraction, land use has often dominated and overwhelmed criteria such as long-term community development.

The Complex Landscape of Coal

Petroleum may strike readers as an unexpected chapter in Appalachia's energy story. Coal is the resource most identified with the region and its development has followed a similar trajectory. However, coal has proven less flexible and portable and its supplies more persistent and bountiful. In other words, coal culture has not been effaced. In recent decades, coal companies have intensified their extraction practices to keep pace with Americans' growing demand for energy. In the United States, one hundred tons of coal are extracted every two seconds and the residual effect can be seen very clearly on the energy landscape of Appalachia. Around 70 percent of that coal comes from surface mines, which tear away vegetation and soil to access layers of the earth's crust. In recent years, an increasing amount of this coal comes from sites in which entire mountains have been leveled in a process called mountaintop removal.

"Not since the glaciers pushed toward these ridgelines a million years ago have the Appalachian Mountains been as threatened as they are today," notes journalist Erik Reece. When viewed from the air, this mining technique is described by Reece as "ecological violence": "Near Pine Mountain, Kentucky, you'd see an unfolding series of staggered green hills quickly give way to a wide expanse of gray plateaus pocked with dark craters and huge black ponds filled with a toxic byproduct called coal slurry. The desolation stretches like a long scar up the Kentucky-Virginia line, before eating its way across southern West Virginia. Central Appalachia provides much of the country's coal, second only to Wyoming's Powder River Basin."[23]

The ethic of extraction drove the coal industry and helped create the energy landscape described by Reece. Throughout the region and, indeed, the nation, for years smokestacks from electrical and industrial plants emitted pollution into the air but were viewed as a sign of economic progress. In remote areas with few other economic opportunities, coal mining offered the entire community a livelihood. Throughout the nineteenth century and deep into the twentieth, the energy landscape primarily required tunneling into the earth to extract the strips of coal that might be found in the earth's crust. Although inefficient, cheap labor made this mining method cost effective for more than a century. The ethic of extraction did not necessarily prioritize the long-term livelihoods of human workers. From this fairly limited impact on the land, though, the ethic of extraction drove more intensive mining efforts. An interest in efficiency and the cost of mining drove far-flung companies to adopt new technologies and thereby adjust the ethic of extraction to accept more intensive impacts on the coal-bearing Appalachians.

The first innovation allowed miners to strip the top off the land in order to mine into the earth. By decreasing labor costs, surface mining allowed large companies to invest in huge pieces of equipment that transformed the coal-bearing flatlands and hills of the Appalachians into massive quarries. The equipment became an active element of the energy landscape, moving from site to site as needed. Through the mid-twentieth century, the transformation of the Appalachian energy landscape spread rapidly. It did not go unnoticed; in fact, critics began to question the ethic of extraction. Throughout his writing career, essayist Wendell Berry found inspiration in the rural Kentucky environment in which he grew up and lived. He became an outspoken critic of strip mining and other practices that damaged the natural environment.

Berry's calls for action in the 1970s helped fuel the drive to regulate the coal industry. This passage comes from his essay "Mayhem in the Industrial Paradise":

> I have just spent two days flying over the coal fields of both eastern and western Kentucky, looking at the works of the strip miners. . . . In scale and desolation—and, I am afraid, in duration—this industrial vandalism can be compared only with the desert badlands of the West. The damage has no

human scale. It is a geologic upheaval. In some eastern Kentucky counties, for mile after mile after mile, the land has been literally hacked to pieces. Whole mountaintops have been torn off and cast into the valleys. And the ruin of human life and the possibility is commensurate with the ruin of the land. It is a scene from the Book of Revelation. It is a domestic Vietnam."[24]

Criticism and protest brought regulation and reform but little enforcement. Ironically, the ethic of extraction expanded significantly, moving from strip mining to the most damaging mining technique seen yet in the Appalachians: mountaintop removal.

Mountaintop removal is currently being used to mine coal in Kentucky, Tennessee, Virginia, and West Virginia. The name of the process creates a very clear vision of how the work is actually carried out. Computer models and seismographic sensors are used to create a portrait of the geology that underlies the surface of a given area. This image guides the placement of the new mining equipment and allows companies to gauge the size and potential of each layer of coal.

Once a site has been selected, stripping the overburden (forest, topsoil, and sandstone) is the first step. Almost everything that is not coal is pushed down into the valleys below. Along with the decapitation of the mountain itself, the valley filling has significantly altered the appearance of the Appalachians. Over the past few decades, the new practice has destroyed some 450 mountains and summits and impacted several hundred thousand acres of land. Meanwhile, more than twelve hundred miles of streams were buried or polluted between 1985 and 2001, a figure which has surely grown in the last decade.[25]

The impact of these activities has been transformative to the Appalachians and critics have become more vocal in their efforts to control the ethic of extraction. Social and environmental groups, such as Mountain Justice, work hard to expose the injustice spreading across the coalfields of Appalachia. Their primary goal is to cast light on the social costs of these new technologies that require fewer workers. In addition, they endeavor to show the lengths to which coal companies are willing to go to circumvent or even break existing laws. One of the issues that most concerns Mountain Justice is the residue left from washing the coal, which is another portion of the energy landscape.

Each year coal washing produces thousands of gallons of contaminated water that looks like black sludge and contains toxic chemicals and heavy metals. The sludge, or slurry, is often stored behind earthen dams in huge sludge ponds. In Appalachia today, it is estimated that there are seven hundred such impoundment pools. Variously referred to as slurry ponds, sludge lagoons, or waste basins, they impound hundreds of billions of gallons of toxic black water and sticky black goo, byproducts of cleaning coal, mostly from underground mines but also from surface mines.[26]

In one of the worst examples of the ethic of extraction, a series of impoundments broke on February 26, 1972, above the community of Buffalo Creek, in southern West Virginia. Records showed that the Pittston Coal Company had been warned that the dam was dangerous but had chosen to do nothing. Heavy rains caused the pond to fill up, breaching the dam, and sending a wall of black water into the valley below. More than 132 million gallons of wastewater raged through the valley, killing approximately 125 people and causing millions of dollars of damage.

In short, the life cycle of producing energy from coal has compromised the ability of humans and other life forms to reside in the Appalachian coalfields. There have been some efforts to reign in the ethic of extraction. Among the actions taken in the United States to help mitigate effects of mountaintop removal and valley fill procedures was the Surface Mining Control and Reclamation Act of 1977. An effort to alter the reigning ethic of coal mining, the SMCRA requires: that mining sites be restored to their original contours, particularly the sites of surface mining that have experienced radical alteration; that a mining operator submit a plan for restoring the land and for mitigating acid mine drainage before being granted a permit to begin mining operations; and that a fund be established to finance the restoration of old abandoned mines by imposing a tax on current coal production. In theory, the SMCRA required companies to establish the approximate original contour (AOC) of a site before mountaintop removal so that restoration or development could take place rapidly after mining was complete. Researchers have demonstrated that the majority of permits are not providing AOC information before development.[27]

One of the most problematic features of the Appalachian energy landscape, abandoned mines, can be found in over twenty-nine states and tribal lands. The U.S. General Accounting Office (now called the Government Accountability Office) has estimated that there are 560,000 abandoned mines on federal lands in the United States. In the state of Pennsylvania alone, 5,600 of the 9,000 known abandoned mines are considered threats to human health or to environmental quality.[28] More than $1.5 billion has been spent since 1977 restoring abandoned mines; two-thirds of the funds have been spent in four states: Kentucky, Pennsylvania, West Virginia, and Wyoming.[29]

Another severe problem is <u>acid mine drainage</u>. After a coal mine has been abandoned, the acid runoff can dissolve heavy metals such as copper, lead, and mercury that then leach into ground and surface water. Environmental effects of acid mine drainage include contamination of drinking water and disruption of growth and reproduction in aquatic plants and animals. Treating the problem is time consuming and expensive and creates vast treatment pools that have now been incorporated into the Appalachian energy landscape.[30]

Particularly in the nature of coal's life cycle, we find the full implications of a region's administration through the ethic of extraction. As Americans begin to consider new models of energy development, one view toward the future again passes through these mountains.

Beyond the Ethic of Extraction

We are used to seeing propeller blades spin, whether they are attached to the chassis of a helicopter or an airplane. Nevertheless, it is unnerving today to see the ridges of Pennsylvania's Allegheny Mountains lined with some of the largest propellers humans have ever constructed: Will they be strong enough to lift the long, slight, tree-covered ridges? Is that the intention? After years of being mined to provide coal for energy production, these mountains may now play another role—while still figuring prominently in America's energy future.

During the industrial era, Pennsylvania produced millions of tons of coal and introduced the world to petroleum. <u>The extraction of these two resources helped define the mountain range as a complex landscape of energy.</u> Today, Pennsylvania remains one of the nation's largest producers of anthracite, or hard coal, though its petroleum production has dwindled. Now, however, a new energy source has materialized: hundreds of wind turbines have been built throughout the state and a number of international manufacturers of wind turbines have made Pennsylvania their U.S. headquarters. One university, surrounded on every side by the Appalachians, has begun the nation's first degree program for windsmiths, the professionals who oversee the turbines.

The turbine-decked mountains provide evidence that help to prove a fact about the first decade of the twenty-first century: Americans are fully engaged in a significant and potentially seminal energy transition. The energy transition initiated in the 1970s did not immediately change American attitudes regarding renewable energy. For many observers, this represents a failure of our species to pursue softer energy paths. While correct on one level, this perspective fails to appreciate the cultural nuance of energy transitions.

[handwritten margin note: and started or addiction?]

From a historical standpoint— one that speaks in terms of centuries and even millennia—an intrinsic shift in the habits of the human species can drag on for decades and even centuries. Clearly, we are in the midst of an energy transition that very likely began thirty years ago. And it may continue for decades longer. This transition is clearly reflected in Appalachia's energy landscape.

Recent years seem to have introduced this moment when the energy transition reached its next, more clear-cut path to the future. The primary impetus has been rising energy prices, particularly for petroleum. This time, the scarcity concern grows not from temporary political instability abroad; instead, the bona fide scarcity concern grows from the geological idea of peak oil and an increasingly competitive marketplace as China and India emerge as energy-hungry aspirants to industrial development. Higher prices for traditionally cheap fuels have combined with the increasing likelihood that carbon accounting in future years will raise prices even further, to make renewable energy sources more competitive than ever in the energy marketplace. The paradigm of cheap energy that forced the title *alternative* on renewables decades ago has been shaken to the point of fracture. Our future energy paradigm, most experts agree, is in play and possesses the potential to shift the playing field considerably.

We have learned a great deal from the ethic of extraction and what it has wrought on the Appalachians and other locales. The serious development of the Appalachians as a windfield is one outcome of these lessons. In addition, Appalachian residents, worn by residual pollution from mining, have found reasons to suspect the turbines' impact on their ridges. Visual blight and noise and increased bird deaths have been the primary criticisms leveled against the power-producing turbines. However, even proud residents of the Appalachians must admit that, unlike some other mining techniques deriving from the ethic of extraction, wind development leaves the ridges intact, allowing them to become a vital component of a revolutionary new landscape of energy.

Notes

1. For a full description of settlers' reactions, see Brian Black, *Petrolia: The Landscape of America's First Oil Boom* (Baltimore: Johns Hopkins University Press, 2003).

2. Martin Pasqualetti, "Energy Landscapes and the Growth of Arizona," in *Building to Endure: Design Lessons of Arid Landscapes*, ed. Paul Lusk and Alf Simon (Albuquerque: University of New Mexico Press, 2009), 43.

3. This material is drawn from Theodore Steinberg, *Down to Earth: Nature's Role in American History*, 2d ed. (New York: Oxford University Press, 2009).

4. Quoted in William Cronon, *Changes in the Land: Indians, Colonists, and the Ecology of New England* (New York: Hill and Wang, 2001), 79, emphasis in original.

5. John F. Sears, *Sacred Places: American Tourist Attractions in the Nineteenth Century* (New York: Oxford University Press, 1989), 191–92.

6. Ibid.

7. David Nye, *American Technological Sublime* (Cambridge, MA: MIT Press, 1996), 25–27.

8. George Perkins Marsh, *Man and Nature; Or, Physical Geography as Modified by Human Action* (1864; repr., Cambridge, MA: Harvard University Press, 1965), 29–30.

9. Cronon, *Changes in the Land*, 170.

10. Aldo Leopold, *A Sand County Almanac, and Sketches Here and There* (New York: Oxford University Press, 1987), 240.

11. This is described with more depth in Black, *Petrolia*.

12. John Brinckerhoff Jackson, *Discovering the Vernacular Landscape* (New Haven: Yale University Press, 1984), 12. The natural environment bears little pertinence in Jackson's landscape hierarchy unless it is set off by human boundaries for a cultural reason, such as preservation or conservation.

13. *Oil City Register*, November 24, 1864.

14. Black, *Petrolia*, 35–38.

15. Lease, Thomas Holmden to James Faulkner, Jr. Venango County Deed Book Z, 19, recorded May 2, 1864.

16. *Titusville Morning Herald*, August 16, 1864; *Pithole City Directory*, 1865–66, 6.

17. *Titusville Morning Herald*, July 29, 1865.

18. *New York Herald*, July 20, 1865.

19. *Pithole Daily Record*, throughout early January 1866.

20. Ibid., April 4, 1866.

21. Ibid., August 3, 1866.

22. Jackson, *Vernacular Landscape*, 40.

23. Black, *Petrolia*, 202.

24. Wendell Berry, "Mayhem in the Industrial Paradise," in *A Continuous Harmony: Essays Cultural and Agricultural* (New York: Harcourt Brace, 1975), 174–76.

25. http://ilovemountains.org/resources/ (accessed October 8, 2010).

26. http://www.coalimpoundment.org/aboutimpoundments/facts.asp (accessed September 2010). Discussion of this issue can also be found in the documentary film *Coal Country*.

27. See, for instance, Ken Ward Jr., "Using Documents to Report on Mountaintop Mining," Nieman Reports, http://www.nieman.harvard.edu/reportsitem.aspx?id=100812.

28. Yuri Gorokhovich, Matthew Reid, Erica Mignone, and Andrew Voros, "Prioritizing Abandoned Coal Mine Reclamation Projects within the contiguous United States using Geographic Information System Extrapolation," *Environmental Management* 32, no. 4 (2003): 527.

29. For instance, see the description of these efforts in John Opie, *Nature's Nation: An Environmental History of the United States* (New York: Harcourt Brace, 1998).

30. See, for instance, Chad Montrie, *To Save the Land and People: A History of Opposition to Surface Coal Mining in Appalachia* (Chapel Hill: University of North Carolina Press, 2003).

THREE

Pollution or Poverty

The Dilemma of Industry in Appalachia

NANCY IRWIN MAXWELL

DISCUSSIONS ABOUT ENVIRONMENTAL JUSTICE IN
Appalachia often focus on resource extraction, in particular coal mining and its
legacy of contamination. However, there is general consensus among those who
study Appalachia that residents of the region bear substantial environmental
burdens beyond those associated with coal mining, including heavy industry
and waste management. To date, little quantitative analysis has contributed to
discussions about disproportionate impacts from industry in Appalachia.

Advocates for environmental justice seek to eliminate disparities in exposures, and thus the first step is to identify where these disparities exist. This is
generally accomplished by comparing exposures and outcomes between populations, such as those people who live in Appalachia and those who do not.
While this type of comparison is one focus here, this chapter also contributes
to the discussion of environmental injustice *within* Appalachia. This is accomplished by exploring connections between socioeconomic measures, on the one
hand, and markers of industrial pollution or its estimated health impacts, on
the other. Further, this work broadens the discussion of environmental injustice by incorporating information on overall mortality, as the most basic indicator of population health. In so doing, this work lays the foundation for future
study of relationships between environmental factors and health in Appalachia.

The conclusions below are drawn from an analysis of a data set that includes ten-year-old census data. As most readers know, there have been significant changes in the U.S. economy since 2000. Unemployment has climbed, along with poverty rates, and manufacturing and industrial jobs continue to decline. Though 2010 census data are not yet available, it seems likely that the trends uncovered in this analysis have become more pronounced for people living in Appalachia, where poverty and unemployment rates have reached unprecedented levels.

Like any analysis that rests on data for places and populations rather than individual people, this one is fundamentally descriptive, and even exploratory. As such, it does not attempt to document cause-and-effect relationships. The analytic approach is not "let's formulate a hypothesis and then test it," but rather "let's see what the data can tell us." The result is a detailed portrait of a region, its population, and its environment that can be a starting point for further discussion about environmental justice related to industry.

The Appalachian Context

A large array of publicly available information was compiled into a coherent data set for 3,144 counties of the United States, including the District of Columbia and a number of independent cities that are treated as counties. With this data set in hand, it was possible to undertake a unified set of analyses that spanned a range of topic areas including environmental and health disparities. Most of the discussion that follows focuses on describing the counties in the Appalachian region (AR), which straddles thirteen states and comprises 413 counties plus eight independent cities in Virginia.[1]

In order to examine social patterns in the burden of industrial pollution within the Appalachian region, it is useful to consider how the region has been described by the institutions and organizations most involved in addressing its concerns. Several groupings of AR counties have been put forward by scholars of Appalachia, some defining geographically contiguous subregions and others classifying counties without regard to contiguity. Figure 3.1 classifies the region according to categories developed in 1975, ten years after the Appalachian region was created. In a system that is still in use today, the Appalachian Regional Commission (ARC) classified the region's counties into three geographic subregions for purposes of development planning—the Northern, Central, and Southern subregions.

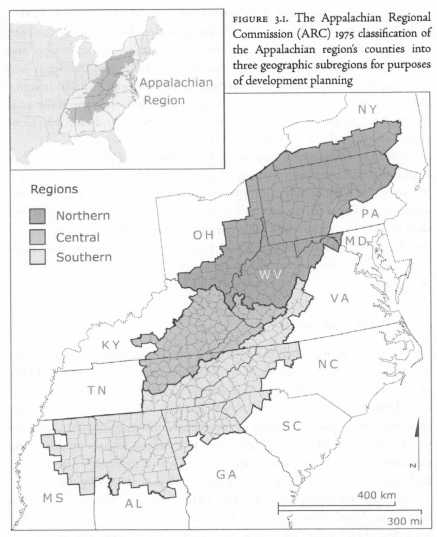

FIGURE 3.1. The Appalachian Regional Commission (ARC) 1975 classification of the Appalachian region's counties into three geographic subregions for purposes of development planning

Taking a different approach, John Alexander Williams relied on environmental and social history to define a core region of 165 Appalachian counties.[2] In Williams's anthropological categorization, the core region comprises the Allegheny/Cumberland, Great Valley, and Blue Ridge subregions (see fig. 3.2). In this map, the Great Valley and Blue Ridge subregions in particular reflect prominent topographic features.

Another categorization is based on a recent analysis by the U.S. Population Reference Bureau, which assessed five subregion classifications, including the

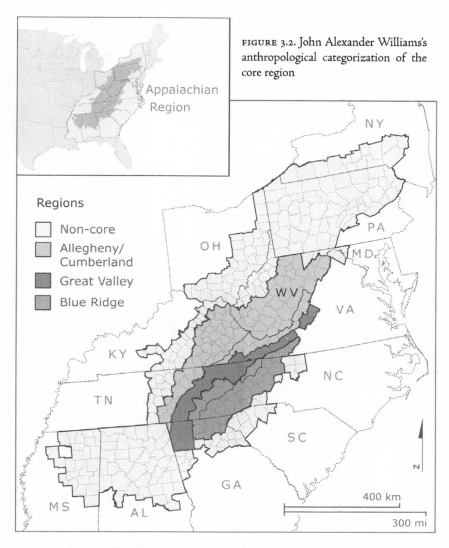

FIGURE 3.2. John Alexander Williams's anthropological categorization of the core region

traditional ARC classification, and identified one of the alternative schemes, which reflects economic patterns in the Appalachian region, as the preferred classification (see fig. 3.3).[3] In defining the West Central subregion in this scheme, the Population Reference Bureau made use of work by the ARC, which has annually classified the Appalachian region's counties by economic status relative to U.S. counties nationwide. The exact method has evolved from year to year, but fundamentally three measures of economic distress are compiled for all counties: three-year average unemployment rate, per

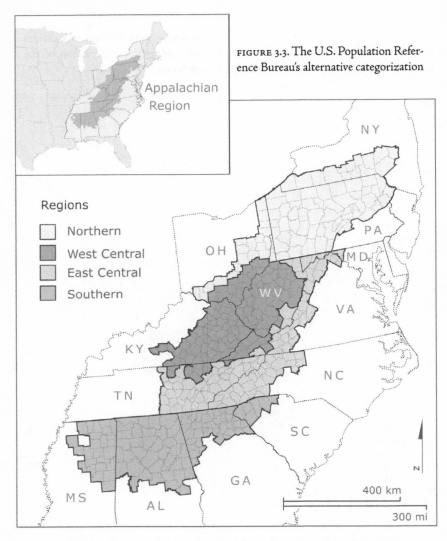

FIGURE 3.3. The U.S. Population Reference Bureau's alternative categorization

capita market income, and poverty rate. Then, based on these three measures, individual Appalachian counties are classified as either distressed, transitional, competitive, or attainment.[4]

The Population Reference Bureau's innovation in defining subregions of the AR resulted in a hub of distressed counties in the West Central subregion, a region that historically depended on coal mining and has suffered from that industry's decline.[5] The use of economic data in this classification scheme also results in a string of nondistressed counties in Ohio being assigned to the

Northern subregion. Like the traditional subregion classification, the bureau's scheme defines Northern and Southern subregions, but it sets their boundaries differently—specifically, it mirrors the intuitive understanding that the heart of Appalachia does not extend either into the states of the old Deep South (Alabama, Georgia, Mississippi, South Carolina) or those north of the Mason-Dixon Line (which runs westward along the southern border of Pennsylvania). The East Central subregion embraces many of the counties in Williams's Blue Ridge and Great Valley subregions. Finally, a strictly economic classification from the USDA's Economic Research Service categorizes all U.S. counties according to the economic sector on which they are most dependent: farming, mining, manufacturing, government, services, and a residual nonspecific category.

Among the three classification systems that create geographically contiguous subregions (see figs. 3.1–3.3), both the Population Reference Bureau and Williams classifications offer the advantage of splitting the Western subregion, as traditionally defined by the ARC, into two subregions. However, the noncore counties of the Williams classification do not themselves form a meaningful group. Thus the remainder of this chapter makes use of these two schemes for classifying the counties of the Appalachian region into subgroups:

The U.S. Population Reference Bureau's set of four contiguous geographic subregions: Northern, West Central, East Central, and Southern Appalachia (fig. 3.3); and

The Economic Research Service's grouping by economic sector on which the county is most dependent.

The Appalachian region now embraces 421 (or 413) counties. The last three counties, all in Ohio, were added in 2008, after the regional classifications described above had been completed. In subgroup analyses, these three counties have been assigned to the Northern subregion in the Population Reference Bureau classification, since their location makes this unambiguous; however, they are omitted from the analyses based on economic status, since they entered the Appalachian region after the most recent economic classification of counties by the ARC.

Because the analysis uses publicly available data, the measures used to represent the burden of environmental pollution or occupational exposure are neither exposure estimates nor measured concentrations of chemicals in environmental media. Rather, these variables are used as proxies for pollution and, indirectly, for exposure. For example, assuming that pollution levels are related to production amount and value, the total value of manufactured products shipped in a given year serves as a rough proxy for manufacturing pollution. Similarly, the percentage of workers who are employed in a specific industry serves as a proxy for possible workplace exposures in a county.

Research quantifying environmental injustice generally involves analyzing demographic variables in the context of the geography of environmental burdens. In this case the geographic context is defined as the Appalachian region of the United States. The data used here represent information in five key areas: (1) urbanization, (2) demographic markers of social disadvantage, (3) the burden of environmental pollution or occupational exposure, (4) the estimated health impacts of air pollutants, and (5) overall mortality rate.

URBAN INFLUENCE

Urban influence is a measure used by regional planners to distinguish between economies of different sizes. This concept is useful because counties that are in or near urban centers have access to a wider range of economic activities than those located in areas with less urban influence. Some of those activities, of course, create pollution. It is important to take account of differences in urban influence when comparing measures of industrial activity or pollution in AR counties to those in other U.S. counties. Since the AR counties, as a group, are less urban than the counties that make up the rest of the country, we might expect to see less industrial activity and pollution in AR counties overall, especially in terms of vehicle pollution. Thus, the question of interest is, how do industrial activity and pollution compare in AR and non-AR counties *with the same degree of urbanization?*

To make such a comparison, these analyses make use of an existing classification of U.S. counties by degree of urban influence. Using 2000 census data, the Economic Research Service (ERS) has classified all U.S. counties into twelve categories representing degree of urban influence based on population size.[6] The twelve categories can be further reduced to three: large metropolitan (located in a large metropolitan area of 1 million or more residents), small metropolitan (metropolitan area of less than 1 million), or nonmetropolitan. Nonmetropolitan counties are categorized as either micropolitan or noncore, based on their proximity to metropolitan areas and the size of their population. For the purpose of this discussion, the nonmetropolitan counties are considered rural, even though there may be some urban influence.

SOCIAL DISADVANTAGE

Social disadvantage is a function of numerous societal influences that may be reflected in demographic data. Table 3.1 summarizes data on demographic characteristics, compiled and made available by the U.S. Census Bureau.[7] Basic demographic data, including population and median age in each county, are the starting point for a description of the region's population. Socioeconomic measures including per capita income, poverty and unemployment rates, and education are indicators of social disadvantage. In addition, characteristics of the housing stock that reflect economic realities in communities are included. Because environmental justice is the theme of this book, data on the presence of racial or ethnic minorities and immigrants are included in the analysis of social disadvantage. Finally, the data set also includes variables that represent the presence of vulnerable subpopulations—the percentage of the elderly population who live in poverty, and the percentage of children and youth who live in poverty.

TABLE 3.1. **U.S. census data used in environmental justice analysis**

Basic population data

    Resident population, 2000 (complete count)
    Median age of resident population, 2000

Socioeconomic status

    Per capita personal income, 1999
    Percentage of population living below poverty level, 1999
    Percentage of civilian labor force unemployed, 2000
    Percentage of persons 25 years and over with high school diploma or higher, 2000
    Percentage of persons 25 years and over with bachelor's degree or higher, 2000
    Percentage of housing units that are owner occupied, 2000
    Percentage of housing units that are mobile homes, 2000

Race/ethnicity/immigrant status

    Percentage white, 2000
    Percentage black or African American, 2000
    Percentage American Indian and Alaska Native alone, 2000
    Percentage Hispanic or Latino, 2000
    Percentage Asian, Native Hawaiian, or Other Pacific Islander, 2000
    Percentage of population foreign born, 2000

Vulnerable subpopulations

    Percentage of population 65 years and over living below poverty level, 1999
    Percentage of children under 18 years living below poverty level, 1999

ENVIRONMENTAL POLLUTION

Environmental and health data were compiled from a variety of sources including the U.S. Environmental Protection Agency (EPA), the U.S. Census Bureau, the Economic Research Service, and the U.S. Energy Information Administration. Table 3.2 groups the environmental health indicators into three types: measures that relate to environmental pollution or potential occupational exposures; measures that relate to population-level health impacts, such as cancer, that have been estimated for specific air pollutants; and measures of mortality as a direct, if crude, indicator of overall population health. All measures of industry represent not only manufacturing industry, but also electricity generation.

In addition to data on manufacturing production and employment, the Toxics Release Inventory (TRI) gives more direct indicators of industrial pollution. The TRI is an annual report published by the EPA that summarizes self-reported releases of several hundred toxic chemicals from industrial facilities. The intent of the TRI is to pressure industry to reduce chemical releases simply by making data on those releases available to the public. The TRI presents pounds of pollution emissions to air, surface water, land, and underground injection, as well as total emissions, in each county.

Even though some of the pollution is emitted on the sites of the facilities that report in the TRI, and other pollution is moved from those sites, it is the total amount emitted that is of interest to environmental justice advocates. These advocates often use the TRI data as evidence that there are disproportionate exposures to pollution that affect the areas closest to the facilities. With this in mind, the total reported releases are used as a simple marker of the scale of industrial pollution in each county.[8]

Another source of environmental data is the U.S. law commonly known as Superfund (originally the Comprehensive Environmental Response, Compensation, and Liability Act of 1980, and heavily amended in 1986 as the Superfund Amendments and Reauthorization Act). This law set up a system to manage inactive and abandoned hazardous waste sites and created a registry of sites called the National Priorities List (NPL). The NPL identifies sites that are considered the worst hazardous waste locations in the country because of their potential for environmental and human health risks. Each site on the NPL undergoes a long process by which human health risks are estimated and the site is then scheduled for cleanup, with the goal that the cleaned up site would ultimately be removed from the list. Thus the number of sites in this pipeline is ever changing, and sites that have been fully remediated and removed from the list could not readily be included in these analyses. Of the more than twelve

TABLE 3.2. **Data related to environmental and health burdens used in EJ analysis**

Burden of environmental pollution or potential occupational exposure

Intensity of manufacturing
   Total value of shipments (North American Industry Classification System 31–33), 2002

Employment in manufacturing
   Percentage of industrial workers employed in manufacturing, 2002

Releases of toxic chemicals (Toxics Release Inventory)
   TRI on- and off-site disposal or other releases, all chemicals, 2000 (pounds)
   TRI air emissions, all chemicals, 2000 (pounds)
   TRI surface water discharge, all chemicals, 2000 (pounds)
   TRI on-site land releases, all chemicals, 2000 (pounds)
   TRI underground injection, all chemicals, 2000 (pounds)
   TRI transferred off-site to disposal, all chemicals, 2000 (pounds)
   TRI on-site disposal or other releases, all chemicals, 2000 (pounds)

Presence of Superfund site(s), early 2009
   Number of Superfund sites
   Superfund site indicator (0 = no sites; 1 = one or more sites)

Coal-fired power plants
   Total megawatts, coal-fired electricity generation, 2003
   Coal-fired power plant indicator (0 = no plants; 1 = one or more plants)

Estimated health impacts of air pollutants

Nonattainment of federal standards for selected Criteria Air Pollutants
   County attained (0) or did not attain (1) Criteria Air Pollutant standard (PM$_{2.5}$), 2006

Estimated cancer risk, neurological hazard, and respiratory hazard from hazardous air pollutants, 1999
   Total estimated cancer risk
      Percentage of cancer risk attributable to major stationary air pollution sources
      Percentage of cancer risk attributable to other stationary air pollution sources
      Percentage of cancer risk attributable to mobile air pollution sources
      Percentage of cancer hazard attributable to background air pollution
   Total estimated hazard index for neurological effects
      Percentage of neurological hazard attributable to major stationary air pollution sources
      Percentage of neurological hazard attributable to other stationary air pollution sources
      Percentage of neurological hazard attributable to mobile air pollution sources
      Percentage of neurological hazard attributable to background air pollution
   Total estimated hazard index for respiratory effects
      Percentage of respiratory hazard attributable to major stationary air pollution sources
      Percentage of respiratory hazard attributable to other stationary air pollution sources
      Percentage of respiratory hazard attributable to mobile air pollution sources
      Percentage of respiratory hazard attributable to background air pollution

Mortality as an indicator of population health

Overall and infant mortality rates
   Average annual deaths per thousand population, 1997–2003
   Average annual infant deaths per thousand live births, 1997–2003

hundred NPL sites, fifteen straddle two or more counties; in this data set, each of the affected counties is designated as hosting a Superfund site. More often, however, individual counties are host to more than one Superfund site.

The final environmental indicators represent the presence of coal-fired electric power generation, which is an important source of air pollution nationwide. One indicator is a simple yes-no variable indicating the presence of any coal-fired generating capacity in a county. A second variable represents the total generating capacity (in megawatts) in 2003 of coal-fired power plants located in the county—on the assumption that total generating capacity is related to actual power generation, which is related in turn to the amount of coal burned, which is related in turn to emissions.

HEALTH-BASED INDICATORS OF AIR POLLUTION

Air quality is among the most measured environmental indicators, and data are available on common air pollutants such as carbon monoxide as well as hazardous air pollutants, most of which are volatile organic compounds. Furthermore, health risks from exposure to air pollution have been the subject of much research, and known health effects include asthma, chronic obstructive pulmonary disease, and lung cancer. Recently, asthma has become the subject of environmental justice discourse due to its rising prevalence, especially in low-income children, and numerous studies have identified a relationship between asthma and exposure to fine airborne particulates.[9] Because of the known health impacts of fine particulates, a variable representing a concentration of fine airborne particulates that exceeds a health-based standard is used in this analysis. Additional air pollution variables represent estimated health impacts associated with exposure to hazardous air pollutants, including cancer risk and hazard indices for both respiratory and neurological effects.

The health-based limits for air pollution are set by the EPA, and most states have adopted these limits for airborne particulates, along with several other common air pollutants, together designated criteria air pollutants. The limits apply to measured levels of air pollutants, and states work with the EPA to monitor attainment of these levels. A given location, such as a county or a group of adjacent counties, is designated a *nonattainment area* for a given air pollutant if the concentration of the pollutant exceeds the national standards. Monitoring data are readily available for particulates as is the location of nonattainment areas across the country. To give a sense of whether people who live in Appalachia are exposed disproportionately to high levels of particulate air pollution, the data set includes a variable that represents nonattainment status in 2006 on the standard for fine airborne particulates. Because this standard is health-based, the variable represents an exposure that has been deemed unacceptable on public health grounds.

The Clean Air Act also designates 187 hazardous air pollutants (HAPs), which are generally less common and more localized than the criteria air pollutants. These HAPs are considered toxic by the EPA, based on evidence that exposure may cause cancer or other serious health effects. The EPA has completed three national assessments that provide a rich source of data for each U.S. county of the total cancer risk, respiratory hazard index, and neurological hazard index of these airborne pollutants, taken as a group. The present study uses the 1999 national assessment data, which became available in 2006, to match the census year as closely as possible. The data represent the estimated share of the total risk (or hazard) that was attributable to major stationary air pollution sources, other stationary air pollution sources (including coal-fired power plants), mobile air pollution sources, and background air pollution.

In keeping with standard approaches in environmental health, cancer risk is presented as a probability: the estimated lifetime risk of cancer that is attributable to a given exposure. In contrast, the hazard index for a noncancer health effect is the ratio of an estimated dose to a reference dose, which is a dose expected to pose no health hazard. For example, a hazard index of 2.0 means that the estimated dose of chemical X is two times the reference dose for chemical X. It is less clear how to interpret a hazard index that represents the combined effects of multiple chemicals—or how to compare such hazard indices for different locations. Nevertheless, as part of the 1999 assessment, the EPA published summary hazard indices (the sum of the individual hazard indices for multiple air pollutants) for respiratory and neurological effects for U.S. counties. These summary hazard indices are the values included in this data set.

MORTALITY AS AN INDICATOR OF POPULATION HEALTH

Because mortality data is the most basic indicator of the overall health of populations, the data set includes two measures of mortality from U.S. census data. One is the overall death rate (deaths per one thousand population per year) and the other is infant mortality (infant deaths per thousand live births per year). Each of these variables represents average annual mortality between 1997 and 2003, a seven-year period centered on the year 2000. The multiyear period is used because death rates for single years are unstable in small populations and thus the annual fluctuations in the death rate may be substantial. Such instability in the rate makes it difficult to discern patterns in mortality.

A Comparison of AR and Non-AR Counties

The county-level data related to emissions, exposure, and health effects allowed a look at the differences and similarities between the more than four hundred AR counties and the three thousand or so non-AR counties. Not surprisingly, the larger and more geographically widespread set of non-AR counties is much more diverse than the set of AR counties. Although the AR counties are themselves somewhat diverse, they also share certain traits, so it is useful to think of these counties as a discrete group for the purpose of research. The comparison confirmed that AR counties are socioeconomically disadvantaged compared to other U.S. counties. It also revealed that the burden of industrial pollution and the estimated burden of ill health associated with such pollution are surprisingly high in this traditionally rural region. Further, in Appalachian counties located in metropolitan areas, overall mortality is higher than in comparably urban counties elsewhere in the United States.

URBAN INFLUENCE

It should be no surprise that the data show Appalachia to be less urban overall than the rest of the United States. However, it is interesting to note that the proportion of counties designated nonmetropolitan is similar in AR and non-AR counties, at about two-thirds. The difference between the two sets of counties is found in the proportion of large metropolitan counties. Approximately 26 percent of AR counties are small metropolitan and about 8 percent are large metropolitan, compared to 21 percent and 14 percent, respectively, of non-AR counties. This pattern is reflected in the population distributions of the two groups. The population distribution for non-AR counties is highly skewed by those with very large populations, including the home counties of Los Angeles (Los Angeles County, 9.5 million) and Chicago (Cook County, 5.4 million). The AR's most populous county is Allegheny County, Pennsylvania (1.3 million), home to Pittsburgh.

SOCIAL DISADVANTAGE

Appalachian counties are socioeconomically disadvantaged compared to non-AR counties. Within each of category of urban influence, the populations of the AR counties have lower income and less education, higher unemployment, and also higher poverty—not only overall, but also among the elderly and children. According to the 2000 census data there was roughly a $5,000 deficit in per capita income in large metropolitan AR counties (see table 3.3). This difference is significant because greater urban influence suggests more opportunity for economic development, yet even AR counties that are influenced by large metropolitan areas suffer from lower wages than non-AR counties. In addition, in all three strata of urban influence, there is an education deficit and a higher burden of poverty among the elderly in AR counties compared to non-AR counties. The overall consistency of the disparate burden on AR counties is also striking.

Table 3.3 Socioeconomic indicators in AR and non-AR counties

SES indicator (1999–2000)	Large metropolitan counties				Small metropolitan counties				Nonmetropolitan counties			
	AR counties (n = 421)		Non-AR counties (n = 2,723)		AR counties (n = 421)		Non-AR counties (n = 2,723)		AR counties (n = 421)		Non-AR counties (n = 2,723)	
	Mean	Median	Mean	Median	Mean	Median	Mean	Median	Mean	Median	Mean	Median
Per capita income ($)	24,935	23,797	30,179	28,359	22,799	22,938	24,838	24,390	19,691	19,594	21,593	21,366
Population in poverty (%)	11.2	10.8	9.4	8.7	13.8	12.7	12.6	11.6	18.1	16.4	15.2	13.9
Civilian unemployment (%)	3.8	3.7	3.4	3.3	4.3	4.2	4.0	3.7	5.4	5.1	4.5	4.2
Adults with HS education (%)	75.9	77.5	81.7	82.4	75.6	76.5	80.3	81.6	69.0	69.4	77.0	78.9
Adults with bachelor's degree (%)	16.5	15.4	23.6	21.9	15.8	14.6	19.6	18.0	11.6	10.6	14.8	13.7
Elderly in poverty (%)[a]	12.3	10.0	9.1	8.1	12.1	11.3	10.6	9.0	16.5	16.0	13.1	11.6
Children in poverty (%)[b]	13.7	13.2	11.9	10.5	17.3	16.6	15.8	14.2	22.9	20.3	19.3	17.5
Housing units owner occupied (%)	78.1	78.3	72.0	75.5	74.5	75.7	71.6	72.4	77.0	77.7	74.5	75.3
Housing units mobile homes (%)	17.0	15.9	8.3	4.7	16.3	15.8	13.0	10.4	21.2	20.6	15.7	14.2

[a] Over 65 years old.
[b] Under 18 years old.

Housing is another indicator of socioeconomic status, and owner-occupied housing is indicative of higher status levels. The percentage of housing units that are owner-occupied is slightly higher in the Appalachian region, across all three categories of urban influence (table 3.3). At first this may seem counterintuitive because poverty levels are so much higher in the AR counties; however, this pattern is partly explained by the higher percentage of housing units that are mobile homes in the AR.[10] The prevalence of mobile homes in AR counties suggests a lower quality of housing stock than in other counties.

THE BURDEN OF INDUSTRIAL POLLUTION AND OCCUPATIONAL EXPOSURE

The counties of Appalachia bear a substantial burden of pollution related to the presence of manufacturing and the toxic wastes it produces, and of coal-fired power plants. Manufacturing is widespread in Appalachia, and U.S. census data for 2002 indicate that more than 70 percent of AR counties have at least some manufacturing output while only about 56 percent of non-AR counties do. This fact suggests the possibility of a disproportionate burden of industrial pollution in these counties.

Reflecting the broader presence of manufacturing across AR counties, the percentage of workers employed in manufacturing is generally higher in the AR counties than in non-AR counties, both metropolitan and nonmetropolitan. Considering manufacturing employment as a proxy for exposure, this pattern suggests that workers' exposures to occupational hazards associated with manufacturing may be higher in the AR counties.

As expected, the quantity of chemicals released into the environment, as captured in the Toxics Release Inventory, is generally higher—in some cases, much higher—in non-AR counties than in AR counties in most categories. Table 3.4 compares TRI data for AR and non-AR counties, providing mean and median total reported releases and reported releases into the air, into surface water, and on-site. This table breaks down the TRI data by category of urban influence in order to identify the role that proximity to metropolitan areas might play in pollution emissions.

A comparison of TRI releases in AR and non-AR counties by degree of urban influence shows mixed results (see table 3.4). Among large metro counties, the mean total of releases is higher in the AR counties, whereas the median value—which is less influenced by extreme values—is higher in the non-AR counties. Among the small metro counties, the reverse pattern appears. Among the nonmetro counties, both mean and median total releases are higher among

TABLE 3.4. TRI releases in AR and non-AR
counties by degree of urban influence, 2000 (pounds)

		Large metro /AR	Large metro/ non-AR	Small metro/ AR	Small metro/ non-AR	Non metro /AR	Non metro /non-AR
Number of counties		30	310	98	495	209	1,132
Total releases	Mean	6,759,680	3,051,930	2,826,150	4,824,990	1,087,680	2,657,210
	Median	287,360	486,364	1,005,350	500,707	109,113	123,071
Air	Mean	2,496,670	1,227,420	1,970,690	1,223,880	769,992	352,642
	Median	165,003	287,759	417,731	250,503	63,154	60,912
Surface water	Mean	1,308,340	170,593	105,191	108,259	58,380	80,061
	Median	6,812	149	1,889	249	5	—
On-site	Mean	1,030,060	909,526	288,546	2,918,930	175,307	2,023,840
	Median	608	10	100	250	—	—

the non-AR counties. Both mean and median releases are higher among the AR counties in two subcategories: surface water and on-site releases in large metro counties; and air releases in small metro and nonmetro counties.

Within the Appalachian region, there are some counties that have very large quantities of total reported TRI releases. The individual AR counties with the highest total TRI releases in 2000 are roughly evenly divided across the Northern and West Central subregions; none are located in the East Central or Southern subregion. The following counties have the highest levels of total releases as reported in the 2000 TRI:

Northern Appalachian subregion: Jefferson County, Ohio; Butler, Armstrong, and Beaver Counties, Pennsylvania.

West Central Appalachian subregion: Adams and Washington Counties, Ohio.

Like the burden of chemical releases, the burden of Superfund sites is generally heavier outside the Appalachian region. Some 541 non-AR counties (about 20%) and 68 AR counties (about 16%) host one or more of these sites. A total of 18 Appalachian counties are home to more than one site on the list. For example, Broome County, New York, hosts 5 Superfund sites and Cattaraugus

County, New York, and Ashtabula County, Ohio, each host 4 sites. All three of these counties are in the Northern subregion. On the other hand, some non-AR counties bear a much heavier burden of abandoned hazardous waste sites: Santa Clara County, California, has 23 Superfund sites, 12 non-AR counties have 10 to 15 sites each, and 210 non-AR counties have 2 to 9 sites each.

The proportion of counties that host at least one coal-fired power plant is similar in the Appalachian region (17.3%) and outside the AR (14.2%). However, within each category of urban influence the mean coal-fired capacity for AR counties is greater than that for non-AR counties. For example, in large metropolitan counties, the mean generating capacity in the AR counties is 601 megawatts, versus 193 megawatts in non-AR counties. This suggests that the coal-fired plants in Appalachia are much larger than those outside the region. The individual AR counties with the highest coal-fired generating capacity have varied economic bases and are geographically scattered throughout the Northern subregion (Indiana County, Pennsylvania, and Jefferson County, Ohio), West Central subregion (Gallia County, Ohio), and Southern subregion (Bartow County, Georgia).

HEALTH-BASED INDICATORS OF AIR POLLUTION OR ITS EFFECTS

Turning to measures that more directly reflect health, a considerably higher percentage of counties in the Appalachian region, compared to non-AR counties, were classified as nonattainment on the air pollution standard for fine particulates ($PM_{2.5}$, or particulates smaller than 2.5 microns) in 2006. This was true within each category of urban influence and may well be related to the magnitude of coal-fired power in the Appalachian region. Nationwide, 19.7 percent of counties that host at least one coal-fired power plant were out of compliance with the $PM_{2.5}$ standard in 2006, compared to only 4.2 percent of counties with no coal-fired plant.[11]

Overall, the distributions of incremental lifetime cancer risk associated with exposure to HAPs are comparable in AR and non-AR counties. However, the maximum values are somewhat higher in the more numerous and diverse large metropolitan and nonmetropolitan groups of non-AR counties than in their AR counterparts (see table 3.5). The values for the estimated lifetime cancer risk are noted as the chance in one million of getting cancer. So table 3.5 shows, for example, that among large metropolitan counties the median risk of getting cancer from exposure to HAPs is similar in AR counties (24 in one million) and non-AR counties (28 in one million). Although there is no consistent regulatory definition of an acceptable level of cancer

TABLE 3.5. Cancer risk and respiratory hazard index
estimated for exposure to hazardous air pollutants, 1999

| Counties | Estimated lifetime cancer risk (chance of cancer in 1 million) | | | | Respiratory hazard index | | | | |
	25th percentile	Median	75th percentile	Max.	Counties >1.0 (%)	25th percentile	Median	75th percentile	Max.
Large metro/AR	14	24	31	78	94.1	1.82	3.04	5.43	9.63
Large metro/non-AR	18	28	42	140	95.5	2.04	3.67	6.3	29.37
Small metro/AR	17	25	32	76	98.2	1.82	2.42	3.32	8.75
Small metro/non-AR	14	23	31	77	86.6	1.43	2.34	3.47	78.53
Nonmetro/AR	11	13	17	33	76.5	1.02	1.35	1.76	5.87
Nonmetro/non-AR	9	11	15	110	39	0.45	0.83	1.34	14.38

risk, a risk of one in one million has been considered "acceptable" in various environmental health contexts. Thus a median risk of twenty-five in one million, though not a high risk in absolute terms, is twenty-five times greater than might be considered acceptable from a public health standpoint.

As described above, a hazard index is a ratio that compares an estimated dose to an established reference dose for noncancer health effects. The hazard indices listed in table 3.5 are summed across multiple chemicals, but represent a single class of health effect. The respiratory hazard index for exposure to HAPs in 1999 is greater than 1.0 for most U.S. counties. Outside large metropolitan areas, a respiratory hazard index greater than 1.0 is more common in the Appalachian region, especially in nonmetropolitan counties (76.5% of AR counties; 39% of non-AR counties).

The maximum respiratory hazard index for exposure to HAPs is higher in non-AR counties, in each category of urban influence. Tooele County, Utah, is an extreme outlier, with a respiratory hazard index of 78.5. The respiratory hazard index for eight other counties, all outside the AR, is between 15 and 30; all these counties are in New York, New Jersey, or California. Five AR counties have respiratory hazard indices between 7 and 10; all of them are in Georgia, and all except Whitfield County are located on the fringes of metropolitan Atlanta.

In all kinds of communities, mobile sources (vehicles) were the largest contributors to the respiratory hazard index for HAPs in 1999. Major stationary sources (including coal-fired power plants) contribute a larger share of the respiratory hazard in small metropolitan and nonmetropolitan AR counties than in their non-AR counterparts. However, it is clear that coal-fired power does not drive the respiratory hazard associated with HAPs in the same way that it drives nonattainment of the $PM_{2.5}$ standard.

The picture is very different for the estimated neurological impacts of hazardous air pollutants. Hazard indices for neurological effects of exposure to HAPs in 1999 were less than 0.5 for almost all counties nationwide. However, seven counties showed hazard indices ranging from 0.9 to 2.8. One of these, Massac County, Illinois, is outside the Appalachian region. The other six are AR counties that form two geographic clusters, each of which straddles the Ohio River, and thus a state line.

MORTALITY AS AN INDICATOR OF POPULATION HEALTH

Differences in mortality—used here as a proxy for a population's overall health status—suggest that the AR counties bear a somewhat heavier burden of ill health than do their non-AR counterparts. In large metropolitan counties (in both overall and infant mortality) and small metropolitan counties (in overall mortality only), median death rates for AR counties from 1997 through 2003 ran 13 to 17 percent higher than those for non-AR counties.

The Focus within Appalachia

Taking a broad view of all the counties within the Appalachian region, the burden of industrial pollution and its estimated health effects is more pronounced where socioeconomic status is higher. This pattern contrasts with the classic paradigm of environmental injustice, in which poorer populations are more heavily burdened. Further, a comparison of subgroups of AR counties shows that the burden of industrial pollution and its estimated health effects is heaviest in the Northern subregion and among the set of counties that are economically dependent on the services sector.

THE DEMOGRAPHICS OF POLLUTION WITHIN APPALACHIA

A generally consistent pattern of associations emerges in table 3.6, a pattern that is maintained even where the associations are weak: measures of industrial production, its environmental impacts, and its estimated health hazards are all positively associated with indicators of *higher* socioeconomic status, and negatively associated with indicators of *lower* socioeconomic status.[12] That is, within the Appalachian region, industry brings both economic benefits and environmental detriments.

TABLE 3.6 Correlations between select socioeconomic indicators and environmental health indicators in AR counties

	Burden of pollution or occupational exposure			Estimated health impacts			Burden of mortality	
	Value of manufacturing shipments, 2002	Industrial workers in manufacturing, 2002 (%)	Total TRI disposal/ releases, all chemicals, 2000	Total estimated cancer risk	Total estimated respiratory hazard index	Total estimated neurological hazard index	Mean annual overall mortality rate, 1997–2003	Mean annual infant rate, 1997–2003
Per capita income	.57	.14	.45	.64	.5	.49	-.2	-.14
Population in poverty (%)	-.46	-.26	-.3	-.42	-.35	-.34	.27	.17
Elderly in poverty (%)[a]	-.4	.1	-.42	-.56	-.23	-.42	.14	.1
Children in poverty (%)[b]	-.4	-.23	-.25	-.36	-.33	-.27	.36	.23
Civilian unemployment (%)	-.36	-.21	-.13	-.36	-.51	-.26	.46	.21
Adults with HS education (%)	.42	-.3	.46	.6	.26	.47	-.16	-.12
Adults with bachelor's degree (%)	.48	-.2	.36	.6	.46	.43	-.23	-.9
Housing units owner occupied (%)	-.48	-.16	-.33	-.53	-.37	-.38	.7	-.1
Housing units mobile homes (%)	-.47	-.6	-.45	-.57	-.23	-.46	-.03	.12

[a] Over 65 years old.
[b] Under 18 years old.

Because the number of counties in each group is large, even modest correlation coefficients attain statistical significance—that is, they are not likely to be due simply to chance. For this reason, the focus here is on the strength of an association, which reflects its practical significance. Correlation coefficients range from 0 (completely unrelated) to 1.0 (so closely related that one value predicts the other). Using community-level data like these, strong associations (>.7) are unusual except between closely related indicators, such as income and poverty. In this description, correlations with a coefficient of .7 or higher are referred to as *strong*, correlations of .4 to .69 as *moderate*, and correlations in the narrower range of .25 to .39—which in these analyses is the boundary zone where most correlations also shade into statistical nonsignificance—as *weak*. Using this yardstick, the associations between income and education and the environmental impacts are all moderate; indeed, no strong associations emerge from this assessment.

Even though no strong correlations are noted, a consistent relationship between income, education, and industry emerges. Industrial impacts are positively associated with higher income and higher education, and negatively associated with the percentage of the population living in poverty. That is, where income and educational attainment are higher, the value of manufacturing shipments is also higher, as are TRI releases and the estimated health impacts of exposure to hazardous air pollutants.

The pattern seen for markers of *lower* socioeconomic status is just the opposite—and thus the two sets of findings are consistent. For example, where the percentage of the population in poverty is higher, the value of manufacturing shipments is *lower*. The percent of the elderly population living in poverty is negatively associated not only with manufacturing shipments, but also with TRI releases and two indicators of the health impacts of HAPs. Only the civilian unemployment rate is associated with a higher overall death rate.

Associations between a demographic characteristic and an environmental burden that is represented by a yes-no variable must be assessed differently. Boxplots (sometimes called box-and-whisker plots) like those in figure 3.4 are particularly useful in making side-by-side comparisons of characteristics such as income or educational attainment in two groups of counties. For example, in the first plot of figure 3.4a, the boxplot on the left is a visual representation of the per capita incomes of all the counties without coal-fired power plants (as indicated by a 0), and the boxplot on the right is a visual representation of the per capita incomes of all the counties that have at least one coal-fired power plant (as indicated by a 1). The center plot in figure 3.4a compares counties in attainment on the air pollution standard for fine particulates (0)

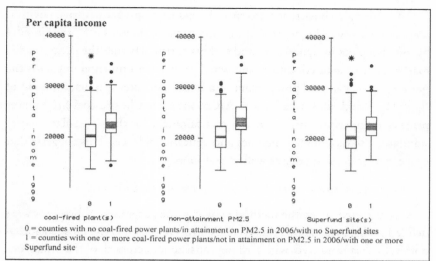

FIGURE 3.4A. Comparison of distribution of income in AR counties without/with coal-fired power plants, in attainment/not in attainment on the PM2.5 standard in 2006, and without/with Superfund sites

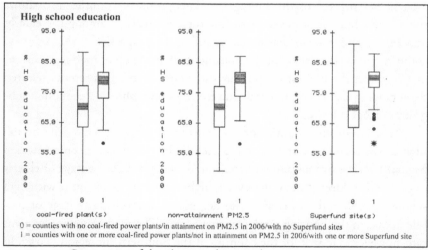

FIGURE 3.4B. Comparison of distribution educational attainment in AR counties without/with coal-fired power plants, in attainment/not in attainment on the PM2.5 standard in 2006, and without/with Superfund sites

to counties not in attainment (1). The right plot shows that the AR counties with Superfund sites (1) have higher per capita incomes, as a group, than the counties without Superfund sites (0).

A strikingly consistent pattern—the association of a negative environmental impact with higher socioeconomic status—emerges from the six side-by-side boxplots in figures 3.4a and b. This is true whether the demographic marker is income or education, and whether the environmental impact is the presence of a coal-fired power plant or a Superfund site, or nonattainment of the $PM_{2.5}$ standard. Overall, those AR counties that host a coal-fired power plant or a Superfund site or are out of attainment for the particulate matter standard, also have higher incomes and educational levels. This suggests that industry breeds prosperity as well as pollution.

SOCIAL DISADVANTAGE WITHIN APPALACHIA

As expected, given the method by which the geographic subregions were defined as discussed above, the West Central subregion is the most socioeconomically disadvantaged, with striking consistency across all of the indicators. These counties, taken as a group, have the lowest per capita income (median $17,844), highest unemployment rate (median 6.0%), and lowest educational attainment (median 63.9% with a high school education, median 9.1% with a bachelor's degree) of the subregions. This group of counties also shows the greatest burden of poverty—in the total population, among the elderly, and among children (medians 21.9, 17, and 27.8%, respectively). Across these counties, the median share of the housing stock made up of mobile homes, at 25 percent, is the highest of the four subregions. Table 3.7 presents selected demographic and environmental data for the geographic and economic subgroups of AR counties.

As a group, the counties of the Northern subregion enjoy the overall highest socioeconomic status, as represented by per capita income (median $22,648), lowest overall poverty rate (11.9%), and lowest percentage of elderly (9.0%) and children (15.6%) in poverty, highest percentage of adults with high school (80.5%) and bachelor's (15%) degrees, and lowest percentage of mobile homes in the housing stock (median 11.9%). The median unemployment rate, however, is lowest for the counties of the Southern subregion (3.9%). In general, the counties of the East Central and Southern subregions are socioeconomically intermediate. However, the Southern counties are more diverse; for example, this subregion includes some high-income counties, as well as most of the counties in the Appalachian region that have substantial African American or Hispanic populations.

Turning to the classification by economic sector, counties dependent on a service economy have the highest socioeconomic status overall, with populations

TABLE 3.7 Selected characteristics of AR counties, by geographic subregion and key economic sector

	Median per capita income, 1999 ($)	Median in poverty, 1999 (%)	One or more Superfund sites, early 2009 (%)	One or more coal-fired power plants, 2003 (%)	Not in attainment on PM$_{2.5}$, 2006 (%)	Median overall mortality rate, 1997–2003	Median infant mortality rate, 1997–2003
By geographic subregion							
Northern	22,648	11.9	37.1	33.7	21.3	10.7	6.9
East Central	21,612	13.8	9.9	15.3	7.2	10.9	7.1
West Central	17,844	21.9	9.4	12.0	12.0	11.4	7.8
Southern	21,074	14.2	12.5	11.5	16.3	10.3	.8
By economic sector on which county is most dependent							
Farming	21,990	13.9	0	0	0	9.5	5.6
Mining	19,032	22.8	3.6	7.1	7.1	11.4	8.7
Manufacturing	21,751	12.9	17.3	14.8	11.2	10.5	7.0
Federal/state government	21,790	15.3	15.2	12.1	6.1	8.8	7.4
Services	25,970	12.1	22.2	27.8	30.6	10.7	6.9
Nonspecialized	21,950	13.0	16.4	23	17.2	10.8	6.7

that are more comfortable economically (median per capita income $25,970; median 12.1% poverty rate overall, 14.5% among children, and 9.7% among the elderly). The populations of service-based counties are also better educated overall (median 81% with high school education and 21% with bachelor's degree). This set of counties also has the lowest proportion of its housing stock in mobile homes (8.2%) and the second-lowest median unemployment rate (3.9%).

Counties dependent on mining stand out as socioeconomically disadvantaged overall, with the lowest median per capita income at $19,032 and the highest median poverty—overall (22.8%), among the elderly (14.4%), and among children (29.4%). Mining counties also have the lowest educational attainment (median 63.8% with high school education and 9.2% with bachelor's degree). Across these counties, a median 25.5 percent of the housing stock is made up of mobile homes.

THE BURDEN OF POLLUTION WITHIN APPALACHIA

The Northern subregion, whose counties enjoy the highest socioeconomic status, is clearly the most heavily burdened by industrial pollution—as represented by manufacturing shipments and TRI releases, as well as the percent of counties hosting Superfund sites and coal-fired power plants, and in nonattainment of the $PM_{2.5}$ standard. Both manufacturing output and manufacturing employment are *lowest* in the West Central subregion. However, the set of six AR counties with elevated neurological hazard indices are all located in the West Central subregion. Among the set of six counties with a hazard index greater than 1.0 for neurological effects, one of the geographic clusters is made up of manufacturing counties (Washington County, Ohio; Wood and Pleasants counties, West Virginia), and the other is made up of economically nonspecialized counties (Lawrence County, Ohio; Boyd and Greenup counties, Kentucky).

MORTALITY WITHIN APPALACHIA

The median overall mortality rate is highest for counties of the West Central subregion, and lowest for counties of the Southern, although the distributions for the four subregions are largely overlapping. The distribution of mortality rates is highest overall among mining counties, and lowest among counties dependent on government services; again, however, there is considerable overlap in the distributions across the six groups. The clearest pattern is the higher annual death rates in less urbanized areas (median 9.35 deaths per thousand per year among the large metropolitan counties, 10.4 among the small metropolitan counties, and 11.1 among the nonmetropolitan counties).

The median infant mortality rate is slightly higher in counties of the Southern and West Central subregions (7.8 per thousand live births per year), and lower in the counties of the Northern and East Central subregions (6.9 and 7.1 per thousand, respectively); again, however, there is considerable overlap in the range of mortality rates across the groups. The median infant mortality rate is lowest in farming counties (5.6 per thousand live births per year) and highest in the mining counties (8.7 per thousand); in all the other subgroups counties, it is between 6.7 and 7.4 per thousand.

Except among the farming counties, the expected associations between mortality and demographic characteristics reemerge sharply when counties are grouped by key economic sector. These clear-cut associations probably emerge because like counties have been grouped together, providing some rudimentary control of variables that might confound the relationship between socioeconomic status and mortality. The overall death rate is positively associated with unemployment and with measures of poverty, and negatively associated with per capita income, as well as with attainment of high school and college education.

Pollution or Poverty

The analysis described here, while confirming the well-known poverty of the Appalachian region, also documents a surprisingly heavy burden of industrial pollution in this generally rural region. In particular, the value of manufacturing output, total chemical releases documented through the Toxics Release Inventory, and some estimated health impacts of hazardous air pollutants are higher than might be expected—and in some instances, they are higher in Appalachia than in the rest of the country. Not surprisingly, the region also bears a disproportionate burden of the effects from large coal-fired power plants, including the associated fine-particulate air pollution.

Perhaps the most striking finding of this analysis is an association, within the counties of the Appalachian region, between a heavier burden of industrial pollution and *higher* socioeconomic status. A similar pattern holds within certain subgroups: specifically, among counties economically dependent on manufacturing, services, or government. Overall mortality, which is somewhat higher for Appalachia than for the rest of the country, is associated with markers of lower socioeconomic status, and these associations emerge more strongly in subgroups of AR counties defined by their economic base.

The association between environmental burden and higher socioeconomic status in Appalachia is somewhat unusual in studies of the demographics of pollution. Early research studies on urban air pollution, for example, generally documented higher exposures to poor and minority populations, and much recent work has shown a similar pattern for residential proximity to hazardous waste sites. However, local and regional forces may play an important role in shaping social inequities. A study of the social distribution of pollution across the 351 cities and towns of Massachusetts, for example, documented two patterns.[13] Among the traditional manufacturing cities and towns, the burden of manufacturing was heavier in locations with poorer and higher-minority populations. In contrast, among the set of relatively well-to-do suburban cities and towns that came to host the emerging high-tech industries, with their largely invisible pollution, a heavier burden of manufacturing was documented in the more prosperous communities.

A similar association between pollution and higher socioeconomic status appears in the present analysis. However, it takes on a different meaning in the context of Appalachia—a region that is generally rural, with a population that is relatively poor overall. Manufacturing industry, which generates pollution, also brings much-needed money into a county. This dilemma represents a different brand of injustice, a forced choice between pollution and poverty in a disadvantaged region of the American landscape.

Notes

1. In federal data sources, the AR comprises 421 counties, eight of which are independent cities. In contrast, the Appalachian Regional Commission (ARC) rolls each of the eight independent cities of Virginia into a neighboring county and reports data for the combined units. In this view, the AR comprises 413 counties, of which six are city-county combinations. Because of the difference between the federal and ARC definitions, the number of counties included in these analyses is most often 421 but sometimes 413, depending on the source of data. When the number is 413, the six counties and eight independent cities are treated as missing values; when the number is 421, the six county-city combinations are treated as missing values.

2. John Alexander Williams, *Appalachia: A History* (Chapel Hill: University of North Carolina Press, 2002).

3. K. M. Pollard, *Defining Subregions in Appalachia: Are There Better Alternatives?* Demographic and Socioeconomic Change in Appalachia, no. 11 (Washington, DC: Appalachian Regional Commission/Population Reference Bureau, 2005).

4. M. Partridge, L. Lobao, P. W. Jeanty, L.J. Beaulieu, S. Goetz. *Final Report: An Assessment of Alternative Measures for Determining Economically Distressed Counties and Areas in the*

Appalachian Region, report prepared for Appalachian Regional Commission (Washington, DC: ARC, 2008).

5. Ibid., 6.

6. U.S. Department of Agriculture, Economic Research Service, "Data Sets: Urban Influence Codes," http://www.ers.usda.gov/Data/UrbanInfluenceCodes/; USDA, Economic Research Service, "Data Sets: County Typology Codes," http://www.ers.usda.gov/Data/TypologyCodes/ (accessed November 4, 2008).

7. All other nationwide county-level data are from U.S. Census Bureau, "USA Counties Basic Information," http://www.census.gov/support/USACdata.html (accessed October 16, 2008).

8. For data on individual facilities and chemicals, as well as aggregated data, see U.S. Environmental Protection Agency, "Toxics Release Inventory (TRI) Program," http://www.epa.gov/tri/tridata/index.htm (accessed October 7, 2008).

9. L. Tecer, O. Alagha, F. Karaca, G. Tuncel, and N. Eldes, "Particulate Matter ($PM_{2.5}$, $PM_{10-2.5}$, and PM_{10}) and Children's Hospital Admissions for Asthma and Respiratory Diseases: A Bidirectional Case-Crossover Study," *Journal of Toxicology and Environmental Health: Part A*. 71, no. 8 (April 2008): 512–20, (accessed September 25, 2010); S. Babin et al., "Medicaid Patient Asthma-Related Acute Care Visits and Their Associations with Ozone and Particulates in Washington, DC, from 1994–2005," *International Journal of Environmental Health Research* 18, no. 3 (June 2008): 209–21, (accessed September 25, 2010); M. Wilhelm, M. Ying-Ying, R. Rull, P. English, J. Balmes, and B. Ritz, "Environmental Public Health Tracking of Childhood Asthma Using California Health Interview Survey, Traffic, and Outdoor Air Pollution Data," *Environmental Health Perspectives* 116, no. 9 (September 2008): 1254–60, (accessed September 25, 2010).

10. M. Maher, "Housing and Commuting Patterns in Appalachia," report prepared for Appalachian Regional Commission, http://www.arc.gov/assets/research_reports/HousingandCommutingPatternsinAppalachia.pdf (accessed October 15, 2008).

11. A similar pattern holds within the Appalachian region: 43.8 percent of AR counties that host at least one coal-fired power plant, but only 7.7 percent of AR counties with no coal-fired plant, were out of attainment on the $PM_{2.5}$ standard in 2006 ($p < .0001$).

12. The Spearman (rank) correlation coefficient (*rho*) represents the association between the ranks of the values for two variables, rather than the actual values of the variables. Spearman's correlation was used here in lieu of the Pearson (linear) correlation because demographic variables are often not normally distributed and relationships between them are often not linear.

13. Nancy I. Maxwell, "Land Use, Demographics, and Cancer Incidence in Massachusetts Communities" (DSc diss., Boston University School of Public Health, 1996).

Data Sources

Coal-fired power plants: U.S. Energy Information Administration, "Electricity/Existing Capacity by Energy Source," http://www.eia.doe.gov/cneaf/electricity/epa/epat2p2.html (accessed October 15, 2008).

HAPs: U.S. Environmental Protection Agency, Technology Transfer Network, "1999 National-Scale Air Toxics Assessment: 1999 Data Tables," http://www.epa.gov/ttn /atw/nata1999/tables.html.

PM$_{2.5}$: U.S. Environmental Protection Agency, "Green Book: Non-Attainment Status for Each County by Year," http://earth1.epa.gov/air/oaqps/greenbk/anay.html (accessed October 22, 2008).

Superfund sites: U.S. Environmental Protection Agency, "National Priorities List," http:// www.epa.gov/superfund/sites/npl/index.htm.

TRI: U.S. Environmental Protection Agency, "Toxics Release Inventory (TRI) Program," http://www.epa.gov/tri/tridata/.

PART TWO

Citizen Action

FOUR

"We Mean to Stop Them, One Way or Another"

Coal, Power, and the Fight against Strip Mining in Appalachia

CHAD MONTRIE

DESPITE A WEALTH OF MINERAL RESOURCES, THE PEOPLE of southern Appalachia are by most measures poor. For over a century now, miners have extracted coal from bountiful reserves and loaded it on train cars to be used somewhere else, in factories or at electric utilities typically beyond the region, with little in the way of a fair return. Property and severance taxes were and are still minimal, while the number of jobs that might pump wages into the local economy has been in steady decline, mostly due to ever more sophisticated methods to increase production with fewer miners. This was, in fact, the main reason coal operators shifted to surface mining after World War II. Simply removing the layers of "overburden" on the side of a mountain or removing the whole top of a mountain, to get at a seam underneath, requires only a fraction of the labor force to extract the same amount of coal as deep mining. Additionally, operators can treat many of the adverse environmental and social impacts this type of mining causes as "externalities," leaving state or federal governments and individual property owners to deal with the cost of acid mine drainage, ruined roads, dry wells, cracked home foundations, insufferable dust, burst slurry dams, and devastating flooding.

Yet this is not to say that mountain residents have been silent and passive in the face of their "colonial" exploitation. During the 1960s and early

1970s resistance was particularly fierce. In Pike County, Kentucky, to cite just one example, people organized and engaged in nonviolent direct action as well as industrial sabotage, challenging not only coal operators but also the local political officials who did their bidding. This happened most dramatically in the summer of 1967, when the Puritan Coal Company threatened to advance on farmer Jink Ray's land. The company was authorized to do so because Kentucky courts had ruled that broad-form deeds, separating mineral and surface rights, gave mineral owners the right to extract coal without a landowner's consent and without compensation for most damages. To stop the mining, antipoverty activist Joe Mulloy put Ray and his supporters in touch with the Appalachian Group to Save the Land and People. They established their own AGSLP chapter, and when a Puritan bulldozer crossed Ray's property line a group of nearly twenty-five people stood in the way and forced it back. Shortly afterward, someone set off dynamite near the mine machinery. "We mean to stop them," explained retired deep miner Bill Fields, "one way or another."[1]

In the latter part of July, when a Puritan bulldozer tried once more to clear Jink Ray's land, activists blocked the path again and convinced the governor to cancel the permit, but that was not the end of the matter. In retaliation for the protests, the Pike County sheriff and the president of the Independent Coal Operators Association (ICOA) visited antipoverty activists Joe Mulloy and Alan McSurely to question them about their role in the actions. Several days later, the commonwealth attorney and past ICOA president Thomas Ratliff returned with fifteen armed deputies to arrest the two men, as well as McSurely's wife. When longtime civil rights and antipoverty activists Carl and Anne Braden came to bail them out of jail, they arrested them too. The charge was attempting to overthrow the government of Pike County, a violation of a 1920s sedition law. "From what I have seen of the evidence in this case," Ratliff said, "it is possible that Communist sympathizers may have infiltrated the antipoverty program not only in Pike County, but in other sections of the country as well." The objective of the antipoverty workers, he claimed, was "to stir up dissension and create turmoil among our poor."[2]

After the Kentucky Court of Appeals ruled the sedition law unconstitutional, coal operators pressured Governor Edward T. Breathitt to end antipoverty work in the region, which he did by making a phone call to the federal Office of Economic Opportunity. The next year, a new governor, Louis Nunn, worked with legislators to establish a Kentucky Un-American Activities Committee, which held hearings to investigate communist infiltration in activist-minded groups, either to tie up their resources and impede organizing or to shut them down entirely.[3] Meanwhile, the Kentucky Court of Appeals made clear that it was still a friend of coal by reaffirming an earlier decision about the unrestricted rights of mineral owners under broad-form deeds. "It appears to us that if, as we in substance are holding, the mineral owner bought and paid for the right to destroy the surface in a good faith exercise of the right to remove the minerals," the justices concluded in *Martin v. Kentucky Oak Mining Co.*, "then there is no basis upon which there could rest an obligation to pay damages for exercising that right."[4]

Revealing the proverbial iron fist inside the velvet glove, reaction to the Pike County insurgency demonstrated that the struggle there and elsewhere was, fundamentally, about a balance of power. When mountain residents and their allies opposed strip mining for the poverty and environmental devastation it caused, they challenged a long-established arrangement of social injustice and political domination, one that worked quite effectively to facilitate the extraction of resources and wealth from Appalachia. That same arrangement is also what led experience-hardened activists to protest outside the law, using various forms of direct action, and to demand abolition rather than regulatory legislation, which could be and was so easily undermined by coal operators. "We are here to consider and evaluate our position under the power of industrial corruption," Warren Wright declared at a 1971 People's Hearing on Strip Mining. Because judges and legislators were too crooked and heartless, he insisted, "we must attempt to bypass them."[5]

With a keen sense of the stakes in the battle, however, coal operators did not respond to the opposition solely with belligerent tactics. In fact, they were much more successful in defending their interests by showing calculated support for minimal regulation. Like their opponents, they understood that any control laws would be largely ineffectual, despite public statements that this or that bill would make surface mining completely unfeasible, and they knew that the only real threat was the demand for a surface mining ban. Consequently, trade association representatives, coal company executives, and their allies in state legislatures and Congress strategically altered their position on regulatory bills as abolition efforts waxed and waned. This approach ultimately paid off, in 1977, with passage of the Surface Mining Control and Reclamation Act. The law was weak and poorly enforced, as expected, but it provided legal sanction and cover for coal operators' continued and even more devastating destruction of the land and its people. For activists it was a resounding defeat, and the opposition movement has only recently reformed and recovered.

A Movement and Its Decline

The militant drive to end stripping in Appalachia began in eastern Kentucky, in the mid-1960s, and quickly spread to other parts of the region. Kentucky was relatively late in establishing even minimal controls on contour, area, and auger operations, and it did as little as any state to enforce regulations. This gap in oversight, as well as a combination of steep hillsides and high average rainfall, which increased the potential for landslides and flooding, are what pushed local residents to act. In 1960, Whitesburg lawyer Harry Caudill introduced the first bill in the Kentucky legislature to ban strip mining, and Letcher County resident Raymond Rash complemented that with petitions calling for prohibition, signed by one thousand supporters. These efforts accomplished little, however, and a 1963 revision of the state's control law also made an imperceptible difference in how stripping was done. Then, in the spring of 1965, coal operators Richard Kelley and Bill Sturgill began a job in Clear Creek valley, Knott County, provoking a storm of active resistance throughout the area that did not let up for several years.

The critical confrontation with strippers happened when bulldozers began threatening to cross onto property owned by Dan Gibson's stepson (who was doing military service in Vietnam), at which point Dan and his neighbors stood in the way. The next day, as clearing resumed, Dan went up to the site with a rifle and again shut down the operation, until he was arrested. When he got to jail a large crowd formed outside, charges were dropped, Dan was released, and a "big gang of outlaws" gathered to block bulldozers once more, finally getting a promise from Bill Sturgill that he would not try to mine the family property.[6] A few weeks later, local residents from Knott, Perry, and Letcher Counties held a meeting in Hindman, where they declared their intention to resort to sit-ins, lie-ins, and even guns to keep strip mine operators off their land. "We feel we have been forsaken," they explained, "that we have no rights when a county sheriff can order a man off his own property and tell him he is trespassing; that he will be jailed if he doesn't readily comply."[7] With this in mind they formed the Appalachian Group to Save the Land and People, which in its name spoke to dual concerns for the environmental destruction caused by stripping as well as the impact this devastation and the inevitable reduction in coal mine employment had on communities.

One of the first initiatives by the AGSLP was a fifty-car motorcade to the state capital, where activists demanded a meeting with the governor (which he reluctantly consented to), and delivered petitions against stripping with three thousand signatures. That night, Governor Breathitt told a symposium on strip mining that operators would have to improve their methods and reclamation practices or he would have to ask the state legislature for a ban. In the fall, the AGSLP also came to the aid of Ollie Combs and her extended family, facing encroachment on their land by a Sturgill operation in Honey Gap, Knott County. The group ran the bulldozers off with guns but the workers eventually returned when only Combs and her two sons were at home. The three sat down in front of the machinery and were arrested and jailed, but they embarrassed the governor into public support once again when a photograph of the Widow Combs eating her Thanksgiving dinner behind bars appeared on the front page of the *Louisville Courier-Journal*, the state's main newspaper. Breathitt urged all citizens of the state to obey the law but noted that "history has sometimes shown that unyielding insistence upon the enforcement of legal rights by the rich and powerful against the humble people of a community is not always the quickest course of action." And he had regulators revoke the permit for the strip operation.[8]

Early in 1966, Kentucky legislators answered the "clamor" in the coalfields with an updated regulatory law, yet at the same time they failed to pass a measure that would have required operators working on a broad-form deed to get surface owner consent and pay damages. The still inadequate controls and uneven enforcement, besides the troubles caused by mineral owner primacy, further demonstrated to activists the need for prohibition. So they continued to organize, establishing new AGSLP chapters, and they continued to resist, fighting with petitions, lawsuits, nonviolent direct action, and, by the spring of 1967, industrial sabotage. That April, someone dynamited a diesel shovel at a Kentucky Coal River strip mine in Knott County, and, in the eighteen months that followed, shovels, bulldozers, trucks, and other equipment at several other Knott and Perry county operations were destroyed under cover of night.[9]

Counseling against the use of "violence," but assisting coalfield residents in a variety of important and critical ways, were antipoverty activists, most of them not from Appalachia. Initially they were college students sponsored by the Council of the Southern Mountains, doing service projects like painting one-room schoolhouses, very much in line with a long history of well-meaning outsiders who had come to the region to help the supposedly isolated mountaineers. By the summer of 1965, however, the antipoverty workers were part of the War on Poverty, most employed through the Office of

Economic Opportunity's (OEO) Volunteers in Service to America (VISTA) program, with a few others placed by the Southern Conference Education Fund (SCEF), and they shifted to community organizing, taking literally the OEO's mandate to encourage "maximum feasible participation of the poor." Until Kentucky VISTA funding was cut in the wake of the Jink Ray protest, the young activists helped AGSLP with research, press releases, and strip mine tours, as well as publishing regular issues of *Strip Mining Bulletin*, distributed to four thousand people.

Meanwhile, people in other parts of Appalachia built on years of dealing with under regulated and laxly enforced stripping and organized their own campaigns for a ban. With the help of antipoverty workers, for example, West Virginia activists formed the Citizens' Task Force on Surface Mining and, later, Citizens to Abolish Strip Mining (CASM). These efforts had support throughout the state, although the strongest base was undoubtedly in Boone, Fayette, and Raleigh Counties, where militant mineworkers were already engaged in a battle with their corrupt union leadership and immersed in an epic fight to call attention to black lung. They understood the threat stripping posed not only to the hills and streams where they lived but also to their jobs. Despite mineworker involvement, however, CASM was ultimately thwarted by the coal industry's divisive rhetoric, pitting jobs against environment, and by its control over the House of Delegates and Senate, which made legislators primarily accountable to operators and equipment suppliers. When their prohibition bill finally died, in 1971, CASM closed up shop, and its leadership helped nurture a regionwide initiative to work toward redress at the national level.

In line with the new approach, in October of that same year, at a meeting in Huntington, West Virginia, representatives from various groups gathered and established the Appalachian Coalition, dedicated to achieving a ban on stripping by federal law. They chose a very outspoken and brash activist, Jim Branscome, as the coalition's lead coordinator, and they made Richard Cartwright Austin, CASM's former head, the new organization's secretary. Later that fall, a number of mainstream environmental groups, particularly the Sierra Club and Friends of the Earth, also joined forces to establish the National Coalition against Strip Mining (NCASM), which was not strictly abolitionist in its outlook or goals. NCASM pledged to work with the Appalachian Coalition to lobby members of Congress and arrange effective testimony at hearings, but its formation was the beginning of an ominous division within the movement.

The United Mine Workers underwent some big changes too, with equally important implications for the stripping struggle. Control of the union had passed from John Lewis to Tony Boyle in the early 1960s, after which it became anything but responsive to the membership, often colluding with coal operators to negotiate sweetheart contracts as well as to block meaningful health and safety legislation. When Boyle hired thugs to murder his opponent in the 1969 election for president, mineworkers in southern West Virginia formed Miners for Democracy. They chose Arnold Miller, a Black Lung Association leader as well as an advocate for banning stripping, to run in the 1972 election, which he only narrowly won. With a growing surface mining membership in the UMW, though, Miller had to hedge on abolition and put the union behind strong regulatory legislation, setting up a potential conflict with activists.

For coalfield residents throughout southern Appalachia, the main argument against stripping was the threat it posed to the land and people. In particular, they objected to its infringement on the rights of small-property owners (ruined gardens and orchards, dried up wells, cracked foundations, flyrock missiles in the air) and the way it eroded what remained of mining employment in the region (since surface methods were much more efficient than underground methods). Framing these concerns, as well as providing legitimacy for resistance, was a tradition of natural rights, elaborated by John Locke and enshrined in the Declaration of Independence by Thomas Jefferson. This tradition established rights like life, liberty, and property as inherent and inalienable, not revocable privileges granted by a monarch or any other authority, and it defined the purpose of government as protecting these rights, granting people the right to alter or abolish the government when it failed in this primary purpose. Faced with the tyranny of the coal industry, which had taken over their legislatures and courts, Dan Gibson, Bessie Smith, Madge Ashley, and others believed they were duty bound to act, and justified in acting even outside the law.

In fact, it was the spreading uprising in the coalfields that forced operators and trade groups to shift their position on control laws over time. Initially, they claimed that any regulations would be the coal industry's death knell, and some tried to fight all attempts at change, but once local people began pressing for a state ban, state regulations became more attractive. Friends of the coal industry in West Virginia's legislature, for instance, saved surface mining only by agreeing to a two-year halt on all stripping in the state's twenty-two still unmined counties. The final law also increased performance bonds (forfeited by negligent operators), required the construction of approved drainage systems, and mandated delayed blasting techniques. On paper, it seemed like the assembly was getting tough with the industry. Perhaps indicative of the weakness of the legislation and its expected inadequate enforcement, however, the president of the West Virginia Surface Mining Association praised it as "fair and equitable." While signing the bill, Governor Arch A. Moore suggested that, considering "the times and temper," the new control act was a good one.[10]

After West Virginia congressman Ken Hechler introduced the first bill to outlaw stripping at the national level, in February 1971, weak federal regulations earned a new appeal as well. The American Mining Congress "will urge the adoption of realistic surface mining regulation at the state level and will support federal surface mining legislation which is realistically designed to assist the states and the surface mining industry in conducting surface mining operations," the trade industry explained in a statement. "From State to State, from place to place, it can well be said of mining that its only constant is its diversity," insisted AMC chair Joseph Abdnor. "All such diverse realities of mining," he said, "argue eloquently against any effort to devise other than broad, reasonable Federal guidelines." Yet industry representatives made a point to argue against outlawing surface coal mining. Reclamation was possible, said National Coal Association president Carl Bagge, whereas prohibition "would have disastrous results for the Nation and its constantly increasing need for energy."[11]

Despite the connection between direct action, demand for a ban, and the coal industry's steady retreat, however, the groups that made up the Appalachian Coalition began to focus their attention on lobbying lawmakers. The last organized, nonviolent civil disobedience against strip mining (for almost thirty years) happened in eastern Kentucky in 1972. In January more than twenty women occupied a Sigmon Brothers strip operation in Knott County from early morning to late at night, periodically harassed by rock-throwing workers, who also beat up men waiting in support at the company gate below. When a state trooper came up to let the women know that the men had left for a hospital (chased part of the way by strip miners), they decided to end the protest, and found their cars with busted windows and slashed tires, as well as one that was overturned.[12] Later, following spring floods that killed one person and damaged countless homes, gardens, bridges, and roads in Floyd County, activists temporarily shut down a strip mine there as well, blaming the operation for causing an unusual amount of runoff. After that, however, in what was perhaps a strategic miscalculation, opposition to stripping in the southern coalfields largely took the form of writing to members of Congress and sending delegations to provide testimony at hearings.

In line with their modified tactics, the formerly militant activists did what they could to find and connect with allies outside Appalachia, particularly mainstream environmental groups. Their two primary contacts were Louise Dunlap, first at Friends of the Earth and then at the Environmental Policy Center, and Peter Borelli, the Sierra Club's eastern representative. Dunlap started and coordinated NCASM and, with Borelli, they drew on the pressure mountain people could bring to bear in Washington, D.C., but not toward the end of abolition. While people like J. W. Bradley (later head of Tennessee's Save Our Cumberland Mountains) called for "stopping strip mining as soon as possible" and invoked the Declaration of Independence as a warning that people would take matters into their own hands if Congress failed to protect their inalienable rights, the professional environmentalists took a hard line only as a foil to win federal regulation.[13] "Though no one seriously expects [the abolition bills] to win committee approval," Borelli wrote in the *Sierra Club Bulletin*, "the abolitionists and their legions have been the first to budge these traditionally mineral-oriented committees. As a result several milder but potentially effective measures that might otherwise have been ignored have earned some credibility."[14]

After a couple more years of hearings, Dunlap and Borelli began to make no pretense about supporting a ban and talked instead about "minimum requirements" that they expected to see in any final regulatory legislation.[15] Consequently, with the "environmental lobby" backing off, support in Congress for a bill to ban stripping began to erode. Representative Hechler responded in frustration, yet he began to waver too. "My people in West Virginia and people throughout the nation," he wrote to activists in January 1975, "are getting more and more cynical about compromising politicians, Washington environmental groups who settle for the lowest common denominator, and those who enjoy the transient glory of winning a few commas or semi-colons while the people and the land continue to be exploited and destroyed." But while Hechler encouraged support for his recently introduced abolition bill, he also noted the importance of defining "the minimum standards you would accept in a regulatory bill." These included a ban on steep slopes (greater than twenty degrees), no mountaintop removal, prohibition of mining in alluvial valley floors, a ban on impoundments for coal waste disposal, and written consent of surface owners in all cases where surface and mineral rights had been separated.[16]

Like members of Congress, once coal trade groups, coal companies, and energy conglomerates saw the movement's decline, they retreated too. After President Ford twice vetoed weak control bills, in 1974 and 1975, their agenda went back to opposing any federal oversight. The American Mining Congress declared that uniform national standards for surface mining and reclamation were "not feasible" and insisted that regulation was best handled at the state level. Anything like the measures just vetoed, it said, would create "a virtual prohibition on surface mining through the imposition of unrealistic and unworkable provisions."[17] Peabody Coal president Edwin Phelps voiced a similar sentiment. "All major coal producing States have their own functioning programs that regulate surface mining and require sound reclamation," he explained. "The debate that has raged over this issue has outlived the need for Federal legislation."[18]

The United Mine Workers moved back to support for state-level regulation of stripping as well. Echoing industry concerns, a sizable number of delegates to the forty-seventh constitutional convention argued that a federal law would not recognize the problems and conditions specific to various regions, and the union's president fell into line. "What works in the hills of West Virginia may not work in the plains of Illinois," Miller explained, "some reclamation standards that would benefit one area could possibly harm another." Surface mining and reclamation were both important to the economy and ecology of the country, he said, and protecting the environment was vital "not only for ourselves but more for the use of our children and our children's children." The UMW would cease working for legislation to establish federal standards and enforcement, however, and instead work for reclamation laws on a state-by-state basis. This position, dictated in part by the growing influence of surface miners in the union, was largely an effort to shore up coalfield employment. The cochair of the committee making the recommendation explained that a state-by-state approach was needed "so that we will not put anyone out of work."[19]

In 1977, Congress enacted—and President Carter signed—federal legislation, although it was not too far from what the coal industry and the UMW wanted at that point. The Surface Mining Control and Reclamation Act (SMCRA) set up a federal-state partnership for oversight, giving most duties to state agencies in good standing, and it was nearly as weak as any bill considered since the start of hearings in 1968. It created an Office of Surface Mining, included a ban against dumping overburden on steep slopes, established an abandoned-mine reclamation program funded by a per-ton tax on coal, and empowered citizens to sue negligent regulatory agencies. Yet the law lacked many of the provisions surface-mining opponents had called for when outlining their own version of a strong bill. SMCRA allowed stripping on steep slopes and alluvial valley floors, said nothing about coal reserves owned separately from the surface and mined without surface owner consent (except federally owned land), and permitted mountaintop removal (with an allowance for a variance from restoration of slopes to approximate original contour) as well as impoundments for slurry waste.

As weak as the law was, the coal industry and its allies in Congress immediately went on the attack to undermine its implementation. The OSM's operating funds were stalled for several months, delaying hiring and the opening of field offices, and the Senate held hearings to investigate industry claims that regulations were confusing and too burdensome. By the spring of 1978 operators also had initiated more than one hundred legal challenges to SMCRA in more than fifteen separate lawsuits. None of this led to modifications in the law, but it was a shot across the bow, and a portent of things to come. SMCRA legalized the destruction caused by strip mining and, in practice, did little if anything to force companies to shoulder responsibility for what had been and continued to be regarded as externalities (ruined land, polluted water, and unemployment). Still, over the next couple of decades operators persistently tried to undermine even the few provisions in the law that seemed to enhance regulatory power.

Resurgence

In the immediate post-SMCRA era, activism against stripping did not stop, but it did change, increasingly attending to land monopoly and tax inequity, an agenda that had considerable potential to revive a struggle with competing claims for power at its center. Just before the new control law was enacted, eastern Kentucky and southern West Virginia were struck by flooding, caused by heavy rains yet made much worse by rapid runoff and silt loads from strip mines. Those left homeless found their plight compounded by lack of available land for resettlement, with trailers for emergency housing standing empty on the road because land and coal companies refused to lease or sell property overlying coal they might want to mine later. Sufficiently incited, residents of Martin and Harlan Counties, in Kentucky, established several community groups to help people in the flood's aftermath and to demand an end to stripping in their area. Across the state line, in Mingo County, West Virginia, the same issues led to formation of the Appalachian Alliance, to "support individuals and communities which are working to gain democratic control over their lives, workplaces, and natural resources."[20]

A year later, in 1978, the Alliance created a Task Force on Land Ownership, to study links between land and mineral ownership, property taxes, and poverty in the region. Martin and Harlan county activists were involved in the part that dealt with eastern Kentucky. They found startling statistics, like the Pocahontas-Kentucky Corporation's $76 annual property tax payment on $7 million worth of coal reserves in Martin County. Subsequently, in 1981, the Alliance established the Kentucky Fair Tax Coalition, which pushed for an increase in the unmined minerals tax and, when that failed, challenged the systematic underassessment of mineral property.[21] In the meantime, the group transformed itself into a membership organization with local chapters, changed its name to Kentuckians for the Commonwealth (KFTC), and expanded its agenda to include opposition to the broad-form deed. As a result of unrelenting grassroots mobilization across the state, by the early 1990s KFTC had not only forced the Kentucky Revenue Cabinet to adequately assess unmined minerals, significantly increasing taxes land and coal companies paid, but also won an amendment to the state constitution to require surface owner consent before mining.[22]

Gradually, though, the fight against strip mining devolved into a mainstream environmental reform campaign, concerned primarily with better enforcement of SMCRA and the Clean Water Act, and lacking any commitment to confrontational tactics. What happened at Tennessee's Save Our Cumberland Mountains (SOCM) is instructive. The group had its origins in the 1960s fight to abolish strip mining, following failed state regulatory efforts, wanton destruction of surface owners' property by mineral owners working under a broad-form deed, and persistent poverty in seemingly mineral-rich coal counties. Leading the organization, from 1972 to 1977, was the outspoken and unwavering J. W. Bradley, a former deep miner who had been forced off his land by the Shemco Coal Company a couple of years before, for interfering with a strip operation. He once described efforts by the federal government to regulate surface coal mining as "short-sighted, unrealistic, and a waste of time," and that seemed to be SOCM's position, at least until 1975. On the eve of SMCRA's enactment, however, there was a definite split in the group's membership, with some favoring federal legislation as a small step forward and others holding out for what they saw as the only real solution.[23]

When abolitionists lost the argument, Bradley stepped down as president and SOCM morphed into a watchdog of the state and federal regulatory agencies (eventually the Division of Surface Mining lost primacy due to inadequate enforcement and the OSM took over entirely). Between 1978 and 1980, wildcat (unpermitted) operations spread throughout East Tennessee and the homes of several activists burned, very likely retaliatory acts of arson.[24] By the mid-1980s, though, SOCM had settled into a comfortable role filing lawsuits, lobbying legislators, and pushing the OSM to improve regulatory standards and do better enforcement. Consequently, the organization stopped being a catalyst for community organizing and increasingly focused on expert intervention, which did little to end the destruction of mountains and communities.

While the opponents of strip mining stumbled, extraction methods evolved beyond the familiar area, contour, and auger operations. More and more operators in eastern Kentucky, southern West Virginia, and East Tennessee engaged in what was called mountaintop removal (MTR), an exceptionally efficient way to get at usually horizontal Appalachian coal seams. The process not only included leveling mountains and destroying the hardwood forests they sustained, but also dumping overburden in huge valley fills, burying hundreds of miles of streams, and building massive slurry ponds to hold millions of gallons of wastewater from washing tons of coal, putting whole communities in jeopardy from disastrous toxic floods.[25] Of course, MTR ate away at the remaining mining jobs in the region as well, allowing for record-high production and record-low employment.

When Congress passed SMCRA, most of its supporters had assumed that mountaintop removal would occur only infrequently, in rare circumstances. And perhaps that explains why the law's provisions defining reclamation after a mountaintop operation are so vague. Operators are required to reclaim the land so that it "closely resembles the general surface configuration of the land prior to mining," or the "approximate original contour" (AOC). This standard could make mountaintop removal mining completely impractical in places like eastern Kentucky and southern West Virginia, where grades often exceed twenty degrees. But it has not been interpreted that way by coal companies, and regulatory officials contend their hands are tied because nobody agrees what AOC really means. SMCRA does allow some exemptions from the standard, if operators submit detailed plans for development of schools, factories, or public parks before permit approval. Regulators have failed to require even that much of operators, however, and the most popular postmining land uses proposed and approved by regulatory agencies are "fish and wildlife habitat" and "timberland."[26]

By the twentieth anniversary of SMCRA, in 1997, even Louise Dunlap admitted that the federal-state regulatory program established by the law had failed. She still believed SMCRA itself was "sound," but cited less than enthusiastic commitment by the White House and Department of the Interior. "Even in the worst-case scenario," Dunlap explained, "I expected the Act to be enforced better than it's been."[27] Yet that had been the abolitionists' point all along, based on the experience they had with a coal industry capturing regulatory agencies or at least significantly influencing implementation of regulations. For some the battle that had raged back in the 1960s and 1970s was about the technical feasibility of strip mining and reclamation, while for many others it was about power and the interest coal companies and energy conglomerates had in making a profit, which they believed doomed any control effort from the start. Louise Dunlap never accepted that, KFTC and SOCM seemed to forget it, and new organizations like the Ohio Valley Environmental Coalition, formed in 1987, missed the point altogether. By the middle of the 1990s, in fact, the campaign targeting strip mining put little or no emphasis on the idea that legislatures, courts, Congress, and regulatory agencies were irredeemably corrupt, and it ceased being a running confrontation with the coal industry and individual operators.

There has since been a rebirth of militancy and activism marked by clarity about the links between the environmental and economic costs of surface coal mining, the factors that undermined even the most well-meant efforts to control it, and the need to use a variety of tactics, including nonviolent civil disobedience. Groups like Coal River Mountain Watch (CRMW), formed by residents of Whitesville, West Virginia, in 1998, are resolutely opposed to mountaintop removal and have been steadily organizing local people in the area. Much of their success is due in no small part to the seemingly fearless Judy Bonds, who came from a long line of coal miners and was initially prompted to get involved battling MTR when Massey Energy strip operation began destroying her family land. Since then, her life was threatened more than once and she was physically assaulted at a demonstration. Nevertheless, she continued to speak out about the true cost of coal and to advocate for active resistance to ban mountaintop removal.

At the same time, exceptionally blunt and forthright leaders have emerged within established organizations, including Maria Gunnoe and Teri Blanton, both of whom have a personal experience with strip mining and are increasingly frustrated by the actions and rhetoric of coal companies and regulators. Like Bonds, Gunnoe is the daughter and granddaughter of coal miners. Born and raised in Boone County, West Virginia, she joined the strip mining fight after an MTR operation commenced above her home in 2000, poisoning her well and leading to devastating floods, one of which destroyed much of her property and covered the yard in toxic sludge. In response, Gunnoe joined the Ohio Valley Environmental Coalition and started organizing her neighbors, in spite of frequent threats and harassment. Blanton first got involved in environmental issues when she was compelled to fight a manufacturing plant poisoning the water supply in her hometown of Dayhoit, Kentucky. Following that, she joined Kentuckians for the Commonwealth, started their Canary Project, and played a leading role in the formation of Alliance for Appalachia, a coalition of more than a dozen groups from several mountain states.

Then there is Larry Gibson. A free spirit in the movement, Gibson became a prominent, vocal critic of strip mining in 1999, when he walked nearly five hundred miles across West Virginia to draw attention to mountaintop removal (which, he pointed out, was equal to the total length of all the streams lost to valley fills in the state). In addition, he founded Keepers of the Mountains Foundation and maintains Stanley Heirs Park at Kayford Mountain, both part of a (dangerous) running battle he has fought with the strip operations that surround his family land. Gibson's homestead and the park he established have become a pilgrimage site for those seeking a firsthand view of MTR's destruction as well as for veterans of the struggle who need a place to come together for relaxation and renewal. This is also true of Bo Webb's homeplace, on Coal River, not far from Whitesville. Bo and his daughter and son-in-law, Sarah and Vernon Haltom, recently waged a successful campaign to force the state of West Virginia to move nearby Marsh Fork Elementary School out from beneath the shadows of a huge sludge impoundment and polluting coal silo.

Augmenting their reach and effectiveness, each of these individuals, if not their organizations or some segment of the organizations they belong to, has begun to work with an entirely new crop of young activists, most originally from outside Appalachia. Their Mountain Justice (MJ) campaign is a response to Bonds, Gunnoe, Blanton, Gibson, Webb, and the Haltoms calling on folks to "seed an uprising" in the coalfields. With links to "deep ecology" and "global justice" struggles, the radically democratic MJ began setting up organizing houses in a number of key mountain states in 2004. From these centers, participants have conducted "listening projects" and outreach, initiated marches and rallies, and planned direct actions, like lockdowns and sit-ins. To recruit new activists and to get them ready for the work at hand, MJ has arranged spring, summer, and fall training camps as well. Dave Cooper, who initially joined the MTR battle through the Lexington KFTC chapter, has played a key role coordinating these camps. He has also logged thousands of miles bringing his multimedia roadshow to colleges, community groups, and others. More recently, Mountain Justice has been joined by activists associated with Climate Ground Zero, which has a strong orientation to nonviolent civil disobedience.

To be sure, there have been questions about the new activism from some corners, particularly for the way it can alienate politicians, regulatory officials, and hesitant or fearful mountain residents. Some mainstream activists continue to insist that SMCRA and other control laws are part of a gradual encroachment on the coal industry's control over political systems, economic development, and the natural environment, affording at least some, if not completely adequate, tools for protecting hills, streams, forests, and wildlife. But anyone sitting through a permit hearing these days could easily call that conclusion into question, since the procedure is so obviously meant to strictly limit discussion and thinking about surface mining, and designed to suggest by the end that due process was offered and carried out. It is tempting, in fact, to think that the whole procedure is a waste of time, and might as well not happen at all. Getting a brief glimpse of the past, when environmental injustice in the coalfields was met with determined resistance and opened up a larger struggle over the balance of power, also brings that kind of clarity to understanding the present.

Notes

1. *Louisville Courier-Journal*, July 9, 1967, 28; July 11, 1967, 20; *Mountain Eagle*, July 20, 1967, 1.

2. *New York Times*, August 27, 1967, 71. Antipoverty workers tried to clarify the situation "because the Appalachian Volunteers are working in Pike and other counties with citizens who are standing up in opposition to strip mining, the Eastern Kentucky stripmine operators seem to have assumed that AVs are responsible for the opposition," the AVs explained in an August 17 press release, but "this is not the case; for us it is clear that the people of Eastern Kentucky would band together against strip mining with or without our help." *Courier Journal*, September 27, 1967, 1; A report by the Federal Bureau of Investigation noted that Ratliff's prime interest was "ridding Pike County of the antipoverty workers . . . [for] reasons economic and political: (1) he has made a fortune out of the coal industry and still had coal interests; and (2) he is running for Lt. Governor in the

Republican ticket and thinks it is a good issue." Paul Good, "Kentucky's Coal Beds of Sedition," *Nation*, September 4, 1967, in *Appalachia in the Sixties: Decade of Reawakening*, ed. David S. Walls and John B. Stephenson (Lexington: University Press of Kentucky, 1972), 192.

3. Albert Whitehouse, Statement on Appalachian Volunteers Situation in Kentucky, September 11, 1967, 1, folder 3, "Strip Mining, Sept. 1, 1967–Dec. 28, 1967," box 20, Harry Caudill Manuscript Collection, Special Collections, University of Kentucky (hereafter cited as Caudill Papers); Harry M. Caudill, *My Land Is Dying* (New York: Dutton, 1973), 89; Calvin Trillin, "The Logical Thing, Costwise," *New Yorker*, December 27, 1969, in Walls and Stephenson, *Appalachia in the Sixties*, 113.

4. *Martin v. Kentucky Oak Mining Co.* (429 S.W. 2d 395), 395–99.

5. Council of the Southern Mountains, *People Speak Out on Strip Mining* (Berea, KY: Council, 1971).

6. Council of the Southern Mountains, *People Speak*; Caudill, *My Land*, 76.

7. *Mountain Eagle*, June 3, 1965, 1–2.

8. Dan Gibson, quoted in *To Look Over the Land and Take Care of It*, Broadside/ Appalachian Video Network, Archives and Special Collections, East Tennessee State University; *Hazard Herald*, November 15, 1965, in folder 4, "Strip Mining, January 10, 1965– December 23, 1965," box 19, Caudill Papers; Caudill, *My Land*, 80–81.

9. *New York Times*, July 30, 1967, 29; Caudill, *My Land*, 87; *Courier-Journal*, August 10, 1967, 1. At the end of the summer of 1968, saboteurs destroyed $750,000 worth of equipment at a Round Mountain Coal Company operation in Leslie County. Later, in December, someone blew up $1 million worth of equipment, including one shovel and six bulldozers, at a Blue Diamond Coal strip operation in Campbell County, Tennessee, near the state border. T. N. Bethell, "Hot Time Ahead," *Mountain Life and Work* (April 1969), in Walls and Stephenson, *Appalachia in the Sixties*, 116–19.

10. *Charleston Gazette*, March 7, 1971, 1; March 10, 1971, 1; March 14, 1971, 1; March 18, 1971, 1.

11. *Mining Congress Journal* 57 (September 1971): 138; Senate, *Hearings before the Subcommittee . . . on S 77* (1971–72), 280–82, 329–32, 620; House, *Hearings before the Subcommittee . . . on HR 60* (1971), 296, 559, 562–63.

12. *Courier Journal*, January 21, 1972; "We will stop the bulldozers—A Statement by the Women of Eastern Kentucky, January 20, 1972 Strip Mining," folder, "Strip Mining," boxes 1–2, West Virginia and Regional History Collection, West Virginia University, Morgantown.

13. House, *Hearings on HR 60*, 690–91.

14. *Sierra Club Bulletin* 56 (May 1971): 8.

15. Senate Committee, *Hearings Before the Committee . . . on S. 425* (1973), 894–96.

16. Ken Hechler to Friends of the Coalition against Strip Mining, January 18, 1975, folder 8, "Strip Mining," box 170, Hechler Papers.

17. "Declaration of Policy," *Mining Congress Journal* 61 (November 1975), 89.

18. House Subcommittee on Energy and the Environment, *Hearings Before the Subcommittee on Energy and the Environment of the Committee on Interior and Insular Affairs on HR 2, Surface Mining Control and Reclamation Act of 1977*, 95th Cong., 1st sess. (1977), 37–38, 185 (pt. 1).

19. *Mountain Life and Work* 52 (October 1976), 41; United Mine Workers of America, *Proceedings of the 47th Constitutional Convention* (Indianapolis: Allied Printing, 1976), 273–76.

20. Melanie A. Zuercher, ed., *Making History: The First Ten Years of KFTC* (Prestonsburg: Kentuckians for the Commonwealth, 1991), 9–11; Beth Spence to Alliance Members, June 28, 1977, folder "Strip Mining," boxes 1–2, WVRH Papers; *Mountain Life and Work*, 53 (August 1977), 46; 54 (January 1978), 23.

21. Melanie A. Zuercher, ed., *Making History: The First Ten Years of KFTC* (Prestonsburg: Kentuckians for the Commonwealth, 1991), 11–13.

22. Ibid., 298–99.

23. J. W. and Kate Bradley returned to their home in May 1977, after a decision by a chancery court judge that included a payment of $2,700 by the company to the Bradleys, for damages to the property and denial of access to the land. *Mountain Life and Work* 53 (August 1977), 35; Bill Allen, "Save Our Cumberland Mountains: Growth and Change within a Grassroots Organization," in *Fighting Back in Appalachia: Traditions of Resistance and Change*, ed. Stephen L. Fisher (Philadelphia: Temple University Press, 1993), 86–87; House Subcommittee, *Hearings on HR 2*, 9 (part 1).

24. Allen, "Cumberland Mountains," 90; *SOCM Sentinel*, October 1978, 3; August 1979, 1; September 1979, 2; October 1979, 4.

25. The earthen dams that made the ponds were notoriously unstable, as the 1972 Buffalo Creek tragedy demonstrated years before and as the more recent Martin County spill of 250 million gallons of toxic sludge showed in 2000.

26. *Charleston Gazette*, May 3, 1998; August 9, 1998; Maryanne Vollers, "Razing Appalachia," *Mother Jones* 7 (July/ August 1999): 36–43.

27. *Reporter* (Citizens Coal Council), special issue, August 3, 1997, 7, 13; At a hearing on the tenth anniversary of SMCRA, Arizona representative Morris Udall, who had played an instrumental role in passing the law, said the act was "fundamentally sound," though hampered by a few states with weak regulatory programs, the change in regulatory philosophy when President Ronald Reagan appointed James Watt as secretary of the interior, and a few recalcitrant coal operators. American Mining Congress representative Ben E. Lusk called SMCRA's standards "demanding, inflexible, often counterproductive and always costly" but also described the law as "fundamentally . . . sound." House Subcommittee on Energy and the Environment, Committee on Interior and Insular Affairs, *Tenth Anniversary of the Surface Mining Control and Reclamation Act of 1977*, 100th Cong., 1st sess. (1987), 1, 65–66.

FIVE

Commons Environmentalism Mobilized

The Western North Carolina Alliance and the Cut the Clearcutting! Campaign

KATHRYN NEWFONT

"THE PEOPLE HAVE SPOKEN WITH A LOUD VOICE," Mary Kelly declared as she and other Western North Carolina Alliance activists delivered an enormous petition to the U.S. Forest Service's Asheville office on Cut the Clearcutting! Day in 1989. "Wow," responded Forest Supervisor Bjorn Dahl, staring at the giant document. Fully unfurled, the petition stretched more than four city blocks. It contained no fewer than 15,500 signatures. More than two hundred people representing at least twelve mountain counties marched the massive ribbon of names through the streets of Asheville to National Forests in North Carolina headquarters. Armed with hand-lettered signs, banners, and a large American flag, they had spent the last two hours listening to speeches and traditional mountain music in the plaza downtown. Hunters, loggers, fiddlers, foresters, biologists, potters, and organizers took turns at the microphone, some with mountain accents and some without. Despite overcast skies and chilly weather, their mood was jubilant.[1]

This April 15 street demonstration built on years of anticlearcutting activism in Appalachian North Carolina. The petition and rally carried local forest watchdogs' best hopes for reversing Forest Service policy in the region, which here as elsewhere favored large-scale clearcut timber harvesting above all other methods. Western North Carolina's widely beloved Nantahala and Pisgah

National Forests contained nearly one million woodland acres. The Western North Carolina Alliance (WNCA), a regional grassroots environmental organization founded in the early 1980s, had organized Cut the Clearcutting! Day as the culmination of an intense four-month campaign of public opposition to clearcutting in these forests. The enormous petition served as a campaign centerpiece. With it organizers intended to showcase the breadth and depth of hostility to clearcutting in the region. They gathered the signatures in a coordinated multicounty effort, knocking on doors and setting up signing stations at convenience stores, supermarkets, and tire shops.[2]

Organizers planned Cut the Clearcutting! Day's spirited events to maximize publicity for the petition's delivery and for the larger anticlearcutting effort. In the rally, they also showcased the WNCA's trademark brand of commons-friendly environmentalism. Many mountain residents valued the Nantahala and Pisgah as commons harvest grounds rather than as untouched wilderness. In the crowd, protesters carried posters reflecting these harvest relationships with the woods. "Stop Clearcutting Says Forester" read one such sign. "Bearhunters against Clearcutting" trumpeted another. "We Oppose Clearcutting NOT Logging," proclaimed a third. Much of the rhetoric from the stage echoed these messages. "We can put those logs on those trucks," thundered Alliance member Bob Padgett in his anticlearcutting speech. Padgett, a U.S. Forest Service retiree and active private forester, delivered one of many addresses emphasizing the productive value of Appalachian forests.[3]

As these signs and speeches demonstrated, the Alliance's anticlearcutting campaign drew its central strength not from wilderness environmentalism but from a different source. The idea of wilderness, emphasizing as it did an absence of people and of human work in the woods, failed to resonate with many longtime mountain residents. It often seemed to them elitist, economically unsound, and historically dishonest. Thus wilderness-inspired environmental campaigns typically gained little traction among mountain people.

Yet as the boisterous Alliance rally and the eventual total of more than sixteen thousand petition signatures clearly proved, mountain people could be passionate, effective, and ambitious defenders of Appalachian forests. In western North Carolina, they fought clearcutting and other industrial development of the region's woodlands with remarkable vigor and tenacity. In Cut the Clearcutting! and in other campaigns, WNCA members championed forest protection goals so far reaching that national environmental groups were unwilling to support them. Yet the Alliance won widespread backing for these bold initiatives from a diverse array of mountain residents.

Just as elsewhere, post–World War II battles over forest resources pitted industrialists against environmentalists. In western North Carolina, however, commons users—who were typically rural and often working class—served as swing voters in these battles. The side that most effectively hitched its wagon to commons culture usually won. Wilderness opponents in the late 1970s, for instance, ceaselessly touted commons concerns as they (quite successfully) fought proposed Pisgah and Nantahala additions to the federal wilderness system.[4]

With its Cut the Clearcutting! campaign, the Western North Carolina Alliance tapped the latent power of commons culture, this time for an environmentalist cause. The WNCA framed its opposition to clearcutting as a form of commons forest defense. The organization decoupled the issue of forest protection from the question of wilderness preservation and hitched it instead to widely shared concerns about the wooded mountain commons. This strategy succeeded in making the Alliance's anticlearcutting position attractive even to many mountain inhabitants who did not ordinarily consider themselves environmentalists. Moreover, with its petition drive, the WNCA provided rural mountain residents with an organized political channel through which to express their protectionist stance. Presented with this opportunity, residents leaped. "Give me that. I'll take it home and get my folks to sign that."[5]

In effect, though they never used the term, WNCA activists pioneered a form of commons environmentalism. As a result, what Mary Kelly told Bjorn Dahl at Cut the Clearcutting! Day was no exaggeration. "The people have spoken with a loud voice. They do not like what clearcutting is doing to our mountains."[6]

The Appalachian National Forest Commons

The concept of the commons has existed in various forms across many human cultures over millennia. Any resource that is widely accessible, used by many people, and communally owned may be considered a commons. Commons resources are not privately owned by any single person or group, though within a commons some specific resources may be reserved for certain claimants. Commons property systems are regulated and managed, either through formal laws and rules or through informal traditions and social sanctions. Illegal or unsanctioned harvest of commons resources is considered poaching, theft, or invasion, and these infractions are punished. Commons systems are dynamic. They are nearly always contested and they are subject to change over time. One enemy to commons property management systems takes the form of "enclosure" moves, or attempts at privatization. Local petty producers typically benefit from commons systems, while enclosure usually benefits elites.[7]

Since their inception the Nantahala and Pisgah forests, like other national forests, functioned as common-property management systems. Significant resources were communally held. The trees, streams, wildlife, minerals, and flora in the forests were widely recognized as valuable resources. They were publicly owned, which is one form of common ownership. Different elements of the forest were held by different government entities—North Carolina state government claimed the opossums, for instance, while the U.S. federal government owned the lichens—but all national forest resources were in the public domain. In other words, citizens and taxpayers ultimately owned them all.[8]

These publicly owned resources were deliberately managed. The United States Forest Service (USFS) had broad authority over resources in the Pisgah and Nantahala National Forests, and it actively managed these resources. And the agency made many national forest resources widely accessible. For a fairly small fee hunters and anglers could purchase rights to take wildlife on hundreds of thousands of forest acres and in thousands of mountain streams. Modest fees also purchased permits to gather various marketable plant species, such as ginseng, galax, mosses, and Fraser fir cones and seedlings. The USFS also sold thousands of moderately priced firewood permits each year. The agency could not say with precision how many people used the woods, but certainly many thousands harvested Nantahala and Pisgah resources every year in the 1980s.[9]

Mountain residents worried about enclosure threats to these commons forests. Enclosure concerns surfaced in every major regional USFS management debate from the 1930s onward. They drew force from a long history of commons forest use in the southern Appalachians, where a commons model of forest thought had roots centuries deep.[10]

Throughout history, recourse to a vast forested commons sustained mountain communities and economies.[11] Although privately owned from the colonial period forward, mountain woodlands nevertheless functioned as de facto commons. As in other field-and-forest regions, local custom treated "improved" farmlands and "unimproved" woodlands differently. It placed cleared and planted lands squarely in the private-property column, but wooded lands inhabited a gray area between public and private. In other words, even privately held forest was considered semipublic—fair game for local hunting and fishing expeditions, not fair game for timber harvesting. A pattern of large-scale absentee ownership emerged early in the region's white-settlement history and strengthened this de facto commons custom by leaving whole sections of the forest largely unsupervised for decades.[12]

After passage of the 1911 Weeks Act, the United States Forest Service inherited both the region's land use pattern and its wooded commons history. High ridges and mid-slopes typically went to the USFS, while richer bottomlands and lower slopes remained in private hands. Thus the pattern of Forest Service ownership replicated in de jure form long-established de facto commons patterns—lowlands were private grounds, highlands public woods.[13]

With major purchases between 1916 and 1918, the U.S. Forest Service established an enormous presence in western North Carolina. By the dawn of World War II it was the largest single landholder in the state's mountain region. By 1970 the Nantahala and Pisgah National Forests encompassed around nine hundred thousand mountain acres—at least one-tenth of the land in nearly every mountain county and over half the land in some. By the end of the 1930s Forest Service holdings also accounted for a substantial percentage of wooded land in the mountains, and that percentage increased as development claimed ever more private woods. The USFS mandate to manage its holdings for "multiple uses"—including small-, as well as large-scale forest extraction—made these tracts de jure as well as de facto commons. In 1982, Macon County's *Franklin Press* noted a pattern that was true throughout the region: "the largest portion of nonposted, available-to-the-public land falls under Forest Service jurisdiction."[14]

During its first several decades in the southern Appalachians, the USFS served largely as a forest caretaker and restorer. Industrial timber harvests of the late nineteenth and early twentieth centuries left many mountain forests in ruins. Formerly verdant slopes were often repeatedly burned over, badly eroded, and, in the worst cases, almost lunar in appearance. Through a rigorous campaign of fire suppression, coupled with erosion control measures, reforestation efforts, and simple benign neglect, the agency helped enable one of the great conservation success stories in U.S. history. Though the ancient forests could not be replaced, lush second-growth forest eventually reclothed Appalachian slopes under USFS management.

In the decades after World War II, however, as these second-growth forests matured, the Forest Service shifted its emphasis to timber harvesting.[15]

Clearcutting

Before the 1960s the Forest Service relied on all-aged management as the chief forest supervision method in the southern Appalachians. All-aged management involved selective cutting, which required foresters to walk through the woods "cruising timber," or assessing trees for their timber potential. Timber cruisers marked mature trees for harvest. Only these designated trees were to be cut. The system was called all-aged management, or uneven-aged management, because after a timber harvest, trees of various ages remained. Because selection cuts took only some trees, the method also left behind a forest canopy.[16]

By the mid-1960s, even-aged management had taken center stage as a forest supervision system, and clearcutting had become the dominant method of timber harvesting in U.S. national forests. With clearcutting, every tree on a given tract was cut regardless of age, size, species, or timber quality. No timber cruising was necessary. Forest managers simply marked the perimeter of a sale area, and timber buyers cut everything within the perimeter. The trees that eventually grew in a clearcut site would all be the same age. By 1969 clearcutting accounted for about 50 percent of timber harvested in the southern Appalachians, and that percentage grew over the following two decades.[17]

To the lay observer, the most obvious difference between clearcutting and selective harvest techniques was the visible aftermath. When carefully done, selective harvesting was all but invisible to the untrained eye. An *Asheville Citizen* reporter looking out over a western North Carolina timber plantation under all-aged management, for instance, noted he could not discern where trees had recently been cut, though he had seen logs come to the sawmill that very day.[18]

Even the greenest of forest novices could never have missed a clearcut, however. Clearcuts left behind desolate landscapes, muddy piles of brush, slash, and debris gashed by huge logging-road scars. They shocked the senses. Critics cast about for words to describe the visual havoc that clearcuts wrought. They were lunar, barren, hideous, denuded, devastated. They looked like the aftermath of an explosion or the end of the world. Even clearcutting advocates readily conceded the method's abysmal aesthetic. After a clearcut "the land has an aura of total devastation," wrote forester Charles E. McGee in 1970, "an appearance of total ruin."[19]

But for many southern Appalachian critics of clearcutting, including Alliance petition signatories, incompatibility with other forest uses was the central issue, rather than ugly aftermath. As one forester noted, local people typically were "used to seeing a tree cut" and as such they did not object to timber harvest. However, whereas traditional timber harvest methods left behind a usable forest commons for hunting, fishing, firewood gathering, berrying, herb digging, and other similar pursuits, clearcutting essentially destroyed the usefulness of the forest. The method transformed a multiple-use forest stand into a single-use timbering site, in effect enclosing the commons forest. Clearcutting removed tracts from commons use and gave over their resources to the exclusive use of a single entity—in this case, a timber company.[20]

Mountain Opposition to Clearcutting

Clearcutting therefore provoked opposition from anyone interested in using the public forests as commons. Madison County hunter Haze Landers explained to Appalshop filmmakers his theory that commons users would even mount financial defenses of the commons forests if allowed. He offered the example of a local clearcut timber sale that had recently gone for $3,500. Hunters like himself would have paid the Forest Service at least as much not to have cut it, he said. "I'd have made up $3,500 and give it to them if they'd have left it there," Landers declared. "I'd have took up a collection and I'd have soon got it off of these hunters here." In Landers's analysis, the forest's commons value was higher—even in dollar terms—than the timber value Forest Service officials assigned to it.[21]

But the rural people who opposed clearcutting on commons grounds were scattered across hundreds of miles and more than a dozen western North Carolina counties. They had no central channel through which to express their opposition. The obvious possible channel, the Forest Service itself, seemed determined to suppress rather than coordinate local opposition. During earlier wilderness fights the Forest Service encouraged local residents (who typically opposed further wilderness designation) to visit district offices and have secretaries transcribe verbal comments for inclusion in the all-important written record. It apparently offered no parallel service to clearcutting opponents. Antipathy to clearcutting in western North Carolina was probably at least as widespread throughout the 1970s and 1980s as antipathy to wilderness, but the agency did little to record or respond to that situation.[22]

Nor did national environmental groups help western North Carolinians express their opposition to clearcutting effectively. Communities in the region poured time, energy, and other resources into contesting particular timber sales, for instance. At Little Laurel, Roaring Hole, Craggy Gardens, Little Prong, Big Rocky, and other sites, local citizens and groups fought national forest clearcutting acre by acre. They filed formal appeals, circulated petitions, and organized public meetings. Throughout the 1980s, however, Sierra Club policy was not to oppose individual sales in the region. The club filed its first appeal of a western North Carolina timber sale in June 1990, more than a year after the WNCA's massive Cut the Clearcutting! campaign. Other national groups followed a similar pattern.[23]

With its Cut the Clearcutting! campaign the Western North Carolina Alliance stepped into the breach left by the Forest Service's and national environmental groups' unresponsiveness to local concerns. The campaign finally provided a central channel for the political expression of the widespread and long-standing but dispersed regional antipathy to clearcutting.

The Western North Carolina Alliance and Opposition to Clearcutting

Since its founding the Western North Carolina Alliance had steadily fought clearcutting, and always with an emphasis on the method's destruction of commons forests. Concerned about early 1980s threats to the Nantahala and Pisgah from oil and gas exploration, Macon County native Esther Cunningham and Cherokee County resident David Liden partnered to establish the WNCA. The organization officially began in 1981. It quickly attracted activists concerned with other dangers to the region's national forests, including clearcutting. These activists formed a Forest Management Task Force within the Alliance, and for years that group spearheaded the organization's anticlearcutting efforts.[24]

Walton Smith, a retired USFS employee and practicing private forester, swiftly emerged as a central figure in the Alliance's task force. Smith and his wife, Dee Leatherman Smith, resided in the Cowee community in Macon County, near the Swain County border. Nantahala National Forest lands were a stone's throw from Cowee. The Smiths lived on a 150-acre tract that had been in Dee Leatherman Smith's family for generations. Walton and Dee Smith called their land Waldee Forest, and Walton managed the property for timber production using selection harvest methods. He operated a small sawmill on the tract, and kept it busy cutting Waldee logs.[25]

Walton Smith became the chief architect of the WNCA's forest management platform, which included strong opposition to clearcutting. Where wilderness opponents had used commons-friendly multiple-use arguments to turn back proposed wilderness designations, Smith used the same arguments to combat clearcutting. He described clearcutting as a single-use threat to the multiple-use commons forest. Addressing the crowd at a 1985 WNCA fundraiser, for instance, Smith criticized the USFS for embracing "wholesale clearcutting at the expense of watershed protection, hunting, recreation, and the continuous production of high quality hardwood trees which make the area so unique," the organization's *Accent* newsletter reported.[26]

Smith and the Alliance were not the first outspoken critics of clearcutting in the southern Appalachians, which had proved a hotbed of resistance to the practice since the 1960s.[27] Yet in the 1980s, clearcutting in western North Carolina's mountains, as in the rest of the nation, continued apace. Then, in October 1984, the National Forests in North Carolina office released its fifty-year draft management plan for the Pisgah and Nantahala forests. The 1976 National Forest Management Act (NFMA) required such long-range forest management plans to be compiled periodically. This was the first plan produced for western North Carolina forests under the NFMA. Five years in the making, it was some four hundred pages long and filled with what one critic described as "technical jargon."[28]

The Forest Service allowed the public ninety days to comment on the draft. Forest activists found small agency announcements soliciting public input buried deep in the pages of area newspapers. Mitchell County clearcutting opponent Will Ruggles remembered that the Forest Service "didn't actually want any public response." Perhaps remembering ardent protests at its wilderness information sessions a few years earlier, the Asheville office arranged no public hearings on the fifty-year plan.[29]

Walton Smith obtained a copy of the plan and deciphered its contents. He grew alarmed when he realized the document called for 389,000 acres— over one-third of the national forest lands in western North Carolina—to be harvested by clearcutting during the next five decades. Access restrictions on 200,000 acres would also be eased to allow mineral and petroleum development, and more than seven thousand miles of new roads would be built. Placed end-to-end, the proposed Forest Service roads would stretch from the North Carolina mountains to the California coast and back, with plenty to spare. "I was jolted into action," Smith remembered. "In spite of public opinion, in spite of legislation, and in spite of the feeling of many in the forestry profession, my prided Forest Service had come up with a plan for almost 100 percent even-aged management with clearcutting as the method of harvesting."[30]

Smith was not the only one jolted into action; the management proposal met with spirited public response. "Somehow—and no one is really sure how," wrote the *Asheville Citizen*, the Forest Service's fifty-year plan draft "touched off the anti-clearcutting movement." The outpouring of public reaction sparked by the plan snowballed to include petitions, letters to the editor, letters to the Forest Service, letters to U.S. Representative Bill Hendon, and newspaper editorials. At one point Congressman Hendon's office reported receiving roughly one hundred anticlearcutting letters a day. The Forest Service had received nearly two thousand responses by the end of its comment period, and these were overwhelmingly opposed to clearcutting. Area newspapers published a steady stream of anticlearcutting letters to the editor, and editorial boards called for revisions to the plan. Thousands of people signed anticlearcutting petitions circulated by the Alliance and other concerned organizations and individuals. Twenty-six different petitions made their way to Forest Service headquarters.[31]

The petition WNCA leaders circulated in response to the fifty-year Pisgah and Nantahala management plan was clearly a commons- rather than a wilderness-inspired document. It opposed both clearcutting and gated roads. In other words, it linked commons concerns about clearcutting with forest access. Antiwilderness commons users could sign the petition comfortably because it carried no whiff of wilderness environmentalism. By coupling clearcutting opposition to concerns about forest access, Alliance strategists broke new and commons-friendly protectionist ground.

Importantly, neither the official WNCA platform nor the organization's petition protesting the fifty-year plan objected to national forest timber harvesting per se. On the contrary, both documents explicitly listed timber harvesting as a legitimate use of the public forests. Platform and petition did not even object absolutely to clearcutting as a USFS timber harvest method. In fact, in its forest management platform the Alliance made a point of recognizing "the need for even-aged management (clear-cutting) on some sites under some conditions." The Alliance and petition signatories opposed "indiscriminate" clearcutting and argued that this abuse of a legitimate technique was "now practiced" by the Forest Service. The problem, according to the Alliance and petition signatories, was that wholesale clearcutting prevented other legitimate uses of the national forests. Large-scale clearcutting could not coexist with true multiple use.[32]

This position again reflected its architects' commons-based understanding of the forest. A wilderness-inspired position would have argued against timber harvesting altogether, since lumbering meant significant human manipulation of the forest. Timber harvesting by any method destroyed wilderness values. Prohibitions against timber harvesting in federally designated wilderness areas reflected that understanding. Of course, they also reflected conservationists' concern to protect some lands from the devastating effects of industrial-scale timber harvests. Those effects were already abundantly clear by the time conservationists began working toward wilderness legislation, in the 1950s. But wilderness ideology had the effect of lumping all harvesting together with industrial timber harvesting. It therefore left little room for legitimate tree cutting, and it seemed hostile to other types of forest harvest as well. Wilderness preservation inevitably alienated those who relied on timber harvesting for a living, but it also repelled commons users, for whom the forest was often more important as a cultural rather than as an economic site.[33]

The Western North Carolina Alliance, by contrast, argued that clearcutting was categorically different from other forms of forest use, including other methods of timber harvesting. By drawing a careful distinction between timber harvesting—including limited clearcutting—on the one hand and wholesale clearcutting on the other, the Alliance staked out environmentalist ground that could be comfortably, even enthusiastically, inhabited by many long-time mountain residents. The timber industry had long been a central pillar of North Carolina's highland economy. Dismissing the industry's economic importance (as many wilderness advocates seemed to do), or failing to grant timber harvesting environmental legitimacy (as wilderness terminology and regulations seemed to do), meant alienating most rural western North Carolinians. By recognizing timber's importance and granting its legitimacy as a use of the forest, the Alliance made environmentalism safe for many of these same rural residents. "You'd come up with petitions, you'd have people grabbing them out of your hand," Mary Kelly remembered.[34]

When local citizens poured out their objections to the large-scale clearcutting called for in the draft fifty-year plan, the Forest Service indicated a willingness to listen. "We were told that our voices were heard," Walton Smith wrote, "we were thanked for our input; and we were assured that the Final Plan would give full consideration to our comments." But when the agency released its final plan, now scaled back from fifty years to fifteen, clearcutting opponents felt they had received only lip service. The new plan showed small amendments but it still overwhelmingly favored clearcutting.[35]

Other groups were also dissatisfied with the Land and Resource Plan for the Nantahala and Pisgah Forests, 1986–2000. Walton and Dee Smith and Alliance activist Taylor Barnhill met with representatives of the Sierra Club, the Wilderness Society, and the Southern Environmental Law Center to discuss the possibility of filing a joint appeal. The parties found some agreement, and the Sierra Club and Wilderness Society joined forces. Eventually the North Carolina Wildlife Federation also enlisted in these groups' appeal. Though they concurred with some of the organizations' objections, the Smiths and Barnhill noted important differences in emphasis and they decided to move the Alliance forward independently.[36]

The WNCA hired the Washington, D.C., law firm of Wilson and Cotter to help it craft an independent appeal of the fifteen-year plan. The Alliance's Forest Management Task Force worked closely with this legal team to develop the appeal. To document widespread local opposition to clearcutting, the Alliance hurriedly gathered sixteen hundred signatures for an anticlearcutting petition it appended to the text.[37]

All appeals went to the Forest Service on September 7, 1987. The Alliance had asked twice for a stay on clearcutting and burning while its appeal was under consideration, but those requests were "summarily denied," Walton Smith wrote. "Clearcutting and burning will go on as usual or maybe be increased while we bite our fingernails." The full Alliance appeal was an immense document two inches thick. Alliance coordinator Mary Kelly described it as "beautifully crafted." But on February 5, 1988 the regional forester's office in Atlanta denied the appeal. He "did not give an inch," Smith reported.[38]

Smith circulated a fifteen-page commentary on the regional forester's forty-page response to the appeal. The Forest Management Task Force planned to resubmit the appeal, this time to federal headquarters—the Washington office of the Forest Service chief. Walton Smith and other Alliance activists raced to fortify the original appeal with further evidence before the May 2 filing deadline. Smith took a team of amateur foresters he had trained to the woods. They did timber assessments on two tracts, one clearcut in 1963–64, and one selectively harvested in 1972. The team's study refuted the Forest Service's claim that clearcutting was the best method for regenerating Appalachian hardwoods. There was more growth on the old clearcuts, the Alliance survey showed, but of lower species diversity and lower timber quality. The task force appended formal results from this study to its D.C. appeal. It also appended statements from local citizens, including area scientists and locally renowned bear hunter and forest expert Taylor Crockett.[39] After the Alliance turned in this final appeal, nail biting began in earnest. As Smith had predicted, clearcutting continued at full speed.

Alliance chapters fought at least three timber sales while the appeal sat in Washington. Bear hunter Clarence Hall, chair of the Jackson County chapter, led the charge against the Forest Service's Roaring Hole timber sale in that area. Hall had actively participated in one of Smith's timber surveys, and Smith worked with another amateur team of volunteers to study the Jackson County site.[40]

Alliance newcomers Mary and Rob Kelly assisted Hall and Smith with the Roaring Hole survey. The Kellys had recently moved to the Hickey Fork area of Madison County, near the Pisgah National Forest. Mary Sauls Kelly was a PhD ecologist and Rob Kelly was a trained forester; both were angling enthusiasts and musicians in the old-time mountain style. Mary joined the Alliance staff as coordinator, and Rob came aboard as a volunteer forester.[41]

Clay County resident Darry Wood organized local opposition to another proposed USFS clearcut, this one on the Clay-Swain county line. Wood arranged a public hearing with Forest Service personnel, and Walton Smith, David Liden, and Mary Kelly spoke at the meeting. Wood also wrote a series of *Timber Targets* columns for the *Clay County Progress*. These columns discussed silviculture in layman's terms, explaining current USFS policy and why Wood and other local residents objected to it. Clearcutting "wastes good timber and tax-payer dollars, and it destroys hard mast supplies for wildlife," Wood wrote.[42]

At roughly the same time, residents of the North Fork Valley, near Black Mountain, fought a clearcut harvest project approved by the Asheville-Buncombe Water Authority. The authority controlled the Asheville watershed, a vast tract that many North Fork families had once called home. The families had been forced to leave when Asheville condemned the land in the 1920s for a dam project to provide the city with water. Resentments over the displacements still lingered. In 1988 residents noticed clearcut scars on the watershed property. They learned the water authority had put a USFS-style timber program in place. It had made one clearcut timber sale already, and had plans for more on a rotating basis. Watershed restrictions prevented local residents even from visiting their families' old homesites, on grounds that human activity in the area threatened water quality. The water authority's decision to allow massive timber harvesting equipment to come in and clearcut, while forbidding area residents to walk or hunt in the woods, infuriated local people. They formed Citizens against Clearcutting in the Asheville Watershed (CACAW), and joined the WNCA as a chapter. Though not a national-forest fight, the controversy over watershed clearcutting raised many of the same issues. Walton Smith came to Black Mountain and spoke at a public hearing CACAW sponsored.[43]

Alliance members fought these and other clearcutting projects, and they waited with growing impatience for an appeal decision from Washington. By late 1988 participants in the organization's Forest Management Task Force were fed up. Mary Kelly remembered one meeting at which "everybody had the same story. 'We're not getting anywhere. We're not getting anywhere.'"

They had painstakingly crafted timber sale appeals, but "the Forest Service had just turned them down, flat out, everywhere around." Years of working on a case-by-case basis, mounting technical challenges to Forest Service proposals, and protesting through official USFS channels had earned the organization's volunteers professional respect but had achieved few concrete forest results. In fact, clearcutting on the Nantahala and Pisgah increased almost every year, even as the task force gained supporters and momentum and stepped up its oppositional efforts. By 1988 the group had concluded that technical arguments alone would never turn the Forest Service away from clearcutting. "So we sat around the table and the people just said, 'What we're doing is not working. We've got to jack it up. We've got to do something else,'" Kelly recalled.[44]

Cut the Clearcutting!

The Alliance now upped the ante, supplementing its technical opposition with a publicity campaign. This campaign, which became Cut the Clearcutting! benefited from the expertise of Monroe Gilmour, a Black Mountain resident and crack social justice organizer who had been a central figure in the Citizens against Clearcutting in the Asheville Watershed fight.[45]

Gilmour brought vast organizational experience to the WNCA. For decades he had worked on a host of social justice causes in the United States and abroad, including racial discrimination in western North Carolina and South Africa. Gilmour was a relative newcomer to environmental work. As he later explained, he had seen environmental concerns as a luxury compared to hunger and discrimination. The watershed fight and his Alliance work on clearcutting made him see environmental issues in a new light. "It became more and more a social justice issue for me," Gilmour explained.[46]

Plans for a four-month Cut the Clearcutting! campaign grew out of task force discussions and a memo Gilmour circulated. The campaign aimed to use publicity and grassroots organizing to put pressure on the Forest Service just as its D.C. chief was deciding how to rule on the Alliance's appeal. Task force members heard from the chief's office that he would likely pass judgment on the appeal in the first half of 1989. As the Alliance newsletter, *Accent*, explained to members, the Forest Management Task Force hoped to use "the sheer weight of numbers of voters opposed to clear-cutting" to influence the chief's decision.[47]

The Alliance launched Cut the Clearcutting! on January 25, 1989, with a press conference in front of National Forests in North Carolina headquarters.

The campaign wedded Monroe Gilmour's organizing and publicity vision to the commons-friendly anticlearcutting platform Walton Smith and other task force members had developed. The street theater was Gilmour's, the rhetoric Smith's. The call for Forest Service responsiveness to local communities belonged to both.

As she kicked off the initial press conference, Alliance steering committee chair Judy Williamson proclaimed, "Clearing in our National Forests has gotten out of hand." Western North Carolinians loved their national forests, she continued, and used them for a variety of purposes including hunting, fishing, sightseeing, and recreation. "We are concerned that clearcut harvesting will ruin large areas of our forest for these other uses," Williamson explained. Current policy called for unacceptable levels of clearcutting. The Alliance did not demand a halt to timber harvesting, Williamson emphasized; it did call on the Forest Service to switch to harvest methods more compatible with multiple uses.[48]

Mitchell County's Douglass Rankin echoed these sentiments when she spoke with reporters. Clearcutting wasted taxpayer money, destroyed wildlife habitat and food supplies, blemished the tourist-attracting mountain landscape, and damaged prime trout streams, Rankin explained. She told reporters that the Alliance was "made up of a real cross-section of folks in Western North Carolina including loggers, hunters, farmers and business people. We don't want to tie up the forest resources; we just want to see them used for the benefit of all in the long run." Rankin's language distanced the WNCA from wilderness environmentalism. Wilderness opponents' frequent charge that wilderness designation "tied up forest resources" resonated with commons users concerned about enclosure threats. By specifically rejecting this language, Rankin made the WNCA's position more attractive to these same commons users.[49]

Press conference participants also unrolled a ninety-foot anticlearcutting petition, and Dick Heywood of Jackson County announced the petition drive. Heywood pledged that by the time the Alliance campaign finished in April, the petition would be long enough to wrap around the federal building in Asheville, which housed National Forests in North Carolina headquarters. "Only Santa Claus may have a list of names longer," wrote one reporter covering the story.[50]

This opening press conference set the tone for the rest of the campaign. It showcased the Alliance's multicounty breadth, it emphasized the organization's pro-timber but anticlearcutting position, and it provided drama. Walton Smith's protégés played leading roles. Dick Heywood was a regular member of Smith's timber survey teams. Douglass Rankin was a longtime Forest Management Task Force activist who had worked closely with Smith for years. She and her husband, Will Ruggles, were stalwarts on Mitchell County's anticlearcutting front lines. Monroe Gilmour's work was also on display. The handmade signs around the stage, the unfurled petition, the promise of more later—all were signature Gilmour publicity strategies. To dramatize their concerns, Alliance members had even hauled dozens of heavy logs and stumps to the streets and placed them beneath a posterboard reading, Your Forest, Compliments USFS.[51]

In the months after its campaign kickoff the Alliance busily continued getting the word out. Monroe Gilmour, Mary Kelly, and other staffers and volunteers put long hours into Cut the Clearcutting! A letter-writing campaign poured letters into editors' offices, and local newspapers around the region covered petition-drive progress. "Anti-clear-cut Drive Picks Up Some Steam," read one typical headline. Organizers photocopied that article and put it on the back of their circulating petitions. Regional media, including the *Charlotte Observer* and Tennessee's *Greeneville Sun*, also covered the campaign. Participants widely posted flyers for the campaign's Ugliest Clearcut Photo Contest ("this one will be tough to judge!"). The contest carried a cash prize and generated yet more press coverage.[52]

Cut the Clearcutting! featured other events designed to attract media attention. In March, the WNCA brought Project LightHawk to Asheville. LightHawk billed itself as the Environmental Air Force. Independent pilots with the organization volunteered their planes and services to fly media representatives, politicians and activists over various environmental sites to view, photograph, and film them. LightHawk had helped document dramatic clearcuts and dam projects in the West, but the Alliance-sponsored trip was its first mission in the East. Pilot Ed Coffman flew several trips over the Pisgah National Forest, carrying reporters, photographers, and activists. Several area newspapers and Asheville's television news team covered his visit and ran striking footage from his flights.[53]

Meanwhile, on-the-ground organizers set up petition-signing stations inside and outside area businesses. Monroe Gilmour worked with Clarence Hall and some of his fellow Jackson County bear hunters in role play exercises designed to help them gather signatures. Black Mountain volunteers sat in front of their local Roses discount store beside a poster bearing a clearcut photo and the message "Stop Clearcutting in WNC Forests." More than a dozen Yancey activists came to a petition-drive meeting called by local organizer Lisa

Loveday. Several were hunters, Loveday reported, and all left carrying copies of the petition. The Yancey team planned to work three weekends in front of the Ingles grocery and the Carolina Tire store in Burnsville. "The people who came to the meeting tonight are energized to collect signatures," Loveday reported. "Most of them have spent a lot of time in the woods, they know where the clear-cuts are, and they don't like them," she added.[54]

Petitions seemed to fly off the tables. "At first we were scared," Mitchell County activist Will Ruggles told reporters, "but everywhere we've gone the store owner has been the first one to sign." He and other county volunteers had collected one thousand signatures in two weekends at a station in front of the Roses store in Spruce Pine. The Mitchell chapter aimed to have two thousand signatures before the drive was over, at the end of March, and they were pleased to be halfway to their goal early in the month. Mary Kelly reported that over one hundred people in her small rural community of Hickey Fork, in Madison County, signed the petition the first day she and Rob left it in the local convenience store. She also remembered people practically grabbing petitions out of her hand. "Everybody had some—or several—big timber sale that they were fighting and could get mad about," Kelly explained. "It was an issue that was deeply felt. It was broad-based." This deeply felt concern translated into ever-growing numbers. By the end of the drive—in a matter of weeks—Alliance volunteers had collected over sixteen thousand petition signatures. "These signatures were collected with ease," Mary Kelly told Bjorn Dahl on Cut the Clearcutting! Day. "We could get tens of thousands if we kept going."[55]

Cut the Clearcutting! Proves Effective

The Cut the Clearcutting! campaign was a political masterstroke. It marked a crucial turning point in the decades-long debate over clearcutting in the western North Carolina national forests. Opposition to clearcutting in the region had long been widespread. It had emerged practically the moment the Forest Service introduced the timber harvest technique, and it had surfaced in nearly every public discussion of forest policy since. Yet levels of clearcut timber harvesting on North Carolina's national forests continued to rise through the 1980s, as they had more or less steadily since the early 1960s.[56]

The WNCA's Cut the Clearcutting! campaign helped to finally reverse this upward trend. In September 1989, Forest Service chief Dale Robertson finally issued his long-awaited decision on the Alliance's appeal of the *Land and Resource Management Plan, 1986–2000*. The document he released also addressed appeals filed by other organizations. Robertson remanded the plan to the Asheville office and ordered important changes. He cited below-cost timber sales as a major problem, and he ruled that planners had not adequately considered "the large public opposition to clearcutting." "The public has won quite a victory with this decision," Mary Kelly announced on behalf of the Alliance. "It has taken a lot of hard, hard work by our foresters and volunteers, but we have finally convinced the chief of the Forest Service that the public has rejected extensive use of clearcutting on our public forests."[57]

Partly this victory reflected national trends. A federal policy shift occurred with the inauguration of a new president in January 1989. The George H. W. Bush White House, though in many ways similar to its fellow-Republican predecessor, was not so hostile to environmental concerns nor so adamant about industrial uses of public lands as the Reagan administration had been. And the USFS began to shift away from wholesale clearcutting partly because mobilized environmentalists nationwide forced it to do so. National-level work on below-cost timber sales, in particular, helped expose the skewed economics behind much of the Forest Service's timber program. Timber sales on North Carolina's national forests, for instance, lost $2.5 million in 1988 alone. Careful environmentalist attention to Forest Service accounting uncovered such numbers nationwide and revealed that taxpayers paid staggering sums to have their publicly owned forests mowed down and hauled off. Amid growing concerns about federal budget deficits, this massive public funding for the timber industry was increasingly difficult to justify. Forest Service chief Robertson noted these concerns in his 1989 ruling on the Pisgah and Nantahala appeals.[58]

Yet important as these national developments were, they could not fully account for all the changes in western North Carolina. When Robertson cited "large public opposition to clearcutting," he referred to the outpouring through Cut the Clearcutting! Mary Kelly recalled Forest Supervisor Bjorn Dahl's calling her office when the chief's ruling was announced. "The Alliance was the first person I had to call because you were the ones that got it," Kelly remembered him saying.[59]

For the WNCA, the chief's decision represented an important victory. Esther Cunningham, David Liden, Bob Padgett, Walton and Dee Smith, Mary and Rob Kelly, and Dick and Gill Heywood celebrated at the Carson Community Center near Franklin, where the Alliance had been born. Mary Kelly rejoiced that Robertson had "told his folks that they'd better listen [to local people], and go back and redo their harvest plans." Walton Smith was more cautious. "We may have won a little on paper," he said, "but we haven't won in the woods yet."[60]

It was not until 1994 that National Forests in North Carolina offices issued a fully revised long-range plan for the Nantahala and Pisgah. This document was far different from the original fifty-year plan it replaced. The new plan represented a clear victory for conservationists.

The Alliance was jubilant. "Public Opinion Makes a Difference! Revised Forest Plan 'Cuts The Clearcutting!'" trumpeted its newsletter. A cartoon of smiling animals—a raccoon, bear, and deer (all popular game species)—dancing above a gravestone accompanied the article. The tombstone read "Here Lies Clearcutting, Died 1994." Forest Management Task Force chairman Bob Gelder thanked everyone who had helped make this happy result come to pass. "None of this would have been possible unless the vast majority of people in our region felt very strongly about this, and were willing to stand up and be counted," he announced. "Everyone who signed a petition, came to a meeting, wrote a letter, or challenged timber sales in their community shares the credit!"[61]

This new plan was part of a larger trend toward more ecologically sensitive national forest management. Democrat William Jefferson Clinton's presidential administration, which began in 1993, was friendlier to environmental interests than the elder Bush's administration had been.[62]

Here again national developments could not fully account for regional particularities, however. The 1994 plan for the Nantahala and Pisgah was one of the most environmentally sensitive USFS regional management plans in the nation. It stood out as a model even among the new wave of more ecologically grounded plans. This was no accident. It was a direct result of the Western North Carolina Alliance's dozen years of tireless forest activism. By wedding Walton Smith's commons-friendly brand of professional forestry to a grassroots campaign tapping powerful regional veins of commons protectionism, the Alliance had reshaped its region's national forest management landscape. It had brought technical credibility to rural residents' brand of forest protection, and political credibility to Walton Smith's version of professional forest management. It had unleashed commons environmentalism.[63]

The forests felt the results. The 1994 plan cut allowable timber harvest levels in the Nantahala and Pisgah forests by more than half, from 72 million board feet per year to 34 million. It nearly eliminated clearcutting as a harvest tool. Clearcutting levels dropped from 4,500 acres per year under the old plan to fewer than 300 under the new plan. The plan removed over 252,000 acres from the 586,000-acre "suitable timber base," declaring these areas too costly, too ecologically sensitive, or too overcut for logging. It made pathbreaking provisions for the first full-scale assessment of bear habitat, forest interior bird habitat, and old-growth forest across the USFS's western North Carolina holdings. And it protected 32,500 acres as Semi-Primitive Non-Motorized areas, a status similar to wilderness.[64]

This victory did not belong only to commons users, but it could not have been accomplished without them. Trained foresters, biologists, ecologists, and botanists lent their expertise to the fight. Wilderness-style environmentalists joined the effort. Ultimately, however, the campaign's success rested on its ability to mobilize commons users in defense of the region's forests. A handful of "outsiders" could be dismissed, but the signatures of sixteen thousand local voters could not.[65] This was especially true because the voters were Republicans as well as Democrats, natives as well as newcomers, housewives and hunters as well as mainstream environmentalists. Western North Carolina commons users gave the pivotal Cut the Clearcutting! campaign the cultural credibility and political clout it needed to succeed.

Cut the Clearcutting! therefore offers lessons to anyone who cares about the future of mountain forests. As the most diverse temperate forests on earth, the southern Appalachian woods are among the world's critically important ecological treasures. The need to protect these forests gains urgency as concerns about species diversity loss and global climate change—and the deforestation that contributes to both—mount. The Western North Carolina Alliance's 1989 Cut the Clearcutting! campaign provides a compelling example of how mobilized commons defense can be a powerful means through which to protect these rich forest ecosystems.

Notes

1. Clarke Morrison, "Clear-Cutting Foes: 'People Have Spoken,'" *Asheville Citizen-Times,* April 16, 1989; Mardell Griffin, "Clearcutting Petition Paraded throughout Asheville," *Mountain Times,* April 20, 1989; "Citizens Gather at Rally to Protest Clear-Cutting," *Hendersonville Times-News,* April 16, 1989; Rusty Sivils, "Clearcut Rally Delivers 1000 Foot Long Petition," *Green Line* 3, no. 7 (1989); "Cut the Clearcutting Campaign," *Accent,* Summer 1989; Anne Lewis Johnson, "Ready for Harvest: Clearcutting in the Southern Appalachians," videorecording (Whitesburg, KY: Appalshop Film and Video, 1993).

2. Griffin, "Clearcutting Petition"; Johnson, "Ready for Harvest"; Mary Kelly, "Alliance Mounts a 'Cut the Clearcutting' Campaign," *Accent,* Spring 1989.

3. Griffin, "Clearcutting Petition"; Walton R. Smith, "Green Paper Number 16," May 10, 1989; "'Cut the Clearcutting' Campaign," *Accent,* Summer 1989, including photo montage; unnumbered photos in the WNCA archival collections (hereafter cited as WNCA). For an excellent exploration of commons culture in the southern Appalachians, see Mary Hufford, "American Ginseng and the Idea of the Commons," *Folklife Center News* 19, nos. 1–2 (Winter–Spring 1997): 3–18.

4. For more on the Roadless Area Review and Evaluation II wilderness controversy in western North Carolina, see Kathryn Newfont, "Moving Mountains: Forest Politics and Commons Culture in Western North Carolina, 1964–1994" (PhD diss., University of North Carolina, Chapel Hill, 2001), esp. chap. 3. See also Newfont, *Blue Ridge Commons: Environmental Activism and Forest History in Western North Carolina* (Athens: University of Georgia Press, forthcoming 2012).

5. Mary Kelly, interview by Kathryn Newfont, Shelton Laurel, NC, November 13, 1998. For a discussion of commons culture in the southern Appalachians, see Hufford, "American Ginseng." For a rich exploration of contemporary commons culture in West Virginia, see American Folklife Center, "Tending the Commons: Folklife and Landscape in Southern West Virginia," American Folklife Center, Library of Congress, http://memory.loc.gov/ammem/collections/tending/index.html (accessed June 20, 2009).

6. M. Kelly, interview; Griffin, "Clearcutting Petition."

7. There is a rich literature on the history and current outlines of commons systems across the globe, only a fraction of which can be addressed here. For an excellent introduction to common property resources, see David Feeney, Fikret Berkes, Bonnie J. McCay, and James M. Acheson, "The Tragedy of the Commons: Twenty-Two Years Later," *Human Ecology* 18 (1990): 1–19. For a thoughtful series of reflections on commons systems, see Bonnie J. McCay and James M. Acheson, eds., *The Question of the Commons: The Culture and Ecology of Communal Resources* (Tucson: University of Arizona Press, 1987). See also John A. Baden and Douglas S. Noonan, eds., *Managing the Commons* (Bloomington: Indiana University Press, 1998). For an illuminating and provocative recent exploration of the commons' role in Anglo-American law and history, see Peter Linebaugh, *The Magna Carta Manifesto: Liberties and Commons for All* (Berkeley: University of California Press, 2008). For especially important examples of U.S. commons history, see Richard W. Judd, *Common Lands, Common People: The Origins of Conservation in Northern New England* (Cambridge, MA: Harvard University Press, 1997); Karl Jacoby, *Crimes against Nature: Squatters, Poachers, Thieves, and the Hidden History of American Conservation* (Berkeley: University of California Press, 2001); Louis S. Warren, *The Hunter's Game: Poachers and Conservationists in Twentieth-Century America* (New Haven: Yale University Press, 1997). For an examination of a present-day U.S. commons, see Brian Donahue, *Reclaiming the Commons: Community Farms and Forests in a New England Town* (New Haven: Yale University Press, 1999). For a widely influential theory of the commons, see Garrett Hardin "The Tragedy of the Commons," *Science* 162, no. 3859 (1968): 1243–48. Hardin's theory predicts dangerous resource depletion as the inevitable result of commons property systems. This theory is typically not borne out by careful studies of specific historical examples of such systems, many of which successfully prevented resource depletion and some of which lasted for centuries. Most commons systems have been regulated or managed; they have rarely allowed the unfettered open access of Hardin's model. Hardin himself has conceded that he might better have titled his piece "The Tragedy of the Unmanaged Commons." See McKay and Acheson, *Question of the Commons*, 1–34.

8. For a discussion of the state and the commons, see McKay and Acheson, *Question of the Commons*, 27–34. See also James C. Scott, *Seeing Like a State: How Certain Schemes to Improve the Human Condition Have Failed* (New Haven: Yale University Press, 1998), 9–24.

9. The U.S. Forest Service shared responsibility for these lands with other federal and state agencies. The North Carolina Wildlife Resources Commission held authority over fish and game animals; it worked cooperatively with the Forest Service on fish-and-game projects on the Nantahala and Pisgah. The federal Bureau of Land Management held authority over minerals on USFS lands. For examples of Pisgah and Nantahala forest use and the fees assigned to them in the early 1980s, see Clyde Osborne, "Moss Thieves," *Asheville Citizen*, March 26, 1981; "Fraser Cones to be Available This Fall," *Franklin Press*, August 20, 1981; "Fish Hides Constructed through Joint Effort," *Franklin Press*, October 22, 1981; "Sutton on Sports," *Franklin Press*, March 4, 1982; "Sale of Green Standing Firewood Is Not Offered," *Franklin Press*, June 3, 1982; "Save Money If You Purchase Lifetime State Hunting License," *Franklin Press*, July 28, 1982.

10. For a history of forest use in the southern Appalachians, see Donald Edward Davis, *Where There Are Mountains: An Environmental History of the Southern Appalachians* (Athens: University of Georgia Press, 2000). For a sweeping case study of one Appalachian range, see Timothy Silver, *Mount Mitchell and the Black Mountains: An Environmental History of the Highest Peaks in Eastern America* (Chapel Hill: University of North Carolina Press, 2003). For history of the Great Smoky Mountains National Park, see Margaret Lynn Brown, *The Wild East: A Biography of the Great Smoky Mountains* (Gainesville: University Press of Florida, 2000). See also Daniel S. Pierce, *The Great Smokies: From Natural Habitat to National Park* (Knoxville, University of Tennessee Press, 2000). For history of the region's industrial timber harvests, see Ronald L. Lewis, *Transforming the Appalachian Countryside: Railroads, Deforestation, and Social Change in West Virginia, 1880–1920* (Chapel Hill: University of North Carolina Press, 1998). For a classic treatment of these harvests and their aftermath, see Ronald D. Eller, *Miners, Millhands, and Mountaineers: Industrialization of the Appalachian South, 1880–1930* (Knoxville: University of Tennessee Press, 1982). For a case study exploration of these harvests and related industrial developments, see Geoffrey L. Buckley, "The Environmental Transformation of an Appalachian Valley, 1850–1906," *Geographical Review* 88, no. 2 (1998): 175–98. For a thoughtful introduction to the forest history of the southern Appalachians, see Chris Bolgiano, *The Appalachian Forest: A Search for Roots and Renewal* (Mechanicsburg, PA: Stackpole Books, 1998). For a discussion of Appalachian forest history in commons context, see Jack Temple Kirby, *Mockingbird Song: Ecological Landscapes of the South* (Chapel Hill: University of North Carolina Press, 2006), esp. 132–55. The idea of a forested commons had great longevity in the region; a case can be made for its existence throughout the period of human habitation.

11. For centuries the mountain forest commons yielded an array of products, including animal skins, medicinal plants, and plant foods. Important products during the long history of the commons included deerskins, ginseng, free-ranging hogs, chestnuts, and galax. Only a sample of this history can be offered here. For the colonial era, see Tom Hatley, *The Dividing Paths: Cherokees and South Carolinians through the Era of Revolution* (New York: Oxford University Press, 1995), esp. sections on hunting and trade, such as 32–33, 163–66, 211–13. For antebellum trade, including forest-foraging livestock and ginseng, see John C. Inscoe, *Mountain Masters: Slavery and the Sectional Crisis in Western North Carolina* (Knoxville: University of Tennessee Press, 1996), esp. 25–58. For history of the commons-based chestnut trade, see Ralph H. Lutts, "Like Manna from God:

The American Chestnut Trade in Southwestern Virginia," *Environmental History* 9, no. 3 (2004): 497–525.

12. Davis, *Where There Are Mountains*, 179; Hufford, "American Ginseng," 5, 7–8; Shelley Smith Mastran and Nan Lowerre, *Mountaineers and Rangers: A History of Federal Forest Management in the Southern Appalachians, 1900–81* (Washington, DC: U.S. Department of Agriculture, 1983), 164–65. For history of absentee ownership, see Wilma A. Dunaway, *The First American Frontier: Transition to Capitalism in Southern Appalachia, 1700–1860* (Chapel Hill: University of North Carolina Press, 1996), esp. 51–86.

13. Bolgiano, *Appalachian Forest*, 106, 110; Mastran and Lowerre, *Mountaineers and Rangers*, 25–29.

14. Quote is from "One Function of Forest Service Is to Uphold Laws," *Franklin Press*, March 25, 1982. For USFS history, see Mastran and Lowerre, *Mountaineers and Rangers*, 30, 48, 53–57; Eller, *Miners, Millhands*, 118–21, Bolgiano, *Appalachian Forest*, 123–230.

15. The shift reflected a nationwide trend. The nation's timber demands skyrocketed in the postwar period, and between 1945 and 1970 national forest timber harvest levels rose—usually dramatically—under every U.S. president. Harvest numbers dipped briefly between 1970 and 1975 but climbed again beginning in 1976 and with accelerating speed in the 1980s. See Paul W. Hirt, *A Conspiracy of Optimism: Management of the National Forests since World War Two* (Lincoln: University of Nebraska Press, 1994), xxi–xxv, xliv, 87–93,113–17, 235–42, 266–67. Also see David A. Clary, *Timber and the Forest Service* (Lawrence: University Press of Kansas, 1986), chaps. 4–7, epilogue (94–199).

16. For discussions of these methods, see Walton R. Smith, "Green Paper Number 15," March 1, 1989; Bob Padgett, "Clearcutting the National Forests: Good or Bad?" January 1987, WNCA.

17. For a useful introduction to the clearcutting issue in western North Carolina, see Johnson, "Ready for Harvest." For a pro-clearcutting forester's view, see Charles McGee, "Clearcutting and Aesthetics in the Southern Appalachians," *Journal of Forestry* 68 (September 1970): 540–44. For discussion of the method's use in western North Carolina national forests, see Pat Cook, interview by Kathryn Newfont, Asheville, NC, July 1, 1999. For national clearcutting critics' views, see Bill Devall, ed., *Clearcut: The Tragedy of Industrial Forestry* (San Francisco: Sierra Club Books and Earth Island Press, 1993), esp. chapters by Herb Hammond, "Clearcutting: Ecological and Economic Flaws," 25–32, and Mitch Lansky, "Myths of the Benign Industrial Clearcut," 47–49. See also Mastran and Lowerre, *Mountaineers and Rangers*, 144; Hirt, *Conspiracy of Optimism*, 131–32, 245–51; Clary, *Timber*, 156–68, 180–94. See also Russ Rymer, "Wilderness Politics," *Atlanta Journal Weekly Magazine*, October 24, 1982.

18. "DeHart, Independent Logger, Typical of Dwindling Breed," *Asheville Citizen*, February 10, 1974.

19. Hammond, "Clearcutting"; Lansky, "Myths"; Monroe Gilmour, interview by Kathryn Newfont, Black Mountain, NC, August 21, 1998; "Citizens Gather at Rally to Protest Clear-Cutting," *Hendersonville Times-News*, April 16, 1989; McGee, "Clearcutting and Aesthetics," quotes 541, 542, 544.

20. Cook, interview; "Cut the Clearcutting," petition, WNCA.

21. Johnson, "Ready for Harvest." See also M. Kelly, interview.

22. M. Kelly, interview; "Large Crowd Protests 'Wilderness,'" *Franklin Press*, July 13, 1978; "RARE II Open House," *Franklin Press*, July 20, 1978; "Get the Facts and Write," *Franklin Press*, July 20, 1978.

23. For examples, see "Clearcut Is Held Up," *Accent*, Summer 1985; Walton R. Smith, "Green Paper Number 1," January 16, 1987; "Madison Residents Question Wisdom of Clearcutting," *Marshall (NC) News-Record*, November 24, 1988; "Craggy Clear-Cut Unpopular," *Asheville Citizen*, January 11, 1989; "Jackson Chapter of WNC Alliance Challenges Roaring Hole Clearcuts," *Sylva Herald and Ruralite*, January 12, 1989; "Clay County Clear-Cutting Opponents Up In Arms," *Asheville Citizen*, February 3, 1989; "Sierra Club, WNC Alliance Challenge Timber Sale," *Asheville Times*, June 26, 1990; M. Kelly, interview. See also Hirt, *Conspiracy of Optimism*, 162–66, 229–33. Of course the Sierra Club and other national groups had limited resources and had of necessity to pick their battles. Wilderness was a cornerstone of their strategy. They stoutly defended wilderness areas and worked to gain protection for more acreage. In general, however, if an area was not wilderness or potential wilderness they did not contest Forest Service management decisions for it. One result of these national-level priorities was that local commons users, whose highly valued forest places did not necessarily overlap with roadless wilderness, had to mount defenses largely on their own. For more on the history of wilderness politics, with particular attention to national forests, see Paul S. Sutter, *Driven Wild: How the Fight against Automobiles Launched the Modern Wilderness Movement* (Seattle: University of Washington Press, 2002); Michael Frome, *Battle for the Wilderness*, rev. ed. (Salt Lake City: University of Utah Press, 1997); Dennis M. Roth, *The Wilderness Movement and the National Forests: 1964–1980* (Washington, DC: U.S. Department of Agriculture, 1984); Kevin R. Marsh, *Drawing Lines in the Forest: Creating Wilderness Areas in the Pacific Northwest* (Seattle: University of Washington Press, 2007).

24. For more on the early WNCA, see Kathryn Newfont, "Grassroots Environmentalism: Origins of the Western North Carolina Alliance," *Appalachian Journal* 27, no. 1 (Fall 1999): 46–61.

25. M. Kelly, interview; Gilmour, interview; Esther Cunningham, interviews by Kathryn Newfont, Carson Community, November 16, 1998, September 9, 1999; Walton Smith, "Green Paper Number 3," April 1, 1987; Johnson, "Ready for Harvest."

26. "Barbeque and Rally a Big Success," "Clearcut Is Held Up," *Accent*, Summer 1985; Walton R. Smith, "Green Paper No. 1," January 16, 1987.

27. Smith was not the first Appalachian activist to use this line of argument to effectively defend mountain forests against clearcutting. West Virginia hunters had made similar arguments on behalf of the Monongahela National Forest beginning in 1964. Their activism led to the landmark 1975 court ruling *West Virginia Division of the Izaak Walton League v. Butz*, which temporarily brought a nationwide halt to clearcutting. Recognizing the renewed clearcutting threat later in the 1970s, some commons forest defenders in the southern Appalachians even hitched the RARE II wilderness initiative to their cause. Western North Carolina's Southern Nantahala Wilderness Area stands as one example of their success. For more on the Monongahela case, see, for example, Clary, *Timber*, 190–94. For more on the Southern Nantahala, see Newfont, *Blue Ridge Commons*, chap. 7.

28. Quote from M. Kelly, interview. For the importance of the NFMA, see Samuel P. Hays, *Wars in the Woods: The Rise of Ecological Forestry in America* (Pittsburgh: University of Pittsburgh Press, 2006), 16–19.

29. "Forest Management," *Asheville Citizen-Times*, October 21, 1984; "Public Reaction to 50 Year Plan," "Alliance Opposes Clearcutting," *Accent* 2 (Spring 1985); Johnson, "Ready for Harvest"; National Forest Management Act of 1976; "WNC Alliance Circulating Anti-clearcutting Petition," *Mountain Times*, March 16, 1989.

30. Walton R. Smith, "Green Paper No. 18," August 21, 1989, 2; Smith, "Green Paper 1," January 16, 1987; M. Kelly, interview; Esther Cunningham, interview by Kathryn Newfont, Carson Community, October 10, 1997; "Public Reaction to 50 Year Plan"; "Alliance Opposes Clearcutting"; "Forest Management," *Asheville Citizen-Times*, October 21, 1984.

31. "Forest Service Revises Plan," *Asheville Citizen*, February 8, 1985; "Public Reaction to 50 Year Plan"; "Alliance Opposes Clearcutting"; "Forest Management."

32. "Cut the Clearcutting Day! The People Have Spoken!" program in Monroe Gilmour, "Cut the Clearcutting" Scrapbook, vol. 1, and in "Cut the Clearcutting" Campaign File, WNCA archival files; Western North Carolina Alliance 1989 Platform in "Cut the Clearcutting" Campaign File and "Cut the Clearcutting" petition, both in WNCA archival files.

33. William Cronon, "The Trouble with Wilderness; or, Getting Back to the Wrong Nature," and Richard White, "'Are You an Environmentalist or Do you Work for a Living?': Work and Nature," both in William Cronon, ed., *Uncommon Ground: Toward Reinventing Nature* (New York: Norton, 1995). Hirt, *Conspiracy of Optimism*, 151–70. For the cultural importance of commons, see Hufford, "American Ginseng"; Kirby, *Mockingbird Song*, chap. 3.

34. M. Kelly, interview. For timber and local economy, see Mastran and Lowerre, *Mountaineers and Rangers*. In Graham County 75 percent of the labor force was employed in timber-related jobs in the late 1970s, for example (p. 169). See also "Forestry Is Important to Economy," *Asheville Citizen*, January 27, 1963; "$19 Million Forest Crop Means Big WNC Payoff," *Asheville Citizen*, June 18, 1972.

35. Smith, "Green Paper Number 18," August 21, 1989.

36. Smith, "Green Paper Number 4," June 1, 1987.

37. Smith, "Green Paper Number 5," August 3, 1987; "In Memoriam: Bob Padgett," *Accent* (Winter 1994).

38. Smith, "Green Paper Number 6," October 1, 1987, "Green Paper Number 8," February 24, 1988; M. Kelly, interview; Catherine A. Cotter to Forest Service Chief Dale Robertson, July 14, 1987, and Supplemental Request for Stay, July 28, 1987, both in WNCA.

39. Smith, "Green Paper Number 8," February 24, 1988, "Green Paper Number 9," April 25, 1988.

40. Smith, "Green Paper Number 13," November 1, 1988; "Roaring Hole Clearcuts"; "Clay County Clear-Cutting Opponents"; "Clarence Hall and Walton Smith Present Data on Roaring Hole Timber Sale," "Mary Kelly Records Data While Clarence Hall 'Calls the Trees,'" "Heywood and Kelly Measure," *Accent* (Spring 1989): 9, 11, 15.

41. M. Kelly, interview; Smith, "Green Paper Number 12," September 28, 1988; "Clarence Hall and Walton Smith Present Data," "Mary Kelly Records Data," "Heywood and Kelly Measure."

42. Darry Wood, "Timber Targets," *Clay County Progress*, January 12, 1989, January 19, 1989, February 9, 1989; "Eyebrows Raising in Clear Cutting Issue," *Clay County Progress*, January 19, 1989; "Clay County Clear-Cutting Opponents"; "Rangers and Residents Square Off over Clear Cutting Issue," *Clay County Progress*, February 9, 1989.

43. Gilmour, interview; Betty Ballew, interview by Kathryn Newfont, Burnsville, NC, September 19, 1998; Roger Brown, interview by Kathryn Newfont, Black Mountain, NC, September 21, 1998; Smith, "Green Paper Number 10," June 20, 1988; "Clearcutting May Be on Hold," *Black Mountain News*, September 21, 1989.

44. M. Kelly, interview; Elizabeth Hunter, "USFS Prefers Clearcutting Method," *Yancey Journal*, March 8, 1989; M. Kelly, "Alliance Mounts"; "Resolution to Commit WNC Alliance to a 'Cut the Clearcutting' Campaign," January 15, 1989, and "Minutes of the WNCA Steering Committee Meeting, Hot Springs, N.C.," January 15, 1989, in "Cut the Clearcutting" campaign file, WNCA.

45. M. Kelly, interview; "Monroe Gilmour Memo to Mary Kelly: Discussion Draft on Stop Clearcutting Publicity Campaign," December 5, 1988, and "Cut the Clearcutting 'Game Plan' Outlined by Forest Management Task Force, December 10, 1988, in "Cut the Clearcutting" Campaign File, WNCA; M. Kelly, "Alliance Mounts."

46. Gilmour, interview; M. Kelly, interview; Johnson, "Ready for Harvest."

47. M. Kelly, "Alliance Mounts," 8; Smith, "Green paper Number 16," May 10, 1989; M. Kelly, interview.

48. "Clearcutting Foes Gather Steam for Continued Push," *Black Mountain News*, February 2, 1989; "'Cut the Clearcutting' Campaign Involves Jackson County Citizens," *Sylva Herald and Ruralite*, February 16, 1989; "WNC Alliance Announces 'Cut the Clearcutting,'" *Asheville Advocate*, January 27, 1989; "Clear-Cutting Foes Express Regret At Champion News," *Asheville Citizen*, January 26, 1989.

49. "Clearcutting Protested by Local Western N.C. Alliance," *Tri-County News-Journal*, February 2, 1989; "'Cut the Clearcutting' Campaign Getting Results," *Mountain Times*, February 9, 1989.

50. "Campaign Getting Results"; "Foes Gather Steam"; "Foes Express Regret."

51. "Foes Gather Steam"; "Foes Express Regret"; "Campaign Getting Results,"; "Heywood and Kelly Measure"; Smith, "Green Paper Number 7," December 1, 1987, "Green Paper Number 8," February 24, 1988, "Green Paper Number 9," April 25, 1988.

52. "Anti-Clear-Cut Drive Picks Up Some Steam," *Asheville Citizen*, March 9, 1989. For examples of broad regional coverage, see Griffin, "Clearcutting Petition"; "Clearcut Rally Delivers"; "Foes Gather Steam"; Hunter, "USFS Prefers Clearcutting"; "Clearcutting Protested"; "Forest Service Clear-Cutting Is Focus of Debate," *Hendersonville Times-News*, February 19, 1989; "Roaring Hole Clearcuts"; "WNC Alliance Announces"; "Eyebrows Raising"; "Madison Residents Question"; "USFS Blasted for WNC Timber Sales," *Franklin Press*, January 4, 1989; "Clearcutting? WNC Alliance Hopes to Make It Dirty Word," *Mountaineer*, January 27, 1989; "Opposition Mounts against Clear-Cutting," *Highlands [NC] Highlander*, March 7, 1989; "Shelton Laurel Residents Oppose Clearcutting Plan," *Greeneville Sun*, January 27, 1989; "War of the Woods," *Charlotte Observer*, February 18, 1989; "Lighthawk Flyover Gives Bird's-Eye View of Forest Service Clearcutting in North Carolina," *Appalachian Reader* 2 (Spring 1989). For photo contest see flyer, "WNC Alliance and

the 'Cut the Clearcutting Campaign' Announce: The Ugliest Clearcut Photo Contest," in Monroe Gilmour, "Cut the Clearcutting" scrapbook, vol. 1; "Contest Held to Find Photo of Ugliest Clear-Cut," *Asheville Citizen*, February 16, 1989; "WNC Alliance Photo Contest Centers on Clearcutting," *Asheville Times*, February 16, 1989; "'Ugliest Clearcut' Photo Contest Set," *Tri-County News-Journal*, February 23, 1989; "Ugly Clearcut Photo Contest," *Black Mountain News*, February 23, 1989; "Ugliest Clear-Cut Photo Contest Now Being Held," *Highlands [NC] Highlander*, March 7, 1989; "Award-Winning Clear-Cut Photo," *Asheville Citizen*, April 17, 1989.

53. "Clear-Cutting Seen from Above," *Hendersonville Times-News*, March 18, 1989; "Environment Guarded Above by Lighthawk," *Asheville Citizen*, March 18, 1989; "Lighthawk Flyover."

54. "Anti-Clear-Cut Drive"; M. Kelly, interview; "WNC Alliance Volunteers Circulated Petitions at Rose's," *Black Mountain News*, March 16, 1989; "WNC Alliance Circulating"; "War of the Woods."

55. "WNC Alliance Circulating"; "Anti-Clear-Cut Drive"; M. Kelly, interview; Morrison, "Clear-Cutting Foes"; Griffin, "Clearcutting Petition."

56. Cook, interview; Hunter, "USFS Prefers Clearcutting."

57. Clarke Morrison, "Forest Management Plan Found Lacking," *Asheville Citizen*, September 30, 1989; "Public Wins a Victory on Clearcutting on NC Forests," *Accent* (Summer 1990); U.S. Department of Agriculture Forest Service, *Land and Resource Management Plan, 1986–2000, for the Nantahala and Pisgah National Forests* (Asheville, NC: USDA Forest Service, Southern Region, March 1987).

58. Hirt, *Conspiracy of Optimism*, 272, 281; Richard N. L. Andrews, *Managing the Environment, Managing Ourselves: A History of American Environmental Policy* (New Haven: Yale University Press, 1999), 256–57, 333; Morrison, "Forest Management Plan." For an excellent analysis of nationwide forest politics in the last third of the twentieth century, see Hays, *Wars in the Woods*.

59. Morrison, "Forest Management Plan"; "Public Wins a Victory."

60. M. Kelly, interview; "Public Wins a Victory"; Morrison, "Forest Management Plan."

61. "Public Opinion Makes a Difference! Revised Forest Plan 'Cuts the Clearcutting!'" and "Here Lies Clearcutting," *Accent* (Spring 1994).

62. "Public Opinion Makes a Difference!"; Hirt, *Conspiracy of Optimism*, 288–92; Andrews, *Managing the Environment*, 312–13, 334–35, 362–66.

63. M. Kelly, interview; "WNC Alliance Members Tell Forest Service Chief How to Reinvent the Agency" and "Public Opinion Makes a Difference!" *Accent* (Spring 1994).

64. U.S. Department of Agriculture, *Land and Resource Management Plan: Nantahala and Pisgah National Forests. Amendment 5* and "Final Supplement to the Final Environmental Impact Statement," *Land and Resource Management Plan: Nantahala and Pisgah National Forests. Amendment 5* (Atlanta: USDA Forest Service, Southern Region, 1994); "Public Opinion Makes a Difference!"; "WNC Alliance Members."

65. On Cut the Clearcutting Day there were around 15,500 signatures, but as stragglers came in the number grew to over 20,000.

SIX

Injustice in the Handling of Nuclear Weapons Waste

The Case of David Witherspoon, Inc.

JOHN NOLT

IN THE FALL OF 1985, DOROTHY HUNLEY DIED OF osteogenic sarcoma, a rare form of bone cancer. Her doctor publicly expressed his opinion that her cancer was the result of occupational exposure to radiation.[1] For over a decade, she had worked for David Witherspoon, Inc., a scrap metal dealer with a history of buying and processing radioactive materials from nuclear weapons facilities.

Hunley's story made headlines in the Knoxville papers, and the publicity brought to light a story of environmental and social injustice that would continue to unfold for more than two decades. It is a tale of two cities—or rather, a city and a neighborhood: the secret city of Oak Ridge and the impoverished South Knoxville neighborhood of Vestal, where Dorothy Hunley lived and worked.

Vestal was settled early in the nineteenth century as a community of farms. It remained largely rural through much of the nineteenth century, until the Tennessee River was bridged, connecting Vestal to downtown Knoxville. Though the fields and pastures are gone, some of the original farmhouses remain. But the newer residences tend to be small, often dilapidated single-story houses. Zoning was long unheard of here. Homes and decaying industrial plants intermingle. Rail lines, still very active, traverse the community.

Through the midst of Vestal flows Goose Creek; a mile or so downstream it empties into the Tennessee River, just across from the University of Tennessee. The land around the mouth of Goose Creek is today the locus of an upscale redevelopment project. But even a block or two to the south, back from the river, visible poverty and hardship remain.

Though now interracial, Vestal was historically mostly white, populated largely by transplanted Appalachian mountain folk. One of the main industries, starting in the 1880s, was the Vestal Lumber Company. Candoro Marble Works, located at the corner of Maryville Pike and Candora Road, was added in 1914. Like many poor communities, Vestal offered cheap labor. Hence it served as a magnet for hazardous and polluting industries, including not only several scrap yards, but an aluminum smelter and an asphalt plant.[2]

The second city of our story, the secret one, lies about twenty miles west of Knoxville. Founded in 1942 as the Clinton Engineering Works, a major facility of the Manhattan Project, it was rechristened in 1943 as Oak Ridge. The federal government appropriated about 60,000 acres of land for the project, displacing thirty-seven thousand people from the farming villages of Elza, Robertsville, Scarboro, and Wheat. Engineers, physicists, and technicians poured in from all over the country to replace them. Almost overnight a remote farming region was transformed into a high-tech, high-security industrial complex focused exclusively on a single urgent task: the creation of the atomic bomb.[3]

But not all who moved to Oak Ridge were highly educated professionals. The weapons plants also employed thousands of industrial workers, many of them black. Segregation was a fact of life. At first blacks lived in very primitive housing; later they were relocated to the Scarboro neighborhood, adjacent to the huge Y-12 weapons plant.[4] Thus, like their mostly white counterparts in Vestal, they endured life in close proximity to industrial operations involving radioactive and other toxic materials.

The management of the Oak Ridge plants was transferred from the Manhattan Project to the Atomic Energy Commission (AEC) in 1946, with Union Carbide Corporation as chief contractor. The AEC was later assimilated into the U.S. Department of Energy (DOE), and the chief contractor eventually became Martin Marietta Energy Systems. Weapons manufacture continued; and after the development of the hydrogen bomb, components for thermonuclear weapons, too, were produced at Oak Ridge.

Over the years, the Oak Ridge plants generated huge quantities of radioactive and other toxic waste. Though much of it was disposed of in burial grounds at or near Oak Ridge (another tale of environmental injustice, but one that cannot be told here),[5] scrap metal and machinery, often contaminated with radioactive materials, was sold to private dealers. Prominent among those dealers was David Witherspoon, Inc.

The firm was founded by David Witherspoon Sr in 1948. It operated on three parcels of land adjacent to rail lines along Maryville Pike, which runs through the center of Vestal:

901 Maryville Pike (also known as the Candora site and as Witherspoon Recycling), an area of about ten acres.

1630 Maryville Pike (also known as the Screen Arts site). This site consists of two parts: the Screen Arts building and surrounding area and the "yard" (also known as the hot field), which is about an acre in area.

The Witherspoon landfill, which covers more than forty acres to the rear of the 1630 site.

Little is known of the company's early history. In 1972 Witherspoon reported to the state that his records had been destroyed in a fire.[6] A spotty paper trail doesn't begin to emerge in the state of Tennessee's files until the 1960s. By that time (some say long before) Witherspoon was regularly buying and processing radioactive scrap metal. In 1966 the company received licenses from the state of Tennessee and from the Atomic Energy Commission authorizing the processing of scrap metal with a uranium surface contamination not to exceed 0.1 percent by weight. The licenses were later amended to allow thorium contamination as well. The state also granted permission for the smelting of radioactively contaminated metals, beginning in December 1968.[7]

During the 1960s and 1970s, the company handled millions of pounds of scrap metal contaminated with radioisotopes (chiefly uranium and thorium), asbestos, and various other toxic chemicals. Much of it came from AEC—later, DOE—nuclear weapons facilities, and especially from the White Wing Scrapyard in Oak Ridge. The company also received "special nuclear material" containing highly enriched uranium from the Babcock and Wilcox Naval Nuclear Fuel Division plant in Lynchburg, Virginia, and handled radioactive materials on site at the Goodyear Atomic Corporation plant in Piketon, Ohio; the United Nuclear Corporation, Chemical Products Division, in Hematite,

Missouri, and AEC facilities at Oak Ridge National Laborator, Paducah, Kentucky; and the St. Louis airport. Tennessee radiological health files also contain references to shipments of radioactive materials from a U.S. Army facility at Weldon Springs, Missouri, and from National Lead of Fernald, Ohio.[8] Sales of scrap metal from DOE contractors to David Witherspoon, Inc., continued at least until April 1984.[9]

Radioactively or chemically contaminated metal in the form of large pieces of equipment, pipes, parts, chips, or tailings was shipped from these facilities to the Witherspoon sites by truck and by rail. At the Candora site, iron was separated from other metals by an overhead magnet. Through the years Witherspoon resold much of the contaminated iron scrap to the Knoxville Iron Company. What became of it after that is not known.

Nonferrous metals were taken to the hot field for sorting.[10] In the hot field, neighborhood women using Geiger counters and working for slightly more than minimum wage—without respirators and often with no protection other than gloves—sorted the radioactive metal by hand, placed it into barrels, and carried it into a warehouse. Workers identified metals by using a grinder to remove the outer layer of rust and dirt and then applying acid to see what color the metal would turn. This grinding operation undoubtedly released radioactive particles into the air workers breathed. Among those workers was Dorothy Hunley.

Hunley labored in the hot field from 1970 to 1983. Shortly before she died, she described conditions there to a news reporter. If the metal to be ground was contaminated with uranium, she said, "it'd throw a spark like crazy. God, it would go right through you." "It was hard work for a woman," she said, "We've had a lot of men come in there and say, 'Lord, what are you women doing in there.' And we'd say, 'Well, we gotta eat.'"[11]

Neighbors and former workers tell stories of large pieces of heavy equipment (including jeeps, trucks, and a crane) being offloaded from trains and buried in the Witherspoon landfill. Workers have reported that transformers shipped from various locations were smashed open with a wrecking ball and the liquid inside (which at the time would have consisted largely of PCBs) was spread on the ground to control dust. The purpose of this operation, they say, was to salvage the copper wiring inside the transformers.

Files on Witherspoon at the Tennessee Department of Environment and Conservation contain numerous records of complaints and safety violations. These begin as early as 1968, when a state inspection found, among other infractions, that Witherspoon was handling material contaminated with yellowcake (a mix of uranium compounds used in the enrichment process at the K-25 gaseous diffusion plant in Oak Ridge) well in excess of the limit stipulated by his state license.[12] Despite these findings, the license for Witherspoon, Inc., was not revoked.

What Witherspoon actually handled during this period went well beyond what his license allowed and what the inspectors found. Records obtained from the DOE in the early 1990s by the Freedom of Information Act reveal that Witherspoon also obtained from Oak Ridge scrap metal contaminated with the artificial and extremely dangerous element plutonium. An internal DOE memo dated April 21, 1969 stated that "the Purchaser [Witherspoon] should emphatically be made aware that the material he is contracting to handle does contain a plutonium potential and we cannot guarantee a specific level below which all the material will read." It further asserts that Witherspoon should be warned of the "possibility that plutonium contamination of his mobile equipment during loading and hauling operations and of the Knoxville Iron Company and environs during smelting operations may occur." A second memo, dated June 4, 1969, said that although most of the potentially plutonium contaminated material sold to Witherspoon remained in Oak Ridge, "four or five pickup truckloads have been taken to Knoxville."[13]

By 1973, David Witherspoon Jr. had replaced his father as the company's president and the landfill had been legally closed—a result of poor management and complaints from neighbors.[14] Nearby residents, however, say that sporadic dumping continued, and Tennessee officials have found evidence of illegal dumping there as late as 1983.[15]

A 1981 investigation by the Nuclear Regulatory Commission (NRC) found that Witherspoon had bought more than two hundred thousand pounds of steel contaminated with uranium 235, never reported the shipment, and then resold the steel to the Knoxville Iron Company, all in violation of NRC regulations. The NRC was unable to determine what happened to the steel after that. No fine was levied against Witherspoon, but his NRC license to handle material contaminated with enriched uranium was eventually revoked. Witherspoon's response to an NRC query as to why he did not know where the metal had gone was, "Iron is iron."[16]

In the early 1980s the state ordered a cleanup of the hot field. In 1983 soil contaminated with PCBs and uranium was removed from the surface of the hot field, placed in barrels, and moved to the Candora site, where it was stored in the near vicinity of neighboring houses. In May 1985 the Tennessee Department of Health and Environment ordered Witherspoon to dispose of these barrels within six months or pay a $50,000 fine.[17] Witherspoon failed to meet the deadline, which was then extended. When the extended deadline passed, Witherspoon argued that no facility in the country was willing or able to accept this sort of mixed waste.

In 1985, largely in response to news accounts of Dorothy Hunley's death, an organization called South Knoxville Citizens for a Better Environment was formed to gather information about the Witherspoon sites and to demand prompt cleanup. The group obtained Tennessee Division of Radiological Health documents indicating that although ten to fifteen violations had been found at each inspection since 1967, this had not resulted in any revocation or alteration of Witherspoon's license to handle radioactive materials. The group also called for fencing of the sites and the posting of warning signs. It continued meeting for a time but ultimately disbanded.

On September 13, 1985, the *Knoxville Journal* quoted Mike Mobley, Tennessee's director of radiological health, as saying of Witherspoon, Inc., "that place has been a very, very consistent violator.""I guess," he added,"it took us a long time to get to the point where we said'Enough is enough.'"[18]

In 1986 the Department of Energy agreed to take the Candora site barrels and 329 tons of contaminated scrap metal back to the Oak Ridge Reservation. The scrap included pipes and centrifugal pumps contaminated with yellowcake. Some of the material also contained asbestos. Removal of the scrap metal was completed on August 8. Some of the barrels were also removed by the DOE, but the department refused to take the others after it discovered that they contained PCBs. DOE officials denied responsibility for the PCBs. Thus more than two hundred of the barrels remained at the Candora site for several years more, rusting and in some cases leaking.[19]

The Community Organizes

In 1989 residents of Vestal and nearby areas formed Project Witherspoon, an organization dedicated to pressuring government agencies to investigate the sites and (ultimately) clean them up. Prominent among the members of Project Witherspoon were Charlie and Wilma Underwood. Wilma Underwood, formerly Wilma Hunley, is the daughter of Dorothy Hunley. Todd Shelton was elected president of the group. I was elected vice president.

As with South Knoxville Citizens for a Better Environment, one of Project Witherspoon's first requests to the state was for secure fencing and posting of the sites. Neighborhood children were known to trespass there, and pets could easily have picked up and carried home contaminants from the sites. Illegal hunting was still common in the landfill, much of which had grown a cover of young woods.

Another problem noted by Project Witherspoon was the nighttime burning of trash, including junk automobiles and piles of tires, at the Witherspoon sites. (This had been occurring sporadically for years and had in the 1950s and 1960s been so intense, according to one former resident of Woodson Avenue, near the Witherspoon landfill, as to turn grass in her yard black.)

Project Witherspoon also asked for removal of the rusting and leaking barrels of mixed waste stored at the Candora site. Finally, the group expressed concern about the possible contamination of Goose Creek, which passes directly through the Candora site and then, less than half a mile downstream, through Mary Vestal Park, a place frequented by children.

As a result of Project Witherspoon's efforts, the Tennessee Department of Health and Environment (TDHE) began an investigation and discovered widespread radioactive contamination in excess of permissible limits in the soil at the Candora site, some of it extending offsite into a nearby ditch. The TDHE also ordered Witherspoon to place the barrels of waste located at the Candora site in land-sea containers where they would not be exposed to soil or weather. Witherspoon eventually complied with this order.

In the meantime, the TDHE once again sought DOE help in disposing of the barrels of waste stored at the Candora site. In an interview published in the *Knoxville News-Sentinel* on July 6, 1990, Mike Mobley, Tennessee's director of radiological health spoke of the DOE's refusal to take the barrels. "We have asked them formally. We have asked them verbally—by phone. We have had many discussions about how they could reasonably deal with the material," Mobley said. He also said, "In fact, we believe they [the DOE] are largely responsible for part of the problem, because Witherspoon should not have been shipped the kinds of materials he was shipped."[20]

On June 16, 1990, Project Witherspoon held a March against Toxic Waste in Our Backyard in the vicinity of the Candora site. The event was attended by well over a hundred people. Albert Gore Jr. at that time a U.S. senator, speaking at Mary Vestal Park after the march, called for an investigation of the Witherspoon sites. Representatives from the U.S. EPA came to Knoxville later that summer, toured the site, decided it was probably not eligible for the National Priorities List (because not enough people in the area used well water), and turned the investigation back over to the state.

Prodded by Gore's office, the state conducted new rounds of tests, as a result of which, all three sites were promulgated for the Tennessee Superfund list. The Tennessee Department of Health and Environment held a public hearing on the Superfund listing in Knoxville on October 11, 1990, and more than one hundred people attended (one news report said 149); all who spoke favored placing the site on the list. The meeting highlighted the considerable anger and emotion felt by the local community. Ken Pointer, enforcement manager for the Tennessee Division of Superfund, was quoted in the *Knoxville Journal* as saying that he was "pretty overwhelmed" by the turnout. "This has by far surpassed anything I've seen since I came to superfund," he said.[21]

On October 17, 1990, members of Project Witherspoon attended a DOE public hearing in Oak Ridge concerning environmental restoration plans for the Oak Ridge Reservation. They asked for DOE help with the investigation and cleanup of the Witherspoon site. Bill Adams, the DOE's assistant manager for environmental restoration, while admitting that the DOE sold radioactive scrap metal to Witherspoon, said there was no evidence that the PCBs found at the site came from Oak Ridge and that the DOE had no responsibility to remove them. Shortly thereafter, Project Witherspoon obtained from the DOE, via Freedom of Information Act requests, bills of sale indicating that DOE contractor Union Carbide had on various occasions sold transformers (which at that time would almost certainly have contained PCBs) to Witherspoon.[22]

On December 4, 1990, the Tennessee Solid Waste Control Board voted unanimously to place all three Witherspoon sites on the Tennessee Superfund list. After the hearing, Dan Hawkins, acting manager of the Knoxville office of the Tennessee Division of Superfund said, referring to all three sites, "This will most likely be one of our top priorities, if not our top priority."[23]

In January 1991, J. W. Luna, commissioner of the Tennessee Department of Health and Environment, issued orders to Witherspoon, Inc., several persons associated with Witherspoon, the DOE, and the DOE's former contractor Union Carbide, to commence further testing, cleanup, and partial fencing of the hot field and landfill.[24] A similar order for the Candora site (which included full fencing) was issued in April.[25]

The DOE, Union Carbide, and Witherspoon all quickly moved to have the order dismissed. Though Witherspoon eventually built a small section of fence at the Candora site, none of the parties complied with either the spirit or the substance of the order.

Members of Project Witherspoon were told by state officials as early as April 1991 that if Witherspoon did not comply with the fencing order at the Candora site, the state would begin construction of a fence there "probably within thirty days." Witherspoon did not comply. Project Witherspoon representatives made repeated inquiries at the Division of Superfund throughout the spring, summer, and fall—and were consistently told that the fence would be erected soon. Finally, in late November or early December the state did build the fence. There were problems, however, with theft of sections of the fence, and still the fence lacked warning signs indicating to potential trespassers the hazardous nature of the site. Members of Project Witherspoon asked the state repeatedly for such signage. These requests produced no action.

In the spring of 1992, Project Witherspoon President Todd Shelton asked the Knoxville Superfund office whether they would post warning signs if Project Witherspoon had them made and the office agreed. A local sign shop donated a number of bright yellow-and-magenta metal signs the size and shape of license plates, which read:

WARNING

TOXIC AND RADIOACTIVE AREA

KEEP OUT

The wording had been suggested to Shelton by Dan Hawkins of the Knoxville Superfund office. The first batch of these signs was delivered to Chris Andel at the Knoxville Superfund office on July 1. A local television station covered the delivery, emphasizing that citizens had made the signs, in the face of the state's refusal to do so.

The following week Hawkins called Todd Shelton and me into his office for a tense meeting. He was angry about the TV coverage and about $15,000 of testing equipment that had been stolen from the sites during well-drilling and core-sampling operations, which had commenced in early summer. His tone betrayed suspicion that we might be responsible for this larceny. (More was stolen or destroyed later in the summer; locks on the well caps were broken and the wells were contaminated with glass and sticks, invalidating further sampling. The vandals were never apprehended.) Finally, Hawkins informed us that the state had a legal problem with the use of the word *area* on the signs. Apparently the term *radioactive area* had a specific definition under the law that the Witherspoon sites may not have met, and the state was concerned about liability in posting the signs. Eventually the state's legal staff decided that the signs would have to be modified by replacing the word *area* by *materials*. They ordered some printed tape to make this change.

Meanwhile, Project Witherspoon, impatient over the repeated delays, decided that if the signs were not in place before August 11, we would post them ourselves, though this meant trespassing and possible arrest. We informed the state and the press of our intentions and held a series of planning meetings and a nonviolence-training session (conducted by Ralph Hutchison and Lissa McLeod of the Oak Ridge Environmental Peace Alliance) to prepare for civil disobedience. Late on the afternoon of August 10, however, state officials posted the signs.

Frustrated as well by the slow progress of the state's efforts against Witherspoon and the DOE, Project Witherspoon sought the aid of Knoxville Legal Aid attorney Cheryl Laubis. In the fall of 1991 Laubis helped Project Witherspoon file a request to intervene in the administrative dispute between these parties, citing the need for citizen oversight to ensure that the state exercises all its options in seeking to resolve the Witherspoon case. The request detailed the long history of delays and inaction or ineffective action by the state.

A week later, Project Witherspoon was informed that the DOE had abruptly reversed its position and agreed to come to the bargaining table with state officials and Witherspoon to discuss possible cleanup and remediation. On March 23, 1992, the state approved a cleanup plan proposed by Witherspoon in response to the state's orders, but Witherspoon then declared that his company was not financially able to implement it.

In December, Martin Marietta Energy Systems and the DOE finally agreed to one of Project Witherspoon's original demands: removal of the barrels of contaminated soil from the Candora site. The state agreed to waive a $96,000 fine against the DOE for unrelated violations at their Oak Ridge operations in return for this "cleanup." In all, 232 fifty-five-gallon drums of mixed waste were to be taken from the Candora site to Oak Ridge, along with twenty-six drums and ten boxes of waste that had been stored in the warehouse at the Candora site. This was done in January 1993 with great fanfare in the media. Many readers and listeners assumed that the Witherspoon sites had finally been cleaned up. But that was far from the truth. Only a relatively small amount of already containerized waste was removed. The soil of all three sites remained contaminated, nothing was done about surface or ground water, and the landfill remained untouched. The total cost for this DOE operation was in excess of $1 million.

Voices of the Community: The Listening Project

In the summer of 1992, two student interns from Vanderbilt University's Service Training for Environmental Progress arrived in Knoxville to assist

Project Witherspoon with the research and design of a long-contemplated project: a community health survey. The interns, Jeff Carter and Lara Setti, spent most of the summer planning and designing the survey.

At an August 4 meeting Project Witherspoon decided to seek the help of Rural Southern Voice for Peace in order to combine with the health survey a listening project to ascertain community concerns. RSVP had considerable experience in conducting listening projects—some in communities dealing with toxic waste.

On October 17, David Grant from RSVP came to Vestal to conduct a training session that initiated the health survey and listening project. Fourteen volunteers went out in pairs into the community that afternoon. The first day's work provided a startling revelation. One of the families surveyed produced a letter from Chris Andel at the state Superfund office informing them that the backyard of a home they owned on Chestnut Avenue near the Candora site was contaminated with PCBs and other toxic materials in excess of acceptable levels for residential areas. The letter warned them not to let anyone into the yard. The family explained that the house's former occupants had included teenagers who had stolen material from Witherspoon and burned some of it in the backyard. The spots on which the burning had taken place were the areas that had been found to be contaminated.

Project Witherspoon completed the listening project and health survey on April 24, 1993, by which time seventy homes had been visited. In the following weeks we analyzed the statistics. The survey did not, as it turned out, detect any unusual pattern of illness. All the illnesses we asked about were within statistical expectations for U.S. averages. In part, this may have been due to the small size of the sample. We had been warned by statisticians that even if there were health effects, a sample of the size we were contemplating would be unlikely to detect them.

In part, the lack of findings may have been due as well to the transient nature of the community. In doing the survey, we discovered that many nearby residents had been in their homes for a few years or less. In the end, the survey left us no wiser with respect to community health effects; it neither confirmed nor disconfirmed their presence. We had hoped that it might help us track down some of the hundreds of former Witherspoon workers as well; but we were able to contact only a few. The listening project did, however, raise community concern and awareness and elicited new information about the spread of the contamination beyond the Witherspoon sites into residential neighborhoods.

Meanwhile, the nighttime fires that had been occurring sporadically on Witherspoon property at least since the 1970s (and, according to some residents, far longer than that) continued.[26] During the night of August 25–26, 1992, the Rural Metro fire department was called to extinguish a pile of burning tires on the Witherspoon sites. When Todd Shelton contacted Rural Metro, the firefighters seemed unaware of the nature of the hazards onsite. Shelton suggested a meeting between Rural Metro and the state Superfund office. It occurred, and received TV coverage, in mid-September. Firefighters would henceforth be required to wear special gear upon entering the Witherspoon sites. State and county officials also met with David Witherspoon Jr. and received his assurance that no more tires remained on site. Astonishingly, yet another tire fire, which set off an explosion audible from Maryville Pike, occurred late in the evening of October 2; this time emergency response teams came in and a helicopter traced the smoke plume as far as Maryville, about ten miles away.[27]

As a result of the tire fires, the Knox County Air Pollution Control Board assessed a $3,000 fine against David Witherspoon Jr.[28] Witherspoon appealed the fine to the board on the grounds that he had not set the fires. The appeal was heard on April 29, 1993, in Knoxville. About twenty members and supporters of Project Witherspoon also attended. At this hearing it emerged that there were still piles of tires on the Witherspoon sites. One of the board members asked Witherspoon if he would remove the tires as a show of good faith to the community. He answered that he would do so only on the condition that he not be required to pay the fine. The board voted unanimously to reject Witherspoon's appeal.

On October 7, 1993, the state of Tennessee filed an action in Davidson County Chancery Court which effectively halted operations at the Candora site. The state charged that even while their Superfund investigation was underway, Witherspoon had allowed additional hazardous wastes to be dumped there. According to documents filed with the chancery court, these wastes included "used motor oil and insulation ash, both contaminated with toxic concentrations of lead, and a drum of corrosive material which ate through its container." (The insulation ash was, Dan Hawkins later explained to members of Project Witherspoon, ash produced by burning the insulation of electrical wires. It was also contaminated with mercury and PCBs.) The state concluded that "defendants operate the site with gross indifference to compliance with environmental laws and efforts of State Superfund and U.S. DOE to assess and remediate" and that assessment and remediation of the site could not go forward while Witherspoon continued to operate there. As a result, it asked for an injunction prohibiting the transportation of anything onto or off the site until such time as Witherspoon could obtain the necessary permits and comply with all relevant environmental laws. The injunction request was granted at a hearing in Nashville on October 19, 1993.[29]

It was not until 1995 that renewed cleanup of any of the sites began, and that was only the Screen Arts site—the least contaminated of the three, having been partially cleaned up in 1983. A 1993 assessment had concluded that the remaining surface contamination there was minor, though there might be some problems with offsite surface drainage. Beginning in May 1995 the Tennessee Division of Superfund removed about a thousand additional cubic yards of soil from the Screen Arts site, about four hundred cubic yards of which was so contaminated with lead that it had to be treated as hazardous waste.[30]

During the mid-1990s the Department of Energy did a new series of field studies to determine the feasibility of remediation at the Candora site and at the landfill. The most highly concentrated contamination was found at the Candora site. Sampling revealed radioactivity as high as 129,700 picocuries per gram. (The applicable state cleanup guideline was thirty-five picocuries per gram.) In places where PCB-contaminated items were burned, the soil contained dioxin, which can be produced by the burning of PCBs, suggesting that workers and nearby residents were exposed to airborne dioxin (a severe carcinogen) while the burning was occurring.

There were also extremely high mercury and PCB levels both in the soil and in the sediments of Goose Creek, which flows through the site. The groundwater at the Candora site was contaminated in excess of state standards with lead, mercury, chromium, beryllium, antimony, and several organic compounds. Particularly striking were the data for beryllium, a highly toxic element widely used at Oak Ridge. Soil samples showed readings as high as 7.5 milligrams per kilogram. The state's health-based limit was 0.143 milligrams per kilogram. In the shallow groundwater the beryllium concentration reached 6.9 milligrams per liter; health based-criteria set the limit at 0.00714 milligrams per liter. The soil and groundwater also contained small amounts of plutonium—an element that normally does not occur in nature.[31] Concerning radiological and chemical risks to the health of human beings at the Candora site (chiefly from PCBs, polycyclic aromatic hydrocarbons, uranium, and thorium), a 1999 DOE report concluded, "In every scenario, the excess cancer risk and/or noncarcinogenic hazard index exceeded EPA thresholds, indicating unacceptable hypothetical and future risk."[32]

Contamination at the landfill, the largest of the three sites, was less concentrated. The landfill contained large amounts of garbage, including medical waste, hazardous waste, and some radioactive waste, and there was groundwater contamination onsite. Radioactive and hazardous materials on the surface were dangerous to humans chiefly through direct contact or inhalation and could have been transported by erosion.[33]

Though remediation studies were complete before 2000, still there was no cleanup at the landfill and Candora sites. On Earth Day (April 22) 2002, the Knox County Commission, frustrated at the lengthening delay, passed a resolution urging the Tennessee legislative delegation to "take any and all steps necessary to cause the Department of Energy to begin serious efforts at cleaning up the Witherspoon hazardous waste sites on Maryville Pike." The resolution (R-02–4-905) incorporated an earlier draft of the history you are now reading.

In July the commission received a response from Congressman John J. Duncan. Duncan enclosed a letter from Jesse Hill Robertson, assistant secretary for environmental management at the U.S. Department of Energy. Robertson's letter stated in part: "The Department of Energy has been actively working with the State of Tennessee to address the South Knoxville Witherspoon sites that are noted in the Knox County Commission resolution. The cleanup plan for these two sites has now been agreed to. We will begin cleanup in 2003, and we plan to complete the work by 2006."[34]

The Candora cleanup was indeed completed in 2006. The cleanup of the landfill, though nearly complete, was still not finished by the end of 2008. As of this writing, more than 15,700 truckloads of contaminated debris have been taken to Oak Ridge, where the waste is being treated by incineration, to destroy organic compounds and to make the remainder more compact. The remainder will be stored in hazardous waste landfills. The total cost of the cleanup has exceeded $35 million.[35] To this day no one has a clear idea of what the Witherspoon operations have cost in human health and human lives.

Despite the history of violations and litigation, as late as 2007 Dan Hawkins of the Superfund division of the Tennessee Department of Environment and Conservation said in a newspaper interview that the many fines levied against David Witherspoon Jr. over the years have still never been collected. "We've been checking his finances for the better part of two decades," he said. "We have never really been able to touch him because he really doesn't have any assets that are reachable."[36]

The injustices engendered by lax handling of toxic and nuclear materials at David Witherspoon, Inc., were in some respects not uniquely Appalachian. Irresponsible offsite disposal of dangerous materials has occurred at many places in the American nuclear weapons complex.[37] But it is unusual that the mishandling of such dangerous materials could persist in close proximity to residential neighborhoods for decades before rousing organized opposition. Certainly the poverty and disempowerment of the Vestal community were typically Appalachian in origin, and they facilitated the perpetration of these injustices.

Notes

1. Randall Beck, "Woman's Cancer May Be Linked to Radioactive Scrapyard," *Knoxville Journal*, September 13, 1985.

2. Some of the historical material for the previous two paragraphs was obtained from Knoxville–Knox County Metropolitan Planning Commission, *Vestal*, 1997, 15.

3. Oak Ridge Education Project, *A Citizen's Guide to Oak Ridge* (Knoxville: Foundation for Global Sustainability, 1992).

4. Ibid.

5. Ibid.

6. Document entitled "David Witherspoon, Inc.," document in files of Tennessee Division of Superfund (47–541).

7. Ibid.

8. Ibid., attachment 1.

9. The April 1984 date is contained in a 1990 DOE memo from Chief Counsel William P. Snyder to G. Wilson Horde Jr., general counsel of Martin Marietta Energy Systems. The memo, entitled "Surplus Sales to David Witherspoon, Inc." was obtained by Project Witherspoon through the Freedom of Information Act.

10. "David Witherspoon, Inc." in files of Tennessee Division of Superfund (47–541).

11. Beck, "Woman's Cancer."

12. "David Witherspoon, Inc." in files of Tennessee Division of Superfund (47–541), attachment 1.

13. Both memos were obtained from DOE using the Freedom of Information Act by Ralph Hutchison of the Oak Ridge Environmental Peace Alliance. The first memo, originating in ORNL's Nuclear Division, was written by J. A. Elkins. It is headed "Subcontract with Witherspoon, Inc., for White Wing yard scrap." The second is a memo headed "Intra-Laboratory Correspondence" from H. E. Seagren to Julian R. Gissel.

14. Beck, "Woman's Cancer."

15. Tennessee Division of Superfund, David Witherspoon Landfill, TND 98084–8311, Fact Sheet.

16. Beck, "Woman's Cancer."

17. Tennessee Commissioner's Order, Division of Radiological Health, May 9, 1985, 82–316; 84–0068A2.

18. Beck, "Woman's Cancer."

19. I observed leakage and spillage from the barrels in the early 1990s.

20. Frank Munger, "DOE Should Take Disputed Wastes, State Official Says: Radioactive Barrels Still in Scrapyard," *Knoxville News-Sentinel*, July 6, 1990.

21. Ralph Dosser, "Angry Crowd Wants Priority Cleanup of Site," *Knoxville Journal*, October 12, 1990.

22. Records of these transformer purchases occur from the 1960s into the 1980s. The earliest record I have found was a 1968 purchase by Witherspoon from Union Carbide (Sealed Bid Invitation No. UCC-ND-984), which included "Approximately 77,400 lbs. Transformers and Rectifiers." The latest was UNCC-ND-2699, dated November 2, 1983. It records the sale of "Miscellaneous Items consisting of Transformers; Teletype machine; Power supply; Motor" to Witherspoon.

23. Quotation is from notes I took at the meeting.

24. Commissioner's Order, Tennessee Department of Conservation, Division of Superfund, case 90–3434, site 47514, January 18, 1991.

25. Commissioner's Order, Tennessee Department of Conservation, Division of Superfund, case 90–3443, site 47541, April 4, 1991.

26. This was widely acknowledged in the community. There is mention of the burning in Leon Stafford, "Representatives Urged to Take Action against Hazardous Chemical Problem," *Knoxville News Sentinel*, February 7, 1990.

27. The October fire was reported in a brief article. "Tire Fire Hits Waste Site," *Knoxville News-Sentinel*, October 3, 1992. Additional details were obtained by Todd Shelton in conversation with members of the Rural Metro Fire Department.

28. A document in the Tennessee Division of Superfund files, bearing the letterhead of the Knox County Department of Air Pollution Control, records the two fires and the fine. However, it mistakenly places the fires in 1993, not 1992. "Penalty Assessment for Open Burning Incidents on 'Witherspoon Landfill.'"

29. See Betsy Kaufmann, "Judge Shuts Down Knoxville Scrap Yard," *Knoxville News-Sentinel*, October 21, 1993.

30. Information in this paragraph is from notes taken at a briefing given by Chris Andell of the Tennessee Division of Superfund at a Mount Olive community meeting, August 22, 1995.

31. Data in this paragraph were obtained from the Tennessee Division of Superfund and from the United States Department of Energy (USDOE), Office of Environmental Management, Oak Ridge, Tennessee, *Remedial Investigation/Feasibility Study for the David Witherspoon, Inc. 901 Site, Knoxville, Tennessee*, vol. 1, main text (DOE/OR/02–1503, V1&D2), 1999, pp. 3–1 to 3–22, and tables 3.22, 3.24, 3.26

32. Ibid., 4–27.

33. Dan Hawkins and Chris Andel, Tennessee Superfund; Billy Freeman, Tennessee Department of Radiological Health; Ken Pointer, Enforcement Division, Mount Olive School, presentation, May 17, 1993.

34. Jessie Hill Robertson, assistant secretary for environmental management, U.S. Department of Energy, to Congressman John J. Duncan Jr., July 11, 2002.

35. Frank Munger, "Atomic City Underground," November 20, 2008, http://blogs .knoxnews.com/munger/ (accessed September 10, 2010).

36. Frank Munger, "Witherspoon Says DOE to Blame for Selling Him Scrap," *Knoxville News-Sentinel*, December 31, 2007.

37. Diane D'Arrigo and Mary Olson, "Out of Control—On Purpose: DOE's Dispersal of Radioactive Waste into Landfills and Consumer Products," Nuclear Information and Resource Service, May 14, 2007, http://www.nirs.org/radwaste/outofcontrol /outofcontrolreport.pdf (accessed September 10, 2010).

PART THREE

In Their Own Words

SEVEN

Housewives from Hell

Perspectives on Environmental Justice and Facility Siting

MICHELE MORRONE AND WREN KRUSE

> On the river he watched barges and a towboat pass,
> engines droning. It was pushing coal. Once the boat was
> gone the air got quiet and the water was slow and muddy
> and the forests ran down to the edge and it could have
> been anywhere, the Amazon, a picture from *National
> Geographic*. A bluegill jumped in the shallows—you
> weren't supposed to eat the fish but everyone did. Mercury
> and PCB. He couldn't remember what the letters stood
> for but it was poison.
>
> Philipp Meyer, *American Rust*

MOTHERS WILL DO WHATEVER IT TAKES TO PROTECT
their children and most won't stand for unfair treatment in any aspect of their
children's lives. The combination of protectionism and demand for justice
makes women in general, and mothers in specific, a group of environmental
activists to reckon with. In the realm of environmental justice, the health of
children is often the first thing that comes to mind. Today's children may not
only suffer disproportionate impacts of environmental harms now, but they
may be forced to live with the consequences for the rest of their lives.

Children who grow up in Appalachia are in the midst of some of the largest coal-fired power plants in the country. In addition to sulfur dioxide, nitrogen oxides, and airborne fine particles, these power plants send millions of pounds of mercury and other heavy metals into the local environment. However, coal is not the only source of mercury that families in the region are dealing with. Appalachia is home to numerous industries, including massive chemical facilities that manufacture products ranging from Teflon to pesticides. All these operations may employ local people as they are creating global products, however, they are also creating local environmental impacts that have frightened many women into action to protect their own health and the health of their communities.

How the poor communities in rural Appalachia became home to so many hazardous facilities that make products used worldwide is one basis of the discussion about environmental justice in the region. Many of these industries targeted Appalachia and other rural regions because it is good for their bottom line. Because poverty is pervasive in Appalachia, there is a labor force that is willing to take almost any good-paying job that comes along despite the risks. In addition, land is cheap and many rural communities are so desperate for economic development that tax incentives are used to lure businesses into the region. The Appalachian Regional Commission noted, "It is well known that the nation's rural manufacturing economy was largely seeded by branch plants seeking lower operating costs and contains many firms that suffer from isolation and less sophisticated management."[1]

The less sophisticated management contributed to industrial operations that peppered the Appalachian region with damaged ecosystems, hazardous- and radioactive-waste facilities, abandoned mines, and air pollution levels that rival major cities. Similar to coal mining, there is no doubt that industry and manufacturing created short-term and concentrated economic gains in Appalachia. Good-paying factory jobs were available for a time, but a large percentage of them have evaporated because of global competition and the worldwide economic recession. Appalachian residents now face some of the highest unemployment in the country.[2] High unemployment combined with severe environmental contamination have led some residents of the region to question the justice in this situation, and women are among the leading questioners.

Research is beginning to point to environmental contamination as playing a role in health disparities in Appalachia.[3] However, even if data do not suggest that people are being treated differently or that health disparities exist, the perceptions of Appalachians are important indicators of environmental injustice. The best way to get a sense of whether environmental justice is an issue in a specific area is to ask those who live there. This is what we did when we interviewed six environmental activists who have long histories of working to improve their communities and protect their children. There are emotional burdens that can be as significant as documented health disparities, especially when it comes to protecting children.

Save the Children

One of the major themes that emerged during our interviews was that these Appalachian activists are concerned about the health of their families and all the families in their communities. Perhaps their greatest incentive to get involved is one that many of these women share, and that is their concern over children's health. A motivation for Teresa Mills, who led a campaign to shut down a trash-burning power plant near her neighborhood, was concern about her children and the children in her community.

Teresa's fight began in the early 1980s when a power plant designed to burn municipal solid waste began operating on the south side of Columbus, Ohio, near a low-income neighborhood. This was right before the discussion about environmental justice hit the national stage with the publication of *Toxic Wastes and Race* by the United Church of Christ.[4] The incinerator was a controversial issue in Columbus for almost ten years, and at one point, environmental activists were so frustrated and angered over the facility that they took over the director's office at the Ohio Environmental Protection Agency.

The activists were led by Teresa Mills, who was afraid and angry that the facility was emitting toxins that were causing acute health problems and would eventually lead to long-term health outcomes. The basis of her anger was the fact that environmental contamination was being thrust on a low-income community that had no political clout when the facility was sited. Teresa sums up why children are often a motivating factor of environmental activism:

> One of the reasons that I started looking into this at all is that there were several children in my community that had strange illnesses or, you know, my daughter had a bone tumor. And another kid, another boy on our court, had bone tumors. And that's how I personally got started, but as time went along that's when people were calling me, that's what they were referring to: "Well my child has this, my child has that, can it be caused by this can it be caused by ___?" So, that's kind of how it affects not only my family, but

other families that I work with. Typically that's how environmental investigations get started. Something happens to trigger that protective instinct in a parent, and they want to know what caused this, was it my fault. And that's how most of your typical . . . you know, when citizens have the fear that either something has happened or something may happen.

The incinerator was shut down in 1994 after several studies indicated high levels of dioxins, chemicals that have been linked to cancer in humans; however, officials indicated that the reason for the closure was financial, not environmental. Because Teresa was concerned about her children and the injustice of pollution on the south side of Columbus, she became the most outspoken activist during the incinerator controversy. The burning of trash by the local power plant was the foundation for more than twenty years of activism, and she has taken her fight from her one neighborhood in Columbus to communities across the state including those in Appalachian Ohio. It is clear that, like other activist-mothers, she seeks to protect the health not only of her own children but of all children.

Suzanne Wisdom is a member of a local chapter of the international environmental group Oceana and has been working to force Olin Corporation to eliminate mercury emissions at its Chlor Alkali plant in Charleston, Tennessee. Olin identifies itself as "No. 1 in industrial bleach production in North America."[5] Since mercury is used in the production of industrial bleach, the Olin plant is also a leading emitter of mercury in Tennessee. Suzanne's task is significant because of the evidence that mercury affects children and unborn babies, and, along with PCBs, it is one of the main reasons that there are fish consumption advisories across the country. For example, pregnant women, nursing mothers, and children are advised not to eat largemouth bass from the Hiwassee River near the Olin plant because of mercury contamination.[6] Suzanne believes that the contamination of the river is one of the most glaring examples of environmental injustice:

> Another way this is an injustice is that the Hiwassee River is something that belongs to everyone. There are many low-income families that use that river for recreation because it is a great family experience plus it is inexpensive. I have also been told that many of the lower income families relied on the Hiwassee River fish for an inexpensive high-protein meal. Now, many still eat the fish from that river even though the levels warrant an advisory. I also know that that mercury poisoning is more likely to affect children, women of childbearing age, those with compromised immune systems, and the elderly.

Suzanne offers some hope about future generations related to the environmental conditions that exist in Appalachia. She argues that because it is unsafe to fish in some of the waters in her community, "people will have to find alternative ways and places to teach their families about the outdoors. At best, maybe some will learn that polluting our environment is such a negative that the future generations will place greater demands on businesses in our area."

In addition to the number-one producer of bleach in North America, Appalachia is the home of the only manganese refinery in the United States and Canada—Eramet Marietta, Inc., just outside Marietta, Ohio, on the Ohio River. In 2008 this facility reported releases of more than 3.5 million pounds of manganese compounds into the environment.[7] With these numbers in mind, and research indicating that exposure to high levels of manganese can affect neurological development in children,[8] Caroline Beidler, an activist from southeastern Ohio, has the right to be concerned. She has been involved in a campaign against the facility for many years, and she was clear about her concerns regarding the health of children and families:

> There are so many little kids around here with asthma. These kids that are on breathing machines and the parents actually have to go into the school in the middle of the day and run these breathing machines for these kids. And you know how scary it is, I don't know if you've ever had an asthma attack, or just that when you've been real stuffy or can't breathe right. Just think how scary it is for a little kid.

Lisa Crawford moved to Ohio from Kentucky to find a home in the country for her kids to grow up. Her home was located across the street from a plant that she thought made Purina dog food because of the red-and-white checkered water tower on the plant's site. Lisa lived in her country home for about five years, raising her son and working hard to make a living, and she remembers the day her life changed forever. Her husband telephoned her and told her he heard there was something wrong with their well that provided the drinking water for their home. She attended her first public meeting not long after that phone call and discovered there that the well was contaminated with radioactive material. The facility across the road did not make dog food, it was the Fernald uranium enrichment facility operated by the U.S. Department of Energy. Even though Lisa was talking about the Fernald site, her words reveal the fear that many parents feel in relation to environmental pollution:

And I think people were really scared, I mean I was extremely scared for my husband and I, and also for our little boy at the time. We lived in a house across the street from the site that we were renting and the water had been contaminated with uranium for five years and we had never been told. So you know there was this really big fear of how is this going to affect my child, how is it going to affect me if I want to have another child.

Anyone who is a parent knows what it is like to be afraid for your child. There are certain milestones that your children reach that compound parental fear. One of the greatest fears for many parents arises when your child starts driving. The constant worry when your teenager takes the car for the evening is magnified with each accident that you hear about that cuts a short young life. Now imagine feeling that kind of fear twenty-four hours every day as you worry about what your child is breathing and eating. You worry about the water he or she is bathing in and if where you live may be having long-term health effects. For the activists that we interviewed, this fear has contributed to a sense of injustice that is often tied to a lack of trust in both government and industry.

Maya Nye is relatively new to activism, having recently taken the helm at People Concerned about MIC (methyl isocyanate), but she has lived in worry about the health of her family and community for most of her life. She remembers an explosion when she was sixteen years old as the defining moment in her drive to get educated about environmental issues. The source of the explosion was a plant owned by the Bayer Corporation near the small, predominantly African American town of Institute, West Virginia. Institute is one community in a region of Appalachia that has been named Chemical Valley because of the prevalence of industry. People Concerned about MIC is speaking out against Bayer, and Maya Nye recently became the group's main spokesperson.

Maya was raised in St. Albans, West Virginia, about four miles from the plant, and returned there after college. In August 2008 another explosion at the plant killed one person and forced local officials to call for everyone in the vicinity to stay inside. Responding to the explosion was one of the first things that Maya did as the new spokesperson for the group. After a fine was levied against Bayer for the explosion, she wrote comments to the EPA with the group's concerns about the penalty:

Bayer CropScience and the chemical companies that precede it have consistently discharged fugitive emission into the air, land and water of our community since the 1940s. While the violations represented in the penalty cover a short amount of time, they do not cover conclusively the years of damage that have been done to health and the environment of our community.[9]

This excerpt summarizes one of Maya's main reasons for engaging in the fight to protect her community. She talks about living every day with a feeling that there is a "ticking time bomb" that may go off at any time. While she has some concerns for herself because she is of childbearing age, she feels that it is her responsibility to do whatever she can to improve the quality of life of her neighbors. She humbly accepts the role as the "ominous new spokesperson" of the activist group when she explains that there are other women who have been fighting for a long time in the valley and she thinks they might be getting tired, so she is ready and willing to step in.

Trust Me

Trust, or the lack of it, is often the basis for people's motivation to participate in environmental decisions. Sometimes activists do not trust any of the organizations involved, including government and business interests. One underlying reason for mistrust in these organizations is the perception of deception. It can take years to build trust and a split second to erode it, and, once eroded, it may be impossible to rebuild. Think about how long it takes for someone to earn back your trust once they do something to lose it. Mistrust is the function of dishonest communication.

Communication is the foundation of trust and this communication must be honest and open and address the needs of an audience.[10] Even though communication is the foundation, follow-through creates the structure that builds trust. This means that behavior must follow the words that are spoken. In the case of environmental justice, perceptions of trust are almost as important as perceptions of health disparities. The women we interviewed identified cracks in both the foundation and structure of trust in government and industry and these cracks motivated them to take action.

THE FOUNDATION OF TRUST

No one likes to be lied to, or to even have the perception they are being lied to. Some people get angry enough about another's lying to do something, which suggests that there clearly is a relationship between trust and activism. Teresa Mills summed up the role trust played in motivating her to act when she felt government officials had lied to her:

Well, probably what made me speak out the most was when I started, I had a city councilman, we had a little meeting, I live on a court of fourteen homes. And we had a little court meeting and one of our elected officials told us to be quiet about it—you know, don't talk about it, it will hurt your property values. Well, some of us had medical bills that were higher than our property values. That kind of angered me, it frustrated me. But then when we started dealing with the agencies, and I'm always the type of person that I kind of know the answer before I ask the question. And when they were not outright lying, but not telling me the truth either, then I just became infuriated. And I've always taken the position I have the right to be in anyone's face that I so choose. And since they're government officials, that doesn't bother me—they put their pants on the same way I do.

Environmental activists do not trust industry to put the environment and human health ahead of profits and production efficiencies. This mistrust is the basis for the environmental movement, which has focused on demanding that governments take the lead to protect the environment. The result of these demands is a long history of laws, regulations, and policies originating from elected officials reacting to concerns of their constituents. There have been successes and failures with these legal interventions; however, activists have generally felt that they can count on their elected officials to at least listen to their concerns.

When elected and government officials stop listening but continue to make decisions that affect communities, mistrust takes over and everything said, or unsaid, becomes the focus of the conflict. Unlike the other activists we interviewed for this chapter, the government, not industry, was the villain in Lisa Crawford's situation. She identifies the impact of trust in mobilizing activism when it appears that information is being withheld from interested parties:

The second piece, I think, is people were really up in arms and furious that our own government could secretively do this to a community and not tell anybody. So it was outrage, and then I think people became very empowered because they were so scared and outraged that . . . I'll just be blunt, you get pissed off. And you ask a lot of questions and you don't get a lot of answers, and this was a group of people who came together and formed this organization and said, Hell no, we're not gonna take this anymore. And pretty much kicked the gate open, kicked the door open on the Department of Energy and really let the country know what was happening in some people's backyards across this country all in the name of national security.

Maya Nye talked about a public meeting that was called after another explosion at the Bayer plant. People Concerned about MIC invited Bayer to attend the meeting, but no one came. Her group saw this as an unwillingness by Bayer to engage with the community because the company had something to hide. She believes that Bayer has a communications strategy that includes marginalizing her group by keeping as much distance from them as possible. This strategy has led to serious trust issues between Maya's group and Bayer, and these issues will cloud any hope of progress in resolving disagreements in the future.

THE STRUCTURE OF TRUST

When it comes to environmental issues, private industry usually bears the brunt of the wrath of activists, who are more inclined to mistrust industry than government. For example, one of the activists interviewed expressed her faith in government but was unwavering in her mistrust of industry. This mistrust leads to feelings of injustice and is grounded in the profit motive of private industry, as Suzanne Wisdom explains:

> It's absolutely unfair. Olin gets all the benefits while the community has the consequences. Olin's biggest way to assert themselves in this community is to donate lots of money to many people and efforts. The high schools, universities, and businesses that would like to get involved in this campaign often can't because of Olin's contributions to their programs. Olin also employs many people in the community. Olin often states that they would have to shut down their plant if they could no longer use mercury in their process.

It is very easy to lose the trust of a person but very difficult to regain it. There are steps that industry can take to build trust, however, and Carolyn Beidler indicates that trust is built on effective and open communication.

> I will say that after ten years of asking the plant manager to sit down and meet with us, whether it be one or two or five or the whole community, finally in the last day of February this year the new plant manager who came on board in May of last year, he finally agreed to sit down and meet with some of us. We've had two meetings, we'll be having our third one in May. So we are making some progress ... It is going ... it's going as well as can be expected. There's distrust on both sides and we've got to kind of build that, we've got to build the trust. But they have definitely, they've been listening

to what we've been saying, and they're presently working on a project to refurbish one of their three furnaces. So it is a step in the right direction. It's been a long haul, though, and there's a long way to go.

Mistrust clearly contributes to feelings of unfair treatment and, while it may be possible for private industry to build trust in communities affected by their practices, in other instances there is probably little that industry can do. This deep-rooted mistrust is based on an ingrained belief system that has developed in response to a long history of industrial development.

Dr. Margaret Janes works with the Appalachian Center for the Economy and the Environment and she has a long history of working for environmental protection in West Virginia. One of the projects she is working on is with a chloralkali plant in the small town of Natrium, an unincorporated area on the Ohio River in Marshall County. As with the Olin plant in Tennessee, this facility is a major emitter of mercury, and Janes is most involved in monitoring the water pollution produced by the plant and responding to citizen concerns about the levels of mercury. In Janes's view industry has played a key role in environmental injustice because of its focus on the bottom line.

> I think environmental justice has a lot to do with disparate power. I think it has to do, particularly in West Virginia, when primarily, not exclusively, but primarily out-of-state corporate entities come into a place like WV that has few resources, low population and basically site various undesirable or harmful, or illness-causing facilities and take advantage of the political climate and the natural resources and people in the area. They frequently create an economic monopoly, and it's easier to control people because of the conflict between environmental harm and economic survival.

In a somewhat ironic twist, an out-of-state entity has been a key player in forcing the plant in Natrium to reduce mercury emissions. In August 2009 the Maryland attorney general announced a settlement with the plant that it will reduce mercury emissions over the next five years or face fines. From the success of the settlement, it may appear to some local activists who are dealing with the local effects of water and air pollution, that they were being ignored by this industry. It was only because of the actions of the attorney general of Maryland that the company agreed to reduce mercury pollution to minimize the impacts on residents in a neighboring state more than seventy miles from the facility.

Love It or Leave It

Is pollution from industry really a problem in Appalachia? Isn't manufacturing dying across the country as the economy shifts to an increased reliance on service and health care professions? Just like resource extraction, as industries shutter their windows and close their doors, they will leave behind an environmental legacy that will affect the communities for years to come. The nonenvironmental result of industrial shutdown is that poverty is certain to increase in the region leading to further injustice.

The death of manufacturing has led to desperate measures as residents seek any means to make a living. Young people are especially vulnerable and pop culture reflects this vulnerability. The Brassknuckle Boys are described as a Kentucky punk rock band, and in 2009 they delivered their second album, *Appalachian Industry*. In the title cut they sing, "Appalachian poverty breeds Appalachian industry," and the industry they sing about includes meth labs and prisons. Their songs and simple lyrics, such as "love it or leave it" in relation to this new type of industry, speak to a whole new generation about the injustice of economic conditions in Appalachia. Jobs have been, and will probably always be, the main concern for Appalachian people. How can they worry about protecting the environment when they cannot keep their heat on or feed their families?

The jobs-versus-environment debate has been a contributing factor in environmental justice because at least some of the environmental degradation in Appalachia is the result of locating facilities in the region with the full support of the residents. Chemical plants, uranium enrichment facilities, and heavy industry have been supported by residents through the promise of jobs, and Teresa Mills explains there is injustice in the broken promises related to jobs:

> No, it's not fair. Typically the community receives very little benefit from these types of facilities. Most of these facilities take highly technical people to run them. If they [local people] do get work in a facility it's as a laborer. . . . So not only are they exposed to it [pollution hazard] in their workplace, but they're also exposed to it [pollution] in their neighborhood. So, workers get a double hit. So while we all need jobs, we need jobs that are safe. It's like dangling a poison carrot in front of a rabbit. The rabbit doesn't realize it is not supposed to eat that carrot because there's something wrong with it. You know, jobs, jobs, jobs. Well, jobs are a necessity of life, but contamination isn't.

Teresa goes on to say that the "desperation" for jobs in the region has led to siting hazardous facilities that would not get a hearing in wealthier regions. In her view, unemployment and poverty make people willing to take risks that they might not take when they are employed. These risks include support for facilities that are bad for the environment but perceived as good for the economy.

Margaret Janes may have never met Teresa Mills, but she shares her opinions about why harmful facilities are located in poor communities. She says that industry "would not site a mercury chloralkali plant near a high-income sophisticated citizenry. They would never allow it and ... they pick areas like West Virginia that have a very lax climate, and boom there they are." Janes further explains the challenges with trying to mobilize local people to act when the major source of employment is the facility that is causing environmental harms: "I think in Natrium the [chloralkali] facility has primarily provided jobs, and we tried to get into that community through very strident environmental advocates, and they were afraid to help us. The community is very pro-PPG [Industries]. Pretty much the whole town is employed there."

The promise of jobs creates challenges for activists who are trying to protect the environment, and Lisa Crawford wants people to see through the promises about jobs: "I think they also dangle jobs, which is the economic piece. I think jobs are dangled in poor communities and, you know, 'We'll come in, we'll have five hundred jobs.' When we know that's a big fat lie. And I think that's deceptive and it's just basically wrong."

Caroline Beidler understands the challenges in trying to protect the environment and human health under the economic conditions in Appalachia:

> Marietta's just like any other community in Appalachia. I mean we're hurtin'. It's tight around here and there are definitely two sides. And, you know, we feel it, we feel the pressure in our jobs. We have chamber of commerce people who have said to us, When I smell that smell and when I see that soot, I think of American ingenuity. And you know when the chamber of commerce president told me that ... I said, Well, we're done here. You know, I really didn't know where to go with that. I thought, We're never gonna see eye to eye on this. So that's some of the mentality you're working against.

It used to be difficult to imagine a time in Appalachia when job creation and environmental protection would be discussed simultaneously. For most of its history, the promise of jobs was enough to convince communities to support the new factory, even if there was uncertainty about the environmental impacts. This has led to numerous cases in which people who live far from the plants try to influence decisions that may not affect them personally. Maya Nye explains that it is not easy, as a lifelong resident of the community, to say, Shut the plant down. Her own father worked at the plant she has been fighting against for twenty-six years, and she knows many people often have to choose between putting food on the table and keeping the heat on.

There is some hope emerging in the economy-environment arguments now because Appalachia is being viewed for its potential for alternative-energy jobs.[11] These new-generation jobs will mean that the workforce in Appalachia will need to be retrained so they can contribute in meaningful ways to new economic development. Even with their environmentally friendly aura today, jobs to create components for wind power and solar energy will still produce goods that are exported from the local communities. Hopefully we have learned something from the environmental injustices associated with resource extraction and existing Appalachian industries and we will not be discussing environmental justice in relation to alternative-energy production in the future.

Homeschooled Activists

There is no escaping the relationship between jobs and educational levels, and educational attainment in Appalachia is lower than in the rest of the country. Furthermore, the poorest counties in the region are also the least educated.[12] With these low levels of education, how is it possible for citizens to understand the highly technical nature of environmental problems? The activists we interviewed did not necessarily have the background in environmental science, chemistry, or medicine, but they had motivation to learn as much as they could. Teresa Mills explains that her concern, fear, anger, and frustration were strong motivators for getting educated:

> Some people, including myself, when I first started this I thought, Pfft, I'm just barely a high school graduate, I'm not smart enough to figure this out. And, you know, I was falling asleep at my kitchen table trying to read a scientific book when I just barely graduated from high school! But it was self-determination and self-education, and that's what some people don't have time to do.

Maya Nye was inspired to learn about the environment after the explosion that occurred when she was sixteen; she wanted to learn more about what was happening to the environment in her community and channel her creative energy into solving environmental problems. She attended a small liberal arts college and earned degrees in environmental studies and theater, eventually writing a play with an environmental theme.

Lisa Crawford views education as empowerment and argues that you must take education into your own hands because there is no outside assistance available that can be trusted:

> So there's health issues, there's outrage, there's getting yourself empowered and organized, and then there's education. Then you get yourself educated so you know what you're talking about, 'cause that's one of the things they'll get you on if you start raising hell about things and you don't know what you're talking about. So we spent a really tremendous amount of time getting ourselves educated so we could consciously know what we were talking about.

When faced with uncertainties about the health and environmental effects of industrial activities, local people will often look to outside experts to help them understand their situation. These experts conduct studies that can be accessed by all sides of the issue, therefore it is very important that they are perceived as objective. For example, an environmental health researcher from the University of Cincinnati has been awarded a grant from the National Institute of Environmental Health Sciences to conduct a study in the Marietta area. The research aims to quantify levels of contaminants, including manganese, in the air.

Caroline Beidler is relieved that there will be some research on the children who live near Eramet, even though the researcher expressed in an October 2008 meeting that she is most interested in "what is in the air."[13] Caroline called the study "really exciting" and has already drawn conclusions about what the study results will show: "This could have national or worldwide impact as far as regulations for the size, the quantity, of manganese emissions that should be or could be let loose and how it affects people."

Never Give Up

The women activists who are working to improve the environment in Appalachia are doing it for the sake of the children, to help local citizens understand that the environment and the economy are not enemies, and because they believe that there is injustice at the root of the environmental problems in the region. Lisa Crawford does not mince words about the role that injustice has played in her life as an activist:

> I think environmental justice is about how companies, whether they're the government or private industry or whatever, think they can just come into anybody's neighborhood and build anything they want and do anything they want under a veil of secrecy. To me that's part of the environmental justice movement . . . to me when something like this touches your life and upsets you, you have the right as an environmentalist, as a mother, as a citizen of this country to fight back and say, No, we don't have to put up with this.

The Appalachian activists who are involved with industrial issues mirror those who are fighting for environmental justice in coal mining. They share common values about the region and strong ties to their communities. They are upset that their environment and culture is being jeopardized by activities that offer few benefits to residents of Appalachia. Nevertheless, they vow to keep fighting the fight, even though it is not easy. As Maya Nye says, you have to "speak up and speak out," because when nobody asks questions, problems will never be solved.

Suzanne Wisdom will not quit fighting to reduce mercury emissions in Tennessee, even though she understands the challenges:

> Working to change attitudes and policies can take a long time. I think it is better to ease a community like ours into a way of thinking rather than make demands. It is easy to get bogged down when the community is non-responsive or disinterested in their own environment's welfare. But when you keep working, you keep meeting people who will help you, and you find them in unlikely places sometimes. Bottom line is to not give up.

Notes

1. Appalachian Regional Commission, "Sources of Growth of Regional in Non-Metro Appalachia," http://www.arc.gov/research/researchreportdetails.asp?REPORT_ID=84.
2. Appalachian Regional Commission, "Appalachian Region Employment Report," http://www.arc.gov/images/appregion/AppalachianRegionEmploymentReport2009Q1.pdf.

3. Michael Hendryx, "Mortality Rates in Appalachian Coal Mining Counties: 24 Years Behind the Nation," *Environmental Justice* 1, no. 1 (2008): 5–11.

4. United Church of Christ Commission for Racial Justice, *Toxic Wastes and Race in the United States: A National Report on the Racial and Socio-economic Characteristics of Communities with Hazardous Waste Sites* (New York: Public Data Access, 1987).

5. See Olin Chlor Alkali Products, http://www.olinchloralkali.com/.

6. Tennessee Wildlife Resources Agency, http://tennessee.gov/twra/fish/contaminants .html.

7. United State Library of Medicine, "ToxMap," http://toxmap.nlm.nih.gov/toxmap /combo/triIdentify.do#number1.

8. Agency for Toxic Substances and Disease Registry, "ToxFAQs for Manganese," http://www.atsdr.cdc.gov/tfacts151.html.

9. USEPA, responsiveness summary, docket CWA-RCRA-CAA-CERCLA-EPCRA -03-2009-0011.

10. USEPA, "7 Cardinal Rules of Risk Communication," http://www.epa.gov/care /library/7_cardinal_rules.pdf.

11. Southeast Energy Efficiency Alliance, "Energy Efficiency in Appalachia: How Much More Is Available, at What Cost, and by When?" Appalachian Regional Commission, http://www.arc.gov/research/researchreportdetails.asp?REPORT_ID=70.

12. John Haaga, "Educational Attainment in Appalachia," Appalachian Regional Commission, http://www.arc.gov/research/researchreportdetails.asp?REPORT_ID=35.

13. Tom Lotshaw, "UC Researcher Visits Marietta to Give Update on Children's Health Study," Marietta Register Online, http://eh.uc.edu/news/pdfs/haynes_marietta _10_22_2008.pdf.

EIGHT

Stories about Mountaintop Removal in the Appalachian Coalfields

GEOFFREY L. BUCKLEY AND LAURA ALLEN

> There was just no way to gauge how tall the thing was because there was nothing natural about it, nothing you could compare it to, and then it dawned on me exactly what I was standing under—Yellowroot Mountain, dead. I knew from Lace and Uncle Mogey that after they blasted the top off the mountain to get the coal, they had no place to put the mountain's body except dump it in the head of the hollow. So there it loomed. Pure mountain guts. Hundreds of feet high, hundreds of feet wide. Yellowroot Mountain blasted into bits, turned inside out, then dumped into Yellowroot Creek.
>
> Ann Pancake, *Strange as This Weather Has Been*

APPALACHIAN RESIDENTS KNOW ALL TOO WELL THE injustice of mountaintop removal (MTR) coal mining. Many people living close to these mining sites are frustrated and angry about the damage inflicted on their homes, communities, and environment.[1] They blame the coal companies, the government, the courts, and the media for thirty years of unchecked abuse. While local residents have spoken out against the practice, their objections have generally fallen on deaf ears—ignored by the public institutions set up to protect them and by others who view them as backward hill folk opposed to modernization and progress.

While many of us who live in urban America benefit from the "cheap" electricity generated at coal-fired power plants, relatively few of us actually know where these plants are located or what it takes to keep them operational. Fewer still have ever visited an active coal mine, let alone a mountaintop removal site. Only rarely are we exposed to the landscapes of mineral extraction and energy production that keep our lights on and our air conditioners running. Interviews with some of West Virginia's most prominent citizen-activists cast light on the day-to-day struggles endured by those who live in the shadow of MTR operations. Their stories, excerpted below, are powerful and compelling.

"A War Zone"

According to U.S. EPA reports, over ninety thousand acres in southern West Virginia were permitted for mountaintop removal mining between 1992 and 2002.[2] Flying over the coal-mining regions of West Virginia, the most obvious impacts of mountaintop removal are the environmental ones. MTR techniques have not only altered the geomorphology of this section of Appalachia, they have had a significant effect on the region's forest and water resources as well.

The first step in the process of mountaintop removal mining involves the clearing of trees and other vegetation. Next, explosives are used to remove what industry professionals refer to as overburden. Vernon Haltom and Jim Foster are familiar with the practice. Haltom, currently codirector of Coal River Mountain Watch, describes what it is like to live near an MTR site:

> I live in an area that gets rocked by blasting pretty frequently. It's just horrendous blasting. It's hard to describe. Unless you're in a war zone there's really nothing to compare it to. It's very much like that sometimes. The sound of it can be heard for miles away. The jolt of it is pretty readily apparent. I live about three thousand feet from the edge of a mountaintop removal site. It's bone rattling sometimes. . . . It's very nerve shattering.

Foster, who is eighty years old, has lived in Boone County, West Virginia, his entire life. He, too, lives next to a mountaintop removal site:

> They claim that they're using 3 million pounds of explosives per day here in West Virginia on these mountaintop removal sites. I sometimes believe that

there's that much used right here in this one county where I live. Right here in Boone County. The coal trucks and the explosives trucks run constantly. They run twenty-four hours a day, six days a week, and sometimes even on Sundays they haul coal.

Once the trees and other vegetation are removed, and the soil and subsoil layers are blasted away to expose the coal seam, bulldozers and heavy trucks are employed to remove the coal. The process is repeated as new seams of coal are exposed.

With the hills laid bare, lands in the immediate vicinity of the mine site become susceptible to damage from floods and erosion. Maria Gunnoe, an activist with the Ohio Valley Environmental Coalition, has lived in southern West Virginia for almost four decades:

> Altogether we've been flooded nine times. It has gotten worse with each flood. In 2003 there was just a huge washout. We had a substantial amount of rain that day. . . . About four and a half inches of rain fell in four hours. But within the first hour of this rainfall I had already been totally, completely washed out. . . . It just devastated our property. And I've lived here about thirty-nine years, and I've seen a lot of rainfalls, a lot of really heavy rainfalls, and we've experienced four-inch rainfalls many times in my thirty-nine years of living here. And I have never seen this little tiny creek that you can step over turn into a raging river like it did in 2003.

Gunnoe attributes the change in the behavior of her local stream to the fact that its headwaters are now buried by a valley fill: "The coal company went in and blasted the mountaintop off to get to the coal seams beneath and put everything other than the coal in the valley that made up the headwaters of the stream that runs through our property. And that's the only thing that's changed."

According to Jack Spadaro, a whistleblower who worked for the National Mine Health and Safety Academy until he was fired, in 2003, some thirty-five hundred miles of streams may well have been buried by mine waste by 2012 and "another five or six or seven hundred mountaintops" leveled. But it is more than mountain peaks and headwater streams that will be lost. The forest that blankets these ancient mountains and valleys will also disappear:

> The forests that are here are the most diverse forests in North America. It's one of the most diverse ecosystems in the world outside the tropics, and that

will all be gone. It'll just be utterly destroyed and we'll get these vast waste-lands of mountaintop removal sites where only a few species are growing. I mean we've got 250 bird species that breed in these hardwood forests and when you get to a mountaintop site you might find two or three bird species.

It will take generations before such biologically diverse forests reestablish themselves, regardless of the reclamation work performed after mining opera-tions have ceased.

"You cannot grow a forest in a pile of rocks"

The Surface Mining Control and Reclamation Act of 1977 requires coal companies to restore land to its approximate original contours (AOC) after it has been mined. In the case of mountaintop removal, however, coal operators can obtain an AOC variance if the postmining landscape can be used for "higher or better uses"—often interpreted to mean commercial or residential development.[3] Thus, coal operators attempt to make the postmining site as flat as possible so it can be used for this purpose. They flatten the land and then cover it with grass seed. Most activists are not satisfied with the results. Haltom explains why:

It's, I mean, to look at, to fly over this area, it's bizarre. I mean it's totally bizarre. You wonder how large swaths of Arizona got placed on West Vir-ginia.... You know, the coal industry will tell you ... that they're making the land better than it was and that we need flat land for development. Well, at the rate of development that we've had going on, we have enough flat land to last for three thousand years, so maybe in three thousand years if they develop that, maybe then you might want to start looking for flat land. But here in this town where I'm at right now, I mean, coal production is, now it's pretty high around this area. But the town is dying. ... So not only do we have plenty of flat land but we have plenty of empty buildings if someone wants to develop the area, but there is no development.

Jim Foster is also frustrated with the "reclamation" process. In his opinion, covering up the problem with a little fertilizer and grass seed will not solve the problems created by mountaintop removal:

They will sow grass and stuff like that and will try and cover up, make people think that it's habitable, can be used again. But after a year or so, everything washes away. You don't have anything but just a desolate waste-land, just like the moon surface or something. There's nothing can live on it. I don't care what anyone says, it can never be used for anything. They talk about flattening out land for businesses and industry. I haven't seen any of that stuff. If they [the government] could force them, give them a permit to mine five acres and say, Now, when you get that five acres reclaimed and get some industry established on it, we will give you another permit for five more acres, I will guarantee you that the first five acres they got would be the only permit they would ever get because nobody is gonna put an industry on top of a site where they've had this mountaintop removal.

Spadaro agrees that the coal industry does not have a very good record when it comes to reclamation and development:

Well, about a million and a half acres have been mined in this area. And a very, very small percentage—less than 1 percent—of the surface area has actually been used for alternative postmining land use. What you have are some grasslands that are far inferior to the original diverse hardwood forests that you had, so you have destroyed the potential for any kind of renewable resource. And there's just nothing really happening on this land. . . . There have been a few golf courses but there can't be a million and a half acres of golf courses in Appalachia! . . . That whole alternative postmining land use is simply bullshit.

Perhaps Maria Gunnoe says it best: "You cannot grow a forest in a pile of rocks."

"Violate, violate, violate, and then negotiate"

For residents living in mining communities, damage to water wells is one of the worst environmental problems associated with mountaintop removal. Community members whose water has been safe for generations now have to purchase bottled water for drinking and cooking. Chuck Nelson, a retired underground miner, describes the process by which coal slurry contaminates local wells:

So I've been going to communities where a lot of people . . . had well water where they had big slurry impoundments. . . . That's the water and the waste from cleaning coal and they put it in a big impoundment, a slurry pond that holds millions and millions of gallons. And they're man-made dams. They just do a dam across from one ridge to the next and that's where they put their ponds in. And after the ponds get filled, what they do is they inject this stuff into abandoned mine workings and so they have trillions of gallons of slurry pumped into our hills. And then with the practice of mountaintop removal where they come in and they use twenty-five hundred tons of explosives every day in West Virginia, and with that type of explosives . . . when they let these explosives off it cracks the rock strata. And it allows this slurry in these abandoned mine workings to get into the aquifer and get into the streams . . . [and] into people's well water.

Haltom notes that a lot of people whose wells have been fouled by coal slurry are experiencing a variety of drinking-water related health problems:

They had it for free and now suddenly this generation the water is starting to come out black and brown and smelling of hydrogen sulfide and corroding their pipes and making them horribly ill. There's family after family after family where people have kidney problems, liver problems, and brain tumors. A five- or six-year-old child should not have to pass kidney stones. That's not a normal five- or six-year-old disease. An eighteen- or nineteen-year-old girl should not have to have her gall bladder removed. That's not normal. . . . It's not normal for a woman in her thirties, who's never touched a drop of liquor in her life, to have severe liver problems. It's a serious problem.

As Haltom readily concedes, it is very difficult to connect the dots: "One of the problems is how do you prove that that company poisoned that water that made you sick, how do you prove that that water is what made you sick, how do you prove that that water came from that company's coal waste? It's very difficult, but empirically, when you look at the evidence, it's pretty overwhelming." In a court of law, however, Haltom admits "there's a good chance you'll die before" a lawsuit is decided in your favor. "Their strategy is to violate, violate, violate, and then negotiate."

Gunnoe views the water contamination problem through the lens of environmental justice: "I mean, it quite honestly really surprises me that there's people out there that would be willing to sacrifice my family so that their family can have play stations and umpteen billion TVs and computers, and drive around in gaudy vehicles . . . and I'm thinking my kids have to drink their water out of a bottle." Unlike most Americans, whose municipal drinking water supplies are deemed safe by the U.S. EPA but who choose to drink bottled water out of convenience or to make a social statement, Gunnoe's family consumes bottled water out of necessity: "We can't drink the water that comes in our home. We can't use the water that comes into our home for any kind of consumption. . . . I feel that if I had water that I could use right now, I'd be rich."

Home and Community

According to residents, the most devastating effects of mountaintop removal coal mining are not environmental. They are the effects to home and community. Indeed, many activists are not comfortable calling themselves environmentalists. In fact, many are not opposed to mining at all. But they draw the line when it comes to mountaintop removal. While they appreciate the beauty of the mountains they maintain that they are simply fighting for their future. In addition to mudslides and contaminated water, many residents in coal country fear their homes will be damaged by blasting or from flying rocks. And the coal companies, they point out, are often slow to pay for the damage they have caused.

In Gunnoe's opinion, the mining industry has not treated the communities where they operate with respect: "They go in and fill the headwaters of these streams with the blasted former mountaintops." It basically devastates the homes and the communities downstream "through water pollution, through subsidence, through flooding, and through blast damages to their homes.""The air quality is horrible," adds Gunnoe."The explosives used in the blasting, we breathe that every day."

Public buildings, too, have been affected by mountaintop removal. Coal River Mountain Watch is currently monitoring the situation at Marsh Fork Elementary School, which is next to a large coal sludge impoundment."It's a bad situation," opines Haltom:

> The school itself is four hundred yards downstream from a 2.8 billion gallon sludge dam. What this sludge is, it is the toxic residue remaining from washing the coal. The coal doesn't just go straight from the ground to market. It's processed at these preparation plants, which are right near the school, and the sludge is pumped up behind by this dam. And this isn't a steel and concrete dam. It's actually made of coal refuse . . . and it's been cited by the Mine Safety and Health Administration numerous times for flaws in construction. Flaws that can be fatal to folks downstream if they were not corrected.

Haltom is also bothered by the fact that state and federal officials have permitted other mining-related structures to be located in the vicinity of the school:

> Also near the elementary school, you've got a preparation plant. The coal produced by the preparation plant goes into a coal silo. It's a tall, cylindrical structure, and a train pulls through the silo and loads and takes it to market. The silo itself was built in the year 2003, and it's within three hundred feet of the school building. It's only 225 feet from the school building, which is a violation of both federal and state laws. The state DEP [department of environmental protection] granted the permit for that (a) without examining the law and (b) without examining the permit boundary for that company. . . . The fact that both of the silos are within three hundred feet of the school is wrong, the fact that they were placed outside the original permit boundary is troubling, and the fact that this company would even consider putting these things right next to an elementary school is just atrocious.

To Haltom and others, there can be no justification for placing 230 students in harm's way.

Economy and Employment

Many people are afraid to speak out against the coal companies because some community members depend on them for jobs. "It's almost a feudal society where the coal industry is king, and the people who live in this area are serfs and peasants," complains Haltom:

> What happens is the industry does hire some people. There's not much in the way of other economic alternatives here because those alternatives have been stifled for many years, so what the companies do is they do hire some people, and when you hire one person, that shuts up a large number of people. So if somebody has a brother or cousin or uncle or nephew or friend that works for the coal company, they're not going to speak out about things because there's the chance that person could be fired. And people don't want to make trouble for their friends, they don't want to make trouble for their relatives, and there's this culture of just taking it. Just sitting down and shutting up.

Haltom believes that a lot of people actually oppose many of the things that the coal industry does but don't believe anything can be done: "They say . . . the legislature is owned by the coal industry, the governor's office and the governor is owned by the coal industry, the courts are owned by the coal industry, there's nothing you can do." And yet, argues Gunnoe, people cannot simply ignore MTR because the effects are everywhere to be seen: "Nobody wants to deal with it and we have to. It's literally in our backyards."

Coal companies launch vigorous media campaigns in West Virginia, trying to convince citizens that they need coal in order for their economy to survive. Many people are afraid to oppose mountaintop removal because they work for the coal companies or they have a brother, father, uncle, cousin, or close neighbor who works in the coal industry. In communities with very limited employment options, losing a coal-mining job of any kind is devastating. Chuck Nelson experienced such a disaster in 2000. He says he was blacklisted for voicing his concerns about coal dust in the community and for organizing a petition drive in his town. His story and the stories of other anti–mountaintop removal activists paint a different picture from the one that coal companies present about the impact of their industry on the economy of the region.

The mining industry often blames environmental activists and environmental laws for job losses in Appalachia. Understandably, residents often sympathize with the coal miners who have lost their jobs. Many are not aware, however, that the major cause of job losses in the mining industry over the past eighty years has been mechanization. According to Nelson:

> The coal industry is pointing a finger at us and saying, You're trying to take jobs, but no, we're not trying to take jobs. In the sixties and seventies, when I worked as a union miner, we had about two hundred thousand miners in West Virginia.[4] Today with the practice . . . [of] mountaintop removal, it takes less manpower. It takes two people to drill, a person on a dragline in a dozer, and people to let the explosives off. And this practice is eliminating jobs. . . . The industry is taking jobs by going to this practice.

A former miner, Nelson does not want to see the coal industry leave the state. Rather, he favors an increase in underground mining: "We tried, we said we want this type of mining [MTR] stopped." With underground mining, "you'll put a lot more citizens in a lot more communities back to work."

Some community members are concerned about what will happen when coal can no longer be mined in their town or their county. "There's gonna come a time when coal's not gonna be there anymore," warns Nelson. "And you have to start planning and transition into where we're gonna get energy in the future. In the meantime we're also concerned about the future of our kids and their kids. What kind of future do they have here in the communities which I was raised up in?" After the forests are clearcut and the coal is extracted using mountaintop removal techniques, citizens like Jim Foster worry about the degraded landscape left behind:

> What are they gonna do for wood and lumber if they destroy all the forests? It's hard to understand why they would let that happen. They use coal one time; they burn it; it's gone; that's forever. But the forests, you can go through and cut . . . timber, and go back thirty to fifty years later, and some of the soft timber like poplar . . . it'll grow back and have monstrous trees in thirty to forty years. And the hardwood forests, the oaks, the hickory, and all the hardwood; it'll grow back about every fifty years, you can get a cutting. That gives something for each generation. But if you allow one generation to destroy it all and leave nothin' for the next generation, I think that's a big sin. I think that's the worst thing that ever happened.

Anyone who doubts Foster's convictions on this matter is referred to the Bible: "Turn to the eleventh chapter of Revelations [sic], the eighteenth verse, and read for yourself what it says about it. 'Those that destroy the earth; they will be destroyed.' And I actually believe that God don't intend for the earth to be destroyed because this is God's creation, the earth is God's creation. And I don't think it's right to allow a handful of people to destroy it. It's not right."

Other community activists propose alternative solutions to resource extraction that would still provide energy and jobs for the region. Nelson talks about a study Coal River Mountain Watch did on wind potential in the mountains:

> We did a study on Coal River Mountain, where they're trying to get a permit to take all of it. Now, we've offered an alternative to take some windmills up there. They can have power, enough power to supply ninety-three thousand homes, and this is forever, it's not like you're gonna run out of it. The wind will always be there. And it will supply permanent jobs, lifetime jobs. With mountaintop removal, they give them a pledge 'cause they know they'll get temporary energy sources. They use that coal and then it's gone. The mountain's destroyed. They're temporary jobs. When the coal's gone, the job is gone. And we're offering an alternative. Whereas they, with this permit, they go ahead and cut the tops off these mountains and cause so

much environmental damage! Not only are they destroying the land, the people, the water, and everything, the air, but then also the potential for wind farms. Once these mountains are torn down, the potential no longer exists. And we're offering alternatives to 'em.

An Energy Sacrifice Zone

Fairly or unfairly, Appalachia is often perceived as an energy sacrifice zone—a place where human lives are valued less than the natural resources that can be extracted from the region.[5] Gunnoe explains why she is fighting as hard as she can to change this perception:

> What they [government and coal industry] don't realize is that the people that they're dealing with right now do not have a choice. They have already taken the lives that we had planned for ourselves. They've already taken that. And we have no choice but to fight what's going on. They've backed us into a corner and we cannot sit down because if we sit down we're giving up on everything that our lives are based on in the past, the present, and the future.

As difficult as it may be to come to terms with broken lives and broken dreams, it is the next generation—and those that follow—that Gunnoe is most concerned with at this stage in her life:

> Then too, as a parent, how do you look at your children and say, Well, people in America need energy, so your life don't matter. You can't do that. You have to say, Your life matters just as much as anybody else, especially the people sitting in DC that's making the decisions that are ruining your life right now. Your life is just as important as theirs. And in my opinion, it's more important because they are our future. And my children very much understand that their lives have been sacrificed so that people can keep their lights on. And don't think for one minute that either of us is content with that.

Loss of Heritage and Culture

People who live in mining communities are used to coal mining, but in the past mining did not prevent them from using other resources available at their doorstep. The mountains possess an abundance of wild animals, plants for food and medicine, clear streams, swimming holes, and favorite hiking trails. Growing up in Appalachia, the mountains figure prominently in the lives of the region's children: "There's times in your life, as a young adult that you go to places, maybe a favorite swimming hole, your favorite little cove to hang out in, you just love it there," reflects Gunnoe. "Well, as you grow up you wanna go back to that place. Imagine that place not being there. It's not there anymore. You can't find it." As for the resources she and her ancestors have relied on for centuries, they too are gone:

> And I know this because growing up here, we depended on this land for our medicine, for our food, and our water especially. I mean when I was a young kid, we ran these mountains all day long, every day. That was what we done. And we never did as kids, we never had to take water with us. And if we got hungry there was things in the woods that you could eat. There's an abundance of greens and mushrooms and roots, and things like this that you can actually eat. That's the reason my family settled here to begin with, because there is an abundance of food in these mountains, and then, the wildlife too, of course, that was our meat when we was growing up. And what they've done, the coal companies have blocked us out, they've fenced in and put up gates and no trespassing signs and they've threatened to put people in jail, and they've basically moved in and taken over.

Gunnoe lives on land that her grandfather, a coal miner earning $18 a week, passed on to her:

> And before he passed on he looks at me and he says, "You're the one I want here." That meant the world to me. I don't see how I'm supposed to walk away. What do I do with the rest of my life? I had a plan for my life. . . . I wanted to raise them [my children] the way that I was raised, knowing the things that I know about the forest, and quite honestly it's been very handy to me as an adult to be able to sustain myself in all conditions. And it's just not happening, and it's not gonna happen because of the fact that everything that our lives are based on has been trashed by the coal companies.

And so, despite the flash floods and mud slides, the blasting and fly rocks, the threats and frustration, Gunnoe and her family cling to their mountain home.

One of the greatest challenges citizen-activists face is the battle against apathy and prejudice. Try as they may, people in power both inside and outside the region are reluctant to help. Many activists blame their plight on the persistence of regional stereotypes that portray residents as ignorant and childlike. Many feel they are not being treated like American citizens or even human beings. "We're people that don't matter, right down to the coal miners and the equipment operators on these mountaintop removal sites," asserts Gunnoe. "They're not important; they're expendable, every single one of them, including the people in the communities. Appalachia has always been the rear end, if you will, of the country."

The way Gunnoe sees it, a future that includes mountaintop removal is a future in which her human rights continue to be violated: "In order to continue mountaintop removal coal mining, the United States government and the coal companies and the energy industry are going to have to be willing to continue to walk on people's God-given human rights to clean air, to clean water, and the right to own land, for God's sakes. The right to control what happens on that land. We don't have those rights here." As far as she is concerned, the battle lines are drawn and the stakes are high: "We're not environmentalists; we're citizens. And we're fighting because we haven't got a choice. Either we fight, or we lose. That's your options, and when you lose you're losing everything forever. You're losing your air, you're losing your water, you're losing your land, you're losing your culture, you're losing your heritage, you're losing everything that made us who we are. It's gone forever."

Failure of the Government; Failure of the Media

Ultimately, mountaintop removal continues to be practiced because local, state, and federal government officials have consistently ignored the complaints of community members. They have failed to act. Spadaro maintains that the federal government weakened the strongest environmental laws so they could be violated without legal repercussions:

> One weakness in the law was that it allowed the states to assume the responsibility for enforcing the law with oversight by the federal government, and what happened was the federal oversight was weakened beginning in the early 1980s. The number of federal inspectors was reduced, the authority for enforcement of the Surface Mining Control and Reclamation Act was given to the states, and in West Virginia, Kentucky, and Virginia the states simply approved, most often, whatever the mining companies proposed for

their mining operations, even if the proposals were in violation of the law. They did a very poor job of enforcing the provisions of the act related to valley fills in particular and also did a poor job of enforcing the Clean Water Act, which is supposed to protect streams. They've allowed valley fills to be dumped into streams and in the region so that about two thousand miles of stream channels are now filled in with valley fills. And that's been done in violation of federal law and in violation certainly of the Clean Water Act and in violation of the National Environmental Policy Act as well.

Spadaro has witnessed the failure of government enforcement up close. In 2000 he was a member of the team investigating the Martin County, Kentucky, coal slurry spill on October 11, 2000:

> And as we were doing our investigation, [which] began in October of 2000, there was an election, the national election, and by January of 2001 there's a new president, President Bush. And on election day we were notified that Tony Oppegard, the leader of our team, had been fired and that we had a new manager of the investigation and that we were to wrap up the investigation. Well we were nowhere near complete with the work that we were needing to do to investigate the root causes of the disaster. And as time went on into the spring of 2001 as we were writing the investigative report, we were interfered with repeatedly by the management of the agency. And finally interfered with by the new head of the agency, a man named Dave Lauriski. Lauriski weakened the writing of the report, the conclusions, and recommendations. And essentially diverted any responsibility away from the Mine Safety and Health Administration, who had allowed the pumping to continue into the reservoir over that six-year period. . . . He weakened the conclusions and recommendations so that it would be difficult to prosecute the mining company for any kind of criminal negligence.

Politicians have frequently passed difficult decisions concerning coal-mining violations to other levels of government. Haltom resents that the state government has forced community members to rely on their local governments to solve complex, expensive problems, such as the one playing out at Marsh Fork Elementary School. The school, located in Sundial, West Virginia, sits in close proximity to a Massey Energy coal-processing facility and an earthen dam that holds back an estimated 2.8 billion gallons of coal slurry in a lake approximately 3,500 feet long and 1,000 feet wide in spots:[6]

The school board actually did, in March or in early 2007, ask the governor for money to build a new school, and he denied that. That's him passing the buck, really is what it is. He can get his feet into just about anything else regarding state business, but when it comes to something that he really does actually have the power and the authority to make something happen, he claims that he has no power or authority to make that happen. He did say it was, like, Oh well, if Raleigh County wants a new school for the kids, they should put it to the vote of the people of Raleigh County. The problem with that is that end of Raleigh County is probably the least populated and poorest area of Raleigh County. That school historically has gotten the dregs of other schools. They get leftovers or used items from other schools. The other schools get newer things. So because it's not in a populated area it's very unlikely that Raleigh County would vote to support that [a new school].

Ironically, Haltom adds, "Our governor brags about having hundreds of millions of dollars in budget surplus, yet that can't go for a new school."

On April 29, 2010—more than a year after our first interview with Haltom—the Annenberg Foundation announced that it would contribute $2.5 million for a new elementary school in Rock Creek, West Virginia, about a ten-minute drive from the school's current location in Sundial. The announcement came as the Raleigh County school board was struggling to raise an additional $4 million to help cover the $8.6 million price tag of a new building. According to Haltom, the effort to relocate the school would have failed had it not been for the Annenberg donation. "The state's plan was for [the project] to fail," states Haltom. He contends that it was only after staff members from Senator Robert Byrd's office visited the area—including the coal silo and coal slurry impoundment—that state officials began to pay attention to the issue. Soon after Byrd's staffers visited Marsh Fork Elementary, the local school board submitted an official request to the School Building Authority (SBA), headed by Governor Joe Manchin's cousin, Mark, to move the school. As part of their proposal, the Raleigh County school board suggested that Massey Energy contribute $1 million to the project to go along with $1 million from the school board. School board officials hoped the remaining $6.6 million would be provided by the state. When the SBA announced it would offer just $2.6 million, the project appeared doomed. When prominent philanthropist Charles Annenberg Weingarten visited the area after the Upper Big Branch mine explosion, he learned of the situation at Marsh Fork and offered to help. In the end, the Annenberg Foundation agreed to donate $2.5 million if the SBA, Raleigh

County, and Massey came up with more money. The school is scheduled to open sometime in late 2012.[7]

Activists are also frustrated by the lack of media attention for environmental issues in Appalachia. Haltom believes he knows why local and state media are so biased in their coverage of mountaintop removal mining:

> There's the fact that the industry has way too much influence down here. They put ads on TV. They spend a lot of money on their propaganda machine, and that's just something that we can't match. Even the news media is, in large part, overly friendly with the coal industry. There's one company called West Virginia Media Holdings that has three or four TV stations and newspaper and radio stations, and they are completely in bed with the industry. They are friends of coal through and through. Their senior editors and their owners make no bones about it, and there's two other TV stations that are supposedly owned by separate companies, but not really, and they ran for about a month ... twice a day ... on two different channels this series of supposed reports called *Coal under Attack*. It was just propaganda. It was completely unbalanced.

It took three years for national media outlets such as the *New York Times* to interview Spadaro about the Bush administration's cover-up of the three-hundred-million-gallon coal slurry spill in Martin County, Kentucky. Although this spill was one of the largest environmental disasters ever to occur in the United States—thirty times larger than the *Exxon Valdez* oil spill, in 1989—there was very little national media coverage. Spadaro explains why:

> I know that when the *New York Times* writer interviewed me—he was interviewing me three years after the Martin County coal slurry spill—he was interviewing me because I'd gone public, and the agency was trying to fire me. So he asked me in the interview, So why did my paper not write about the Martin County slurry spill in the first place? And I said, Why don't you tell me? And I guess it was because it wasn't in Connecticut or New York, or someplace that's considered pristine. Because it was in Appalachia, it was ignored by the national press.

The Martin County spill was not the only disaster ignored by the national news. Haltom remembers a particularly outrageous accident that resulted in the death of a three-year-old boy:

Later in the year, in September, I went to a rally in Appalachia, Virginia. What had happened there was on August 20 of 2004, I believe it was August 20 at 2:30 in the morning, a little boy was killed in his bed—a little three-year-old boy—when a mining company was illegally enlarging what was supposed to have been an access road. They were illegally enlarging it to make it a haul road. At 2:30 in the morning, under cover of darkness, with an inexperienced bulldozer operator, basically what they did was pushed this boulder off a mountain, and it came down the mountain and into this house, killed this little boy in his sleep. That was so outrageous. I mean it's just one of those outrageous things, but the news of that didn't make it out. I think the *Washington Post* finally published a story about it. I don't know if they actually put it in a printed form, but that was like maybe a month or so after it happened. So, stories like that don't make it out. When some blond child in California or Utah goes missing, that's front-page news, all over the talk shows, and all over the news channels every day. But an Appalachian child gets killed in his sleep by a coal company and you don't hear a thing.

The lack of national reporting on environmental disasters in Appalachia is disturbing, but the lack of press coverage does not stop there. National media outlets have also failed to report demonstrations critical of the mining industry. Haltom recalls one demonstration, in particular, that went unnoticed:

It was in March of 2007, during the week of Mountain Justice Spring Break.[8] It was announced that the surface mine board approved of the second silo behind Marsh Fork Elementary School, and two days later we had a major demonstration in the capital. The governor's reception area, which is a really large room, was filled with people, I think around a hundred people or so, of local people, of people throughout West Virginia, and people throughout the mountain justice movement, and also Mountain Justice Spring Break participants. Singing some old-time music, and calling on the governor to get the kids a safe new school in their community. During the course of that demonstration, thirteen people were arrested, some of them pretty roughly. One of our staff members was handcuffed behind her back and carried by the handcuffs, not by the arms, but lifted up by the handcuffs behind her back, and that's pretty painful. Larry Gibson, whose family still maintains and is holding onto fifty acres on Kayford Mountain, he was at that demonstration. His shoulder was injured. He had to stop by the emergency room on the way to jail.

While the event was covered locally—West Virginia Public Radio did a fairly long segment on the protest—the national news media did not pick up the story. "You would think thirteen people getting arrested in a governor's office would make national news," insists Haltom. "If it was Arnold Schwarzenegger's office, it would be all over CNN and all of the major news networks, but not if it's in West Virginia."

"And It Will Happen"

Despite the setbacks and frustration, Gunnoe remains optimistic that political action is the key to the movement's success. She explains the importance of informing politicians and involving young people:

> I think we're ready as a country to make this transition. We've just got to get the right politicians thinking in the right direction to make this happen, and it will happen because the same youth that were in the colleges . . . five years ago when we started visiting the colleges, the same youth in the colleges then are now building wind turbines. They're turbine engineers. It's happening, and it's time for the government to open up their eyes and say this is what the American people want. That's the biggest hindrance right now—the government and the so-called laws that's on the books to protect people's lives. . . . The American people want a better life for their kids. And the government is scared to death that it's going to affect their pocketbooks.

Spadaro is a bit more skeptical but no less committed to securing a more sustainable and just energy future for the region and the nation: "As far as I can see, it's gonna take the people from the region themselves joining with people from outside the region to raise awareness and create the national movement that's necessary to get federal legislation passed that stops these types of mining practices."

Notes

1. Indeed, as Rebecca R. Scott points out, mountaintop removal mining is an extraordinarily complex issue; one that forces us to examine issues of gender, race, and class in twenty-first-century Appalachia and America. Scott, *Removing Mountains: Extracting Nature and Identity in the Appalachian Coalfields* (Minneapolis: University of Minnesota Press, 2010).

2. Shirley Stewart Burns, "Bringing Down the Mountains: The Impact of Mountaintop Removal Surface Coal Mining on Southern West Virginia Communities, 1970–2004" (PhD diss., West Virginia University, 2005).

3. Erik Reece, *Lost Mountain: A Year in the Vanishing Wilderness: Radical Strip Mining and the Devastation of Appalachia* (New York: Riverhead Books, 2006), 38.

4. Coal employment in West Virginia reached an all-time high in 1948 when 125,669 miners removed 168,589,033 tons of coal. Coal production in West Virginia reached an all-time high in 1997 when 18,165 miners removed 181,914,000 tons of coal. In 2009, the most recent year for which data are available, 20,753 miners removed 144,017,758 tons of coal from West Virginia mines. West Virginia Office of Miners' Health, Safety and Training, "Production of Coal and Coke in West Virginia", 1863–2009, http://www.wvminesafety.org/historicprod.htm (accessed March 21, 2011).

5. Jedediah S. Purdy, "Rape of the Appalachians," *American Prospect* 41 (November–December 1998): 218. Purdy attributes the use of this phrase to West Virginia lawyer Tom Rodd.

6. Vernon Haltom, personal communication, March 21, 2011.

7. Ken Ward Jr., "Annenberg Foundation Offering $2.5 Million toward New Marsh Fork Elementary." *Charleston Gazette*, April 29, 2010. http://blogs.wvgazette.com/coaltattoo/2010/04/29/annenberg-foundation-offering-2-5-million-toward-new-marsh-fork-elementary-school/ (accessed September 14, 2010).

8. According to the organization's website, the annual Mountain Justice Spring Break offers coalfield residents, college students, environmentalists, and concerned citizens the opportunity to learn more about mountaintop removal mining. "Through education, community service, speakers, hiking, music, poetry, direct action, and more," participants during the week-long program "learn from and stand with Appalachian communities" in the struggle to protect land and culture; www.mjsb.org (accessed March 21, 2011).

AFTERWORD

An American Sacrifice Zone

JEDEDIAH S. PURDY

    The American relationship with nature is fragmented and divided against itself, and that division has shaped the land. Americans invented the ideal of wilderness, land forever protected against roads, buildings, and engines. Our laws consecrate more than a hundred million acres to that ideal, most of it in the West, where you can wander for days without seeing a sign of "development." Our national parks mark the first time a democracy chose to set aside revered landscapes in the name of all the people—and for their use and pleasure. President Theodore Roosevelt, a macho bully, imperialist, and champion of executive power, created vast acres of wildlife preserves, quite possibly in violation of the Constitution, because he loved birds.

    But joy in nature, and reverence toward it, are half the story at most. The United States was founded on the belief that the natural world exists for human use, and that the noblest activity is to make nature economically productive—to turn it to human needs and human wealth. This idea has always implied a certain mercilessness toward other views of the nonhuman world. Early Americans justified taking the continent from the Indians on the theory that tribes that did not settle and clear the land could not own it, because ownership had to be earned by development. The American Revolution, too, was justified partly by the British government's forbidding the colonials to settle beyond the Allegheny Mountains—denying them, in other words, the human right and duty of development. This view of nature has often been at war with the first: in loggers fighting environmentalists, cattlemen who resisted the parks and wilderness system, and Westerners today who want to kick the federal government out of the national lands in their backyard. Those who work the land for wealth have often felt that preserving it from use is not just inconvenient to them: it is an insult to their way of life.

Then there is a third ideal, which really came into its own in the suburbs and culture of consumption after World War II. This is the clean landscape: unpolluted, free of rank smells and waste, safe for children to run in. The wish for the clean landscape helped inspire the great antipollution laws of the 1970s, including the Clean Air Act and the Clean Water Act, which did indeed make life safer and healthier in much of the country. But this was also a segregating ideal. It drove *working* nature out of sight and out of mind, excluding farming, making things, and burning things for energy from the places where people lived.

The logic of all this is to create *sacrifice zones*—the places where we produce food and energy, with little regard for the health or beauty of the land, to maintain our clean and convenient lives. American farmland has become more and more like an industrial waste system over the last fifty years, and its fertilizers, pesticides, manure, and soil erosion account for much of the country's failure to meet its announced standards for clean air and water.

Since the mid-1990s, central Appalachia has become the country's purest sacrifice zone. Energy from coal runs laptops, iPhones, and supergreen electric cars, plus high-efficiency air-conditioning—all the conveniences of the clean world. At the same time, that energy comes from a use of the land that treats it as disposable. In the Appalachian coalfields, Americans do not treat the land as a people would who expected to live in a place for generations, or for more than a few years. When dynamite blasts apart a hilltop and draglines heap dirt in the surrounding hollows, the land is being classified as a place that we ruin forever, in return for a few years of convenience.

The movement against mountaintop removal has failed again and again in court, though at the time of writing it may be starting to see some success in politics. Its clearer success, though perhaps a pyrrhic one, has been to raise Americans' awareness of the sacrifices their energy economy entails. This comes at the same time that the industrial food system is increasingly visible, so that plastic-wrapped hamburger and pork chops have indelible associations with pools of liquid manure, industrial-scale antibiotics that produce drug-resistant bacteria, and confinement that denies animals the basic pleasures of movement and fresh air and seems to drive them mad. These changes in awareness are beginning to show those who pay attention that there is no such thing as a clean world. Instead, we face a choice between acknowledging our waste and destruction, and trying to deal with them as responsibly as we can, or ignoring them and deepening the logic of the sacrifice zone.

What does all of this have to do with justice? A standard definition of environmental justice is that less powerful individuals and communities should not bear a disproportionate share of environmental harms, from pollution to the destruction of mining. This is an idea based in a certain version of fairness: treating people alike, although they may be different in wealth, region, race, or other ways. It is very clear that mountaintop removal and waste dumps in Appalachia, and the rest of the region's environmental experience, are instances of environmental injustice in this sense.

It is important, though, to be clear about how little power this idea of justice has in American law or American life more generally. We allocate most of the benefits of social life according to wealth: buying land in a clean and safe neighborhood, paying for a good education (at a private school, or by buying a house in a good school district), being able to purchase good medical care (or, for the moment, any medical care at all). Even outside of economic life, the burden of our criminal justice system falls heavily on the poor and racial minorities, who fill prisons, and whose crimes are punished much more harshly than those of the comfortable and privileged. We don't exactly let people starve, and in person we Americans are often compassionate and charitable; but our way of sharing out the world speeds many lives on a road to ruin.

We treat landscapes the same way, along with the people who live on them. There is no equality among American landscapes: some are sacred, some protected against harm, and some sacrificed. As a result, there is no equality among Americans *to the degree that they care about their landscapes, identify with them, and wish to imagine that their children and grandchildren might live there as they have.* If you live in a wooded suburb of Boston and treasure the preserved lands next door, if you live in the dense neighborhoods of Boulder, Colorado, and like to duck into the Rocky Mountain National Park for your summer hikes, your relation to the land is secure, a privilege enshrined in law. But if you love the hills of southern West Virginia or eastern Kentucky, if they form your idea of beauty and rest, your native or chosen image of home, then your love has prepared your heart for breaking.

Today, climate change seems to insure that no one can be sure of growing old, or even growing up, in the landscape they were born into. Change, uncertainty, all parts of modern life, are now acute features of the global environment, with results that we have not really begun to understand. This is not just a physical, practical vulnerability. It is also a vulnerability in memory and hope, in ways of seeing the land, anticipating the seasons, knowing what will grow and what lives there with you, knowing whether it will be habitable at all. Wherever they live, Americans might consider that this is a vulnerability our laws have long imposed on those who live in, and love, the country's sacrifice zones.

CONTRIBUTORS

LAURA ALLEN received her bachelor's degree in cultural anthropology in 2009 from the Ohio University Honors Tutorial College. At Ohio University, in addition to her cultural anthropology coursework, she focused on Japanese, environmental studies, and Appalachian studies. Her departmental honors thesis on environmental advocacy in Appalachia is titled "Stand Up and Fight: Ideologies of Anti-mountaintop Removal Coal Mining Activists in West Virginia." Since 2009 she has been working in rural Japan as an assistant language teacher at two junior high schools, four elementary schools, and a kindergarten.

BRIAN BLACK is professor of history and environmental studies at Penn State Altoona, where he currently serves as head of the Division of Arts and Humanities. His research emphasis is on the landscape and environmental history of North America, particularly in relation to the application and use of energy and technology. He is the author or editor of several books, including the award-winning *Petrolia: The Landscape of America's First Oil Boom* (Johns Hopkins University Press, 2003) and the forthcoming *Contesting Gettysburg: Preserving a Cherished American Landscape.* Currently, he is writing about twentieth-century petroleum consumption.

GEOFF BUCKLEY has a joint appointment in geography and environmental studies at Ohio University. He is the author of *Extracting Appalachia: Images of the Consolidation Coal Company, 1910–1945* (Ohio University Press, 2004) and *America's Conservation Impulse: A Century of Saving Trees in the Old Line State* (Center for American Places, 2010). Over the years his articles have appeared in the *Annals of the Association of American Geographers, Historical Geography, Geographical Review, Urban Ecosystems, Maryland Historical Magazine, Appalachian Journal,* and the *Encyclopedia of Energy.*

A native of northwest Georgia, **DONALD EDWARD DAVIS** is a former professor of sociology at Dalton State College in Dalton, Georgia. The author of six books, Davis has published numerous articles in such journals as *Environmental Ethics, The Ecologist,* and the *Utne Reader.* He has also been a research assistant and consultant to the Foundation on Economic Trends in Washington, D.C., collaborating there with Jeremy Rifkin on the book *Biosphere Politics: A New Consciousness for the 21st Century* (Crown, 1991). A Fulbright fellow, Professor Davis has lectured widely in the United States and abroad, including France, Romania, Ukraine, England, and the Czech Republic. He was coordinating director of the Jacques Ellul Society and has more recently served on the board of directors of The American Chestnut Foundation. His books include *Voices from the Nueva Frontera: Latino Immigration in Dalton, Georgia* (University of Tennessee Press, 2009), *Homeplace Geography: Essays for Appalachia* (Mercer University Press, 2006), *Southern United States: An Environmental History* (ABC-CLIO, 2006), the award-winning *Where There Are Mountains: An Environmental History of the Southern Appalachians* (UGA Press, 2000), and *Ecophilosophy: A Field Guide to the Literature* (R. and E. Miles, 1989).

WREN KRUSE graduated from Ohio University, in 2009, with a master's degree in environmental studies. Her work on *Mountain Justice: Social and Environmental Justice in Appalachia* heightened her awareness of the legal implications resulting from the environmental justice movement and motivated her to pursue her present career path. She currently resides in Connecticut and will graduate with her law degree in 2012. As part of her future legal practice she plans to advocate for wiser and more effective environmental regulation and animal welfare laws.

NANCY IRWIN MAXWELL is a surveillance epidemiologist trained in environmental health. She is currently the director of the Communications and Dissemination Core of the Partners in Health and Housing Prevention Research Center at the Boston University School of Public Health. During her first nine years at BUSPH, she taught both environmental health and surveillance methods, and is the author of an introductory textbook, *Understanding Environmental Health: How We Live in the World* (Jones and Bartlett, 2009). As a staff scientist at the nonprofit Silent Spring Institute from 1996 through 2000, she directed an intensive breast cancer surveillance effort on Cape Cod, Massachusetts.

CHAD MONTRIE is a professor in the History Department at the University of Massachusetts Lowell, where he teaches courses on U.S. History, American Environmental History, the United States in the 1960s, Women in American History, the History of Documentary Film and Documentary Filmmaking, as well as others. His publications include two books, *To Save* *the Land and People: A History of Opposition to Surface Coal Mining* (University of North Carolina Press) and *Making a Living: Work and Environment in the United States* (University of North Carolina Press, 2008). He is currently writing another book, *A People's History of Environmentalism in the United States,* for Continuum Press.

MICHELE MORRONE is an associate professor of environmental health and the director of environmental studies at Ohio University. Dr. Morrone previously served as the chief of the Office of Environmental Education at Ohio EPA. She has authored or coauthored more than forty papers on a variety of environmental health issues. Her first book was *Sound Science, Junk Policy* (2002); her second book, *Poisons on Our Plates,* was published in 2008.

KATHRYN NEWFONT is associate professor of history at Mars Hill College and serves as faculty Chair of the college's Liston B. Ramsey Center for Regional Studies. Dr. Newfont has broad interests in the history of Southern Appalachian forests and the people they have sustained. In 2009–10 she had fellowship support from the National Endowment for the Humanities to complete a book project exploring the history of Appalachian commons forests, covering historical forest economies in western North Carolina, the coming of national forests to the region, and the cultural politics of national forest management. Entitled *Blue Ridge Commons: Environmental Activism and Forest History in Western North Carolina,* the book will appear in February 2012.

JOHN NOLT is professor of philosophy at the University of Tennessee, Knoxville, where he has taught since receiving his PhD from Ohio State University in 1978. He has published widely on both logic and environmental ethics and, as an environmental activist, has worked on issues of toxic waste remediation, wetlands preservation, and (most recently) campus sustainability. He is the editor of *A Land Imperiled: The Declining Health of the Southern Appalachian Bioregion* (University of Tennessee Press, 2005).

JEDEDIAH S. PURDY grew up in Calhoun County, West Virginia, near Chloe. His books include *For Common Things* (1999) and *A Tolerable Anarchy* (2009). He has been an environmental activist, a construction laborer, a journalist, and a lawyer. He teaches at Duke Law School and has been a visiting professor at Harvard and Yale.

STEPHEN J. SCANLAN is an associate professor of sociology in the Department of Sociology and Anthropology at Ohio University. He teaches collective behavior at the undergraduate level and environmental sociology, poverty, and social movements at both the graduate and undergraduate levels. He has published on the multiple determinants of food security and development in less industrialized societies, including links to conflict, democracy, and human rights; gender and development; HIV/Aids; population ecology; resource scarcity; and inequality. Current projects include research on gender and sustainable development; "greenwashing" and global agribusiness; hunger strikes as gendered political protest; and economic opportunity structure in Appalachia and American Iraq War deaths.

INDEX